Teaching History to Adolescents

"John A. Beineke's work brings the broad spectrum of history education and methodology into the light of relevance. His research, comprehensive and current, offers questions and answers to the issues of conveying history with meaning to the next generation. Every teacher reaches a point of self-examination, a plateau, and this work presents the teacher with the evidence to reach for a more effective level of instruction in the all too important work of 'preparing adolescents to make sense of history in their daily lives.'"

—*Rich Wetmore, U.S. History Teacher, Marina Village Middle School,*
El Dorado Hills, California

"John A. Beineke's book, while geared toward middle school history teachers, is a tour de force of the changing nature of the discipline of history as a whole. His practical advice is far-ranging and provides a treasure trove of ideas. Teachers from elementary to college classrooms will learn techniques to make the best use of historical sources, from political cartoons and comic books to utilizing public history venues. Beineke's book captures the theory behind the innovations and provides multiple examples to engage students."

—*Linda K. Pritchard, Professor of History and Department Head,*
Women's and Gender Studies, Eastern Michigan University, Ypsilanti, Michigan

Teaching History to Adolescents

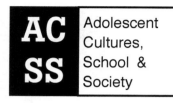

Adolescent
Cultures,
School &
Society

Joseph L. DeVitis & Linda Irwin-DeVitis
GENERAL EDITORS

Vol. 52

The Adolescent Cultures, School and Society series is part of the Peter Lang Education list.
Every volume is peer reviewed and meets
the highest quality standards for content and production.

PETER LANG
New York • Washington, D.C./Baltimore • Bern
Frankfurt • Berlin • Brussels • Vienna • Oxford

John A. Beineke

Teaching History to Adolescents

A Quest for Relevance

PETER LANG
New York • Washington, D.C./Baltimore • Bern
Frankfurt • Berlin • Brussels • Vienna • Oxford

Library of Congress Cataloging-in-Publication Data

Beineke, John A.
Teaching history to adolescents: a quest for relevance / John A. Beineke.
p. cm. — (Adolescent cultures, school and society; v. 52)
Includes bibliographical references and index.
1. History—Study and teaching (Secondary)—United States.
2. United States—History—Study and teaching (Secondary)
I. Title. II. Series.
D16.3.B38   907.1'273—dc22   2011000026
ISBN 978-1-4331-1096-2 (hardcover)
ISBN 978-1-4331-1095-5 (paperback)
ISSN 1091-1464

Bibliographic information published by **Die Deutsche Nationalbibliothek**.
Die Deutsche Nationalbibliothek lists this publication in the "Deutsche
Nationalbibliografie"; detailed bibliographic data is available
on the Internet at http://dnb.d-nb.de/.

Cover illustration used by permission. Copyright Art Parts / Ron and Joe, Inc.

The paper in this book meets the guidelines for permanence and durability
of the Committee on Production Guidelines for Book Longevity
of the Council of Library Resources.

© 2011 Peter Lang Publishing, Inc., New York
29 Broadway, 18th floor, New York, NY 10006
www.peterlang.com

Printed in the United States of America

For the five mentors I have had in my life
—who are also my friends

Dr. Oatess E. Archey
Dr. Jay C. Thompson, Jr.
Dr. Roger H. Sublett
Dr. Robert D. Sparks
and the late
Dr. Robert M. Mitchell

CONTENTS

Introduction

It was as an adolescent that I first became enamored of history. The motivation was a set of novels my mother owned by the now–forgotten historical novelist Thomas B. Costain. Costain was a newspaper man from Canada born in the nineteenth century. He came to the United States to continue his journalistic career as an editor at the *Saturday Evening Post*. Upon reaching the age of fifty-five, Costain shifted careers and ventured into the field of history and historical fiction. Beginning in 1940, until his death in 1965, he wrote bestselling books—eleven novels, six volumes of history, a biography, three young adult books—and edited several collections of short stories. His historical novels were my entrée into the world of history. Costain's works, usually written about little-known historical figures from European and Canadian history, led me to other writers and I became hooked on history.

This book began as an expansion of my chapter in *Adolescent Education: A Reader* (Peter Lang, 2010), edited by Joseph L. DeVitis and Linda Irwin-DeVitis. Using the works of three progressive educators, this book will suggest ways to make history "mean something" to adolescents through how it is taught. John Dewey spoke of "interest and effort"—if there was interest on the part of the student, then effort by the student would follow. William Heard Kilpatrick made his own variation on Dewey's thought with the phrase "activity leading to further activity." This, according to Kilpatrick, should be the primary goal of every classroom teacher. And William Van Til believed the major goal of education was to teach students to solve real problems with real resolutions both inside and outside the classroom. The intention of all three thinkers was to connect the learner to the subject at hand so that the motivation to learn would be, as much as possible, internal rather than external. A quick note on the subtitle to this book—*A Quest for Relevance*. It is borrowed from *Curriculum: Quest for Relevance,* a volume of readings edited by Van Til that I used in graduate school in the 1970s.[1] Van Til was a progressive educator and curriculum specialist from the mid-1930s until his death in 2006. It is my hope that these pages will contain, as Van Til advocated, practical and relevant ideas for educators.

John Dewey, in 1916, also spoke to the issue of how subjects such as history can lose their educational purpose by being reduced to compilations of information. Dewey advocated that subjects like history needed to "enrich and liberate the more direct and personal contacts of life by furnishing their context, their background, and outlook."[2] This is both a lofty goal and serious challenge for those who would teach history to adolescents in the twenty-first century. Another giant of education, Ralph Tyler, wrote in 1949 that even subject matter specialists, such as historians, should be concerned with how "the subject can contribute to the education of young people who are not going to be specialists" in a field, how that subject can "contribute to the layman, the garden variety citizen."[3]

Emily Style has referred to curriculum as both a "window and a mirror."[4] Volts, Sims, and Nelson see Style as saying that for students "windows look into a world that is different than their own and a mirror reflects their own image." They have also suggested that "many students often see school learning as foreign to their everyday concerns, it's our challenge to help learners see how what they study in schools is connected to something that is relevant for them."[5]

Research has established that when teachers focus on the contemporary relevance of history, then students will also see its importance for understanding the present. By the same token, when history teachers center their teaching solely on content, then students follow suit and concentrate on learning a body of information to the exclusion of making connections to present-day issues. Although research on the classroom outcomes of history instruction exists, it has been suggested that even more research is needed on how students engage with the past in less formal or academic settings such as listening to the stories of relatives, visiting museums or historical sites, and discussing politics with peers. In this way it is hoped that students will find relevancy in both their formal and informal study of history.[6]

This book will use recent research and the best in contemporary practices to inform and enrich the teaching of history to adolescents. A plethora of sources on effective schools' research and practice provide often-similar lists of conditions needed for a successful educational experience. In no special order, these include qualified teachers who know their subject matter and the age group they are teaching; a rigorous curriculum; a reasonable teacher-student classroom ratio and usually a small-school setting; time-on-task or significant student engagement in the material being studied; an organized, safe, and fair environment; extracurricular opportunities; supportive parents or guardians; access to health care; and the availability of current learning materials and technology. The list is by no means complete, but it does encompass a variety of essential school-based practices, factors, and resources that provide a foundation for students to succeed.

An underlying assumption of this book is that the academic discipline of history and the act of teaching history should be partners in the endeavor to educate our youth. While I was a program director at the W.K. Kellogg Foundation, we often said that most issues and debates were not a case of "either/or" but of "both." (I have certainly used that piece of wisdom once or twice within the pages of this book.) If we love teaching history, then we need both the subject matter expertise and the pedagogical knowledge to make the endeavor a successful one. Writing this book has simultaneously informed me in both areas. And it has allowed me to engage in my two professional passions—teaching and the study of the past.

One of the overarching aims of education in the United States is to prepare students for life in a democracy. To do this, Nel Noddings notes that students must be allowed to make choices in what they study, especially history and social studies. "Having the opportunity to choose," writes Noddings, "is important in itself because of its connection to motivation." Having students make well-informed choices, she adds, is critical.[7]

This volume is not a methods book per se. It does include, however, numerous ideas, reflections, suggestions, and strategies on teaching history to adolescents. But a major goal of the book is to be a resource for history teachers in gaining professional, intellectual, and resource knowledge for their professional development. The suggestions of resources and ideas are made for the teacher as well as for the learner. The book also will practice what it preaches in terms of the use of history. The teaching of history has its own history and vignettes. These and other examples from history will be drawn from and intertwined with the narrative to shed light on the experience of teaching history and on adolescence itself.

While I intend history to be relevant, at the same time I have been cautious not relate every historical episode directly to a current event. There are in many cases similarities between the past and present, but one needs to be careful when drawing parallels. With the occasional lapse, every effort has been made not to make references to what can be seen on the nightly news, read in daily newspapers or weekly magazines, or viewed over the Internet.

The connections, however, between past and present are readily evident. As the alleged Chinese curse stated, "May you live in interesting times." The times are indeed filled with much that will make history. As this book goes into production, the United States is deeply engaged in two long-lasting wars, with soldiers and civilians being killed every week. We have our first Black president in the midst of his first term, and the two political parties are as deeply and rigidly divided along partisan lines as at any time in our history. The nation's increasing diversity has become politically charged, especially in the area of immigration. The nation finds itself in an economic downturn (the "Great Recession") that has been likened to the Great Depression. We also have a Supreme Court evenly divided and entrenched along ideological lines, making every new nomination to the high court a political mêlée. And with all of this occurring, the nation is dealing with the worst environmental disaster in its history. We do indeed live in interesting times, and most of the above issues and events have similar precursors in our past.

A word about an organizational conundrum that arose during the researching and writing of this book. Chapters usually indicate a logical attempt at coherent divisions, but history and ideas about teaching history do not always occur in orderly fashion, no matter what the author's intentions were. It became apparent on several occasions, that it was not easy to compartmentalize every piece of research, every idea, or every topic into a particular chapter. The reader needs to be aware that autobiographies often found a home in the chapter on primary sources, and the selection of subject matter became entwined with professional development. Higher-order thinking, diversity, and controversial topics seemed to find homes in several chapters. And references to textbooks and film will materialize in various chapters.

For example, the article I used from *Rethinking Education* by Karen Park Koenig, "It Was So Much Fun! I Died of Massive Blood Loss!", raised a number of issues, such as why the reenactments were being done and what did the students take away from the exercise.[8] Should this piece reside in the public history chapter on reenactments, in the controversial issues chapter or in another chapter with a section on simulations and role playing? (It eventually landed in the section on simulations and role playing in the last chapter.)

As a former middle-school educator and also a teacher of high school freshmen and seniors, I have on occasion inserted a few of my own ideas, drawn from my own experiences, into the book. I have also had the opportunity to hold a joint appointment in both education and history at three college-level institutions, teaching survey courses in American history. These courses have allowed me to continue my love of history by teaching freshmen and sophomores. And, as someone has said, the only difference between a high school and a college student is a ten-week summer vacation.

Johnson and McElroy in their *The Eductainer: Connecting the Art and Science of Teaching* echo Van Til's ideas on connecting classroom material with the real world and real problems. Learning must be made relevant, they maintain, and applicable to the students' lives. "It is human nature," they write, "to take an interest in things that are relevant to our own lives. Since practically every aspect of education is in some way relevant to students' lives, it is important for the teacher to make the connection because you can't assume that the students will make the connection of the relevance by themselves." They also contend that teachers should personalize their own stories in their classrooms. Not only should the issues being examined be real, but the teacher herself needs to be real. A final suggestion they make is that teachers have an enthusiasm about the subject and the classroom.[9]

History is about real people, real events, real issues. If history cannot be made relevant for adolescents, then no subject can. Not all students will find history as important to their lives as the author or many who have chosen to read these pages. But it is my firm conviction that many more adolescents can become engaged in history through creative teaching by knowledgeable and energetic teachers in the modern classroom.

Let me mention that what may seem an irregular practice in the area of capitalization has been employed in this work. I have chosen to capitalize the words Black(s) and White(s), drawing on the expertise of two experienced and informed multicultural educators, Sonia Neito and Patty Bode. As they recommend in their most recent book, *Affirming Diversity: The Sociopolitical Context of Multicultural Education*, "We have capitalized the terms *White* and *Black* because they refer to groups of people, as do terms such as *Latino*, *Asian*, and *African*. As such they deserve to be capitalized."[10] I have followed their example.

I want to especially note and thank the contributors to the sections titled "The World of Practice." The contributors were William White, Ruth Baize, Ray Boomhower, Don Maness, Paul Shaddox, Caryn Ellison, Prentice Chandler, Richard Graham, and Linda Merillat. These sections contain not only wise and informed descriptions of current practice but come directly from the real world of practice as related to the study of history. The contributions are from a variety of practitioners closely connected to the chapter topics that contain their work. I have been fortunate to have prize-winning teachers, historians, curriculum specialists, authors, and experts from various fields join in this venture. I am in their debt. The book will be stronger due to their wisdom, knowledge, and expertise.

Others who need special recognition connection here are Christopher S. Myers, Managing Director at Peter Lang Publishing, and Joseph L. DeVitis and Linda Irwin-DeVitis, editors of the series of which this volume is a part. I am deeply humbled by and appreciative of their confidence in the ideas behind the book and also in me as an author. Jimmy Harvey, movie aficionado, kindly read my chapter on film and made a number of enlightening suggestions. Linda Keller, Interlibrary Loan Librarian at Arkansas State University, unflinchingly responded to and secured the dozens of books I requested. Charlotte Foster, a doctoral student at Arkansas State University, reviewed and corrected the formatting of the footnotes and edits, doing a splendid job. I must thank my son, Colin Beineke, a graduate student in English at the University of Nebraska, who led me through the world of comic books and also read and critiqued the occasional chapter when his time allowed. I asked him too many questions, but he was generous with his time and expertise. And to my wife, Marla, who read and proofed the manuscript, word-processed for me as the deadline for completion drew close, and as always supported me in my work. She also allowed me, for much too long a period of time, to turn our dining room into my center for research and writing. The dining room, I am happy to report, is now back in good order.

—John A. Beineke,
December 2010

Endnotes

1   Van Til, William. *Curriculum: Quest for Relevance.* Boston: Houghton Mifflin, 1971.
2   Dewey, John. *Democracy and Education.* New York: Free Press, 1916/1966. 212.
3   Tyler, Ralph. *Basic Principles of Curriculum and Instruction.* Chicago: University of Chicago Press, 1949. 26.
4   Style, Emily. "Curriculum as Window and Mirror." from the *Seeking Educational Equity and Diversity Project on Inclusive Curriculum.* Wellesley Center for Women. Retrieved 21 Aug. 2010. <http://www.ncrel.org/sdrs/areas/issues/educatrs/presrvce/pe300.htm>.
5   Voltz, Deborah L, Michele J. Sims, and Betty Nelson. *Connecting Teachers, Students and Standards: Strategies for Success in Diverse and Inclusive Classrooms.* Alexandria: Association for Supervision and Curriculum Development, 2010. 83.
6   Barton, Keith C. "Research on Student's Ideas about History." Eds. Linda S. Levstik, and Cynthia A. Tyson. *Handbook of Research in Social Studies Education.* New York: Routledge, 2008. 250 and 245.
7   Noddings, Nel. Foreword. *Teaching Social Studies That Matters: Curriculum for Active Learning.* By Stephen J. Thornton. New York: Teachers College Press, 2005. ix.
8   Koenig, Karen Park. "It Was So Much Fun! I Died of Massive Blood Loss!" *Rethinking Education* , 2009, 23. 4.
9   Johnson, Brad and Tammy Maxson McElroy. *The Edutainer: Connecting the Art and Science of Teaching.* Lanham, MD: Rowman and Littlefield Education, 2010. 23–4.
10   Nieto, Sonia, and Patty Bode. *Affirming Diversity: The Sociopolitical Context of Multicultural Education.* 5th ed. Boston: Pearson/Allyn and Bacon, 2008.34.

ONE

The Big Picture

Teaching adolescents and teaching history. There is no more important age group and those who teach history would argue there is no more important subject. As a society we are awash in history, yet how do we prepare adolescents to make sense of history in their daily lives? John Dewey articulated the case for teaching history when in his book *Experience and Education* he asked the question, "How shall the young become acquainted with the past in such a way that the acquaintance is a potent agent in appreciation of the living present?"[1] A group of Stanford University researchers have stated it in plain terms: "The practice of history is a profoundly literate activity that has an important place in the school curriculum."[2]

The purpose of this chapter, as stated in its title, is to provide a wider view of teaching history to adolescents. It will explore the imperative for teaching the subject of history to youth. And then this chapter will turn to four topics, trends, and issues which educators are facing in today's classrooms—competing learning theories, the standards movement, high-stakes testing, and classroom management. These need to be briefly explored before moving to the more specific chapter topics that follow.

This book will look at the context of teaching history to middle school and high school students. The approaches and ideas suggested in these pages are re-search-based and practitioner-tested. The book will not be an attempt to provide a course in pedagogy. "No Easy Answers" might have been the subtitle of the book as easily as "A Quest for Relevance." Hopefully this volume, to use an art metaphor, will be a palette that includes colors, hues, and shades by which to look at the teaching of history. The aim will be to examine ideas that will engage adolescents in 21st-century America while at the same time combining ideas, research, and classroom experiences.

Larry Cuban, after fifty years of teaching, researching, and writing, captured the essence of the goal of these pages with this inclusive statement of purpose:

> I cannot go beyond saying that schools with sufficient resources and teachers fully knowledgeable in the content and skills they teach, armed with a broad repertoire of classroom practices drawn from different traditions of teaching, and the expertise to vary those practices with individual students and groups of students—teachers who hug the middle—have the best chance of succeeding with most students, most of the time.[3]

The late Howard Zinn, whose work and contributions to the exploration of history will be touched on in several places this book, said that his purpose in teaching and writing was "making a connection between history and what is going on today." For him there was no other purpose to history. In speaking of his career in studying and teaching history he said, "I wanted to go into history and come out in the present."[4] Not all history will bring us out "in the present," but what history that does will be much more meaningful to the students we teach.

What do we know about the teaching of history? The answer to that question a mere two decades ago was "not much." Downey and Levstik in a chapter on the teaching of history in the *Handbook of Research on Social Studies Teaching and Learning* wrote: "There is an inadequate body of research on instruction in history. We know little about how interactions among students, teachers, and others are felt in the classroom about how history is taught and learned."[5] Not all the questions have been answered since these two researchers took stock of history teaching twenty years ago. One might even say assessing what we know is an undertaking without end. But we have marched further down the road and the whole endeavor of teaching history, especially to adolescents, is becoming clearer and abounding with ideas.

Author and professor James Loewen has written that "Those who don't remember the past are condemned to repeat the eleventh grade." In a more serious vein, Loewen has noted that students "hate" history, find it "boring," frequently list it as the most irrelevant of twenty-one commonly taught subjects in school, and find it their least interesting subject at all grade levels. A most unflattering jab might be from the rap group Jungle Brothers who declare: "Yeah, I cut class/ I got a D/ 'Cause history meant nothin' to me."[6]

Over a quarter of a century ago, John Goodlad made a similar, though more eloquent, case for the monotony of methods in the modern classroom, especially the history classroom. In his massive study of schooling in the 1980s Goodlad found that history and social studies were the least popular subjects. In high schools, history ranked below math and English and on par with science.[7] Methods could be the culprit in this lack of interest on the part of students, but there seems to be more at work here than how the subject is delivered.

Bringing meaning to the history classroom is a major challenge in today's schools. The teaching of history is challenging because it calls on helping students imagine events and individuals from a past with which they have no connection. Disconnection and lack of engagement by students is evident in many schools. One study found that nearly 40% of students wished they could attend a different school while the same number felt they were an important part of their school community. The same study found two out of three students bored in their high school classes every day. Seventeen percent reported being bored in every class. Reasons for boredom included 1) the material wasn't interesting (75%), 2) material wasn't relevant (39%), 3) work wasn't challenging (32%), 4) no interaction with the teacher (31%), and 5) 27% responded that the work was too difficult.[8]

Terrie Epstein in *Teaching U.S. History: Dialogues among Social Studies Teachers and Historians* echoes these observations. Recent research on the teaching of history indicates "that many history classrooms conform to the Ferris Bueller stereotype of the history teacher." The reference is to actor Ben Stein's portrayal in the 1980s film *Ferris Bueller's Day Off,* where he endlessly drones on with a series of seemingly pointless facts and questions on the Great Depression to a class of dazed and dozing students. Research confirms, writes Epstein, that history teachers ask dry and irrelevant question, are overly reliant on the textbook, and employ worksheets and lead classroom recitations that stress traditional narratives of American history.[9] This approach has led to multiple studies from the 1960s up to the 21st century that the troika of textbook reading, teacher explanation, and testing have become the practices rather than the exceptions in history classrooms.[10]

The term engagement will be used a number of times in this book. What do we mean by engagement? Haudan has written that "People work because they have to. That's why they call it work. But people engage because they want to."[11] The same holds true for adolescents. High and Andrews have written that "Engagement requires students to be emotionally and psychologically invested in their learning." It also calls for students to have a "voice" in their learning. They add that engagement does not equal entertainment, but that "engaging work is motivating work—the kind that will feel more like play and get students 'in the zone.'" The zone is that magical place, they explain, where "students are so absorbed in the task that they forget to check the clock."[12] We know that not all experiences in a history class will be fun or engaging. But the potential to get students engaged is possible when the teachers keep High and Andrews' concept in mind when they select, plan, and implement classroom lessons in history.

Whom do we mean when we use the term adolescent? Susan Eva Porter has provided a detailed description of adolescence through a categorical taxonomy of this stage in human development. Porter has captured four stages of this age group with brief explanations for each. Early Middle School is comprised of grades five and six. They are still concrete thinkers "just beginning to develop the skills that will allow them to reason, organize, and execute complex cognitive functions." While oversight is needed, "Peers are important but kids are not hyper-reactive to their classmates," writes Porter. Separation from parents and teachers has not begun in earnest and peer pressure has not peaked.

Next comes Late Middle School or grades seven and eight. Reasoning capacity increases as adolescents are able to master complex subjects, like algebra, by the end of eighth grade. "Social development and awareness is all consuming during this phase," according to Porter. Social situations become paramount while at the same time there is difficulty in reading social cues and managing feelings of isolation. Early High School, grades nine and ten, is identified by high self-consciousness and preoccupation with peers. In the cognitive arena, academic expectations increase with greater reasoning abilities. Organizational issues also emerge as related to academics. "The search for identity is in full force," states Porter, as questions as to life's meaning and purpose arise. At the same time some adolescents can be idealistic and naïve.

Finally, in Porter's taxonomy, is Late High School or grades eleven and twelve. Mood swings decrease and the world is viewed in terms of black and white. For some adolescents at this stage an element of self-regulation can be seen. As control over their impulses increases, adolescents often relate better to their academic environment as attention spans increase and distractions to the work at hand decrease. What Porter labels the "parallel curriculum" is for her the real work in adolescence. The parallel curriculum is the "set of skills apart from the academic curriculum that teenagers must learn through adolescence in order to grow up." It is apart from the learning that takes place in the classroom, "but is inextricably tied to what happens through the school day."[13] Though seemingly neatly partitioned, this journey to adulthood never follows the same path. But it is a real part of any and all educational experiences adolescents go through.

While the ages of the modern middle school students do not coincide precisely with that of adolescence, the middle school movement cannot be ignored when looking at the dominant areas that impact the teaching and learning of this group. Although there is not a single definition of middle level education, there are a number of characteristics that real middle schools hold in common. Some maintain that middle schools were born in the 1960s with an address by William Alexander. Several of the subsequent distinctive educational practices for ten to fourteen year-olds include attention to the physical and cognitive growth of the adolescent, curriculum approaches such as exploratory and experiential activities, and the integration of subject matter through interdisciplinary teaching. Structural elements found in middle schools are team teaching, advisory programs, and alternative scheduling. The major requirement that encompasses much of the "true" middle school ideal is its being a unique time of growth and exploration for this age group.[14]

It will do no harm for history teachers to be as knowledgeable as they can about adolescents. This would also include being aware of the general socio-economic background of the school's student population. An urban, rural, suburban, or mixed demographic school can have a significant impact on what goes on in the classroom. A tour of the neighborhoods that compose the school's catchment area can be a highly useful part of a teacher interview. Cultural backgrounds such as ethnicity or language can also be important factors, but at the same time educators need to be aware of stereotyping their students. And while it would no doubt be a full-time activity, teachers should have some knowledge of adolescent tastes and trends in reading, music, clothing, and media.

Three researchers have suggested that teachers need to listen to what teens have to say about what it is like to be adolescent. In a sample of over 450 essays, adolescents gave voice to their experiences, dreams, and concerns. The researchers categorized these responses in themes that included fearfulness, risk-taking, boredom, stress, frivolity, and responsibility. From this data researchers concluded the need for teachers to have counseling skills; to allow for risk-taking in the forms of role-playing, goal setting, and defending a personal opinion; to recognize that many adolescents are working hard to be successful both academically and socially; and to allow for independent inquiry and self-exploration. Finally, there needs to be a reinfusion of an ethic of caring, a notion long advocated by Nel Noddings and others.[15]

As educational researchers Johnson and Christensen have pointed out, the history of adolescence itself is instructive when exploring the topic of teaching history. In the 20th century several changes took place that had an impact on adolescence. First, compulsory attendance laws increased school enrollment for fourteen to seventeen-year-olds from six percent in the late 1800s to the significantly higher levels we have today. Second, the juvenile justice system was formed, making distinctions between adolescents and adults. Third, the 1938 Fair Labor Standards Act outlawed hazardous child labor practices, making school rather than work a preferable alternative for youth. And fourth, this age group became a unique field of study during the years 1890–1920, being labeled the "Age of Adolescence" by historian David Tyack.[16]

L.P. Hartley begins his novel *The Go-Between* with the line "The past is a foreign country: they do things differently there." Barton has suggested that while students usually understand that people in the past thought, acted, and lived differently than today, they have only a partial conception as to how and why.

As they move into adolescence, students replace general narrative structures of understanding the past to more specific narratives in order to make sense of historical trends and events. An example would be an adolescent understanding the themes of freedom and progress by knowing that enslaved peoples were freed and technology improved the lives of many. And yet many are unable to fully understand issues such as the inequality between men and women or the social implications of technology such as the shifting of today's jobs from manufacturing to the information sector.[17]

Two logical questions directly connected to the teaching of history are: What is history and what do historians do? There have been volumes written in response to these two questions because there are multiple answers to these questions. For the purposes of this book, Mark Krug's response in the 1960s will be used. He suggested that historians post questions about human interaction in current and past events, seek appropriate sources of data, and attempt to develop an explanation to answer those questions. Krug has written that historians, in doing their work, ask three questions: "What happened? How did it happen? Why did it happen?"[18] The answers to questions about history are actually more questions. And that is how it should be.

Barton examined over a dozen research studies on the development of historical knowledge. He found that while students may at first be highly resistant to historical perspectives that conflict with their own ethical or political beliefs, over time they do grasp that values, attitudes, and beliefs do change. This assists them in creating their own historic perspectives in lieu of previously held unexamined biases. Older adolescents and adults are able to deemphasize personal factors and become more open to entertaining societal and psychological causations to explain historical events.[19]

When advocating the teaching of history to adolescents, the question of "why" should be answered. Berg has identified five reasons for conducting historical research which apply to the teaching of history. They are: 1) to uncover the unknown, 2) to answer questions, 3) to identify the relationship that the past has to the present, 4) to record and evaluate the accomplishments of individuals, agencies, or institutions, and 5) to aid in our understanding of the culture in which we live.[20] All of these elements are essential when teaching history to adolescents.

Furay and Salevouris have contributed additional reasons for the study of history: 1) it brings a sense of our own identity, 2) good history is a corrective for misleading analogies and lessons from the past, 3) it enables us to understand human tendencies, social institutions, and the human condition, 4) it can help develop tolerance and open-mindedness, 5) it can be used as a platform to teach critical thinking skills, and 6) it can be productive entertainment via film, literature, and stories.[21] Further reasons that adolescents themselves give for studying history include its intrinsic interest, a possible hobby (such as genealogy), a future career in heritage conservation or teaching, and its potential to solve future problems from the lessons of the past. One other reason mentioned by youth, but one that most historians would cringe at hearing, was the value of history for contestants on quiz shows.[22] The present then has the promise of helping students make sense of the past while at the same time modern society shapes the history being taught in today's classrooms.

> From his holistic approach to teaching, history and social studies in particular, Andrew Johnson has written: Teaching history to students allows them to touch the lives of people who have lived before them. History is the story of humans. We study it in order to get a sense of who we are and to better understand ourselves. We also study history so that we can learn from the past.[23]

The reasons for teaching history to youth, then, are several. Yet the pedagogical side of the process must also be considered. There are four major trends and issues that underpin and influence—some might even say control—the current educational milieu. These four "Big Picture" elements are competing learning theories, the standards movement, high-stakes testing, and classroom management. In ways interrelated, all four have an impact on the teaching of history in today's schools.

Competing learning theories certainly have an effect on how history is taught. Possibly the phrase "the learning wars" might better capture the debates that surround current teaching and learning strategies. An incomplete list of theories includes constructivism, behaviorism, multiple intelligences, and the brain theorists. Part learning theory, part philosophy, there is also holistic education that attempts to wed multiple levels of meaning and experience that incorporate the emotional, the psychological, the spiritual, the relational, and the experiential.[24] The disciples of all these learning theories are devoted and committed to their beliefs. And some have applied their research to the teaching of history.[25]

The application of these learning theories is essential. For example, Sheryl Feinstein, who has written extensively about brain research as applied to teaching adolescents, has written that the brain, not hormones, is to blame for the inexplicable behavior of teens. In addition, the teen brains are particularly susceptible to novelty. Brain theorists maintain that physical movement helps the cerebellum develop, thereby helping adolescents improve their cognitive skills.[26] While not denigrating brain theorists, the issue is how to formulate what the research reveals and productively utilize it. For example, how can the need for physical movement or the knowledge that the there is a growth burst of the brain's frontal lobes during adolescence be used to teach about the Bill of Rights or the Civil War. Yet, in the broader sense, novelty and the role of emotions in adolescents may very well inform instruction in the history classroom.

The perusal of educational psychology textbooks in any university bookstore can be an enlightening experience. Textbooks each have their own theoretical construct. Constructivist-based texts rarely reference behaviorist theory or vice-versa. These two theories seem to be ships passing in the night, failing to acknowledge that the other theory even exists. A middle level methods text, in discussing learning, provides a paragraph on behaviorism citing Ivan Pavlov and B.F. Skinner and the emphasis on rewards and punishment. The authors then state, "The idea that behavior indicates learning is unsatisfying for cognitive approaches to learning."[27] Behaviorists counter that Skinner has been misinterpreted and that their approach is scientifically based. In literacy and math, claims are made that direct instruction is superior to constructivist and developmental practices.[28] The "learning wars" proceed.

The reasons that various learning theories fail with adolescents vary. Some include seemingly short attention spans, lack of motivation, and competition with various media for a student's interest. And all too frequently, poor attendance and high student mobility mean teaching opportunities are lost. There does seem to be, except for learning theorists at the extremes of the spectrum, an understanding that no single approach works with all students. Therefore, unless demonstrated through incontrovertible evidence to be totally valueless in the educational setting, teachers should have multiple strategies at their disposal for teaching and learning. Therefore, for the purposes of this book, an eclectic approach to learning theories will be the operating presupposition.

Closely aligned with learning theories are ideas on how to build background knowledge in the various disciplines such as history. Marzano and others have confirmed the relationship between background knowledge and achievement. Marzano stipulates it is essential that information become a part of background knowledge. For this to happen information must reach what is called "permanent memory." Direct experiences are often cited as the best way to build and enhance background knowledge in a subject. But it is a reality that real-life experiences, field trips, and first-hand encounters are not always possible, especially in history. In the absence of direct experiences, Marzano has suggested what he calls "virtual experiences." Reading is the most obvious virtual experience. But Marzano posits that this must be undertaken with a clear commitment to build vocabulary so that the reading is done both in context and with comprehension. The final virtual experience that Marzano mentions is educational television, which will be examined in a later chapter on media.[29]

While not a learning theory unto itself, the Effective Schools movement and the research that emerged in the 1970s and 1980s has been able to find commonalities and build a few tenuous bridges among educational psychologists. The Effective Schools "commonsense approach" to teaching practice has included high expectations of students by teachers ("all children can learn" as it is espoused today), focus on the content to be covered, keeping students on task, providing adequate practice time, and monitoring student performance.[30] Although much of the Effective School research is built on constructivism, Oliva, a curriculum specialist, has written that there remains no consensus: "There is some evidence that for certain types of learnings and for certain types of students, direct instruction of the total group by the teacher is more effective than other strategies such as small grouping and inquiry."[31]

While most educators accept the validity of the Effective Teaching research in terms of generic teaching skills, some see these generalizations as limited. Current research on teaching has moved in the direction of case studies, differentiated learning, emphasis on social aspects of learning (collaborative learning), and authentic learning and performance-based assessment. For new teachers especially, there is still much they can gain from the work of the Effective School movement. Oliva concludes that teachers need to be "aware of the wide range of instructional strategies possible and . . . develop proficiency in the use of those strategies."[32]

In the 1990s Howard Johnston investigated the patterns and characteristics of higher achieving students. While more general in its findings, Johnston's work does build on the Effective Schools literature. Some of the characteristics of higher achieving students were:

- Holding more conversations with adults, therefore assignments that require students to interview teachers, parents, and people in their community are helpful.

- Developing skills and interest outside of school, such as hobbies, sports, and music. Middle level schools that incorporate advisory groups (extracurricular groups) have been found to be most effective for this grade level.

- Spending time planning for the future. Students need to think, write, and talk about their futures with responsible adults and plan for life beyond the present moment.

- Spending more time in supervised settings such as home, church, clubs, and sports.

- Spending more time reading. Teachers need to talk about their own reading habits. Reading 30 books per year is suggested as a goal for middle school students.[33]

Many of these characteristics require either parental or other adult involvement in the lives of students. What clearly emerges from this list is the need for a more ordered, consistent, supervised, and adult connected world for adolescents. This means that many of these items are beyond the direct control of students. But teachers connecting through a newsletter, web-page, or other form of communication can provide parents and guardians with ideas to help their sons and daughters. Even sending home Johnston's list might provide the incentive for adults to become more engaged in the lives of their adolescents.

Educational psychologist and teacher educator Jere Brophy in his *Motivating Students to Learn* has given particular attention to what he has termed "comprehensive classroom interventions" to motivate students. These interventions are being given special consideration due to the fact that motivation can be a major challenge when teaching adolescents. Brophy showcases the research of Ames and Epstein who present their findings on a categorical structure of motivational systems represented by the acronym TARGET—Task, Authority, Recognition, Grouping, Evaluation, and Time. Their recommendations are juxtaposed with traditional practices. By "Task" a variety of learning activities are intrinsically connected to students' backgrounds. The tasks are challenging and taught within a construction of goal-setting by the student. "Authority" calls for shared decision-making in the classroom between teacher and learner. The term "Recognition" connotes providing authentic note of all students who are not only high achievers, but make progress toward and demonstrate effort in reaching agreed upon goals. "Grouping" calls for collaborative and community considerations when working on assignments. A variety of assessments are featured in "Evaluation" rather than conventional testing measures. And finally "Time," which represents the flexible and autonomous use of the classroom schedule.[34]

Brophy's other intervention is the Keller Model. Again, synthesizing motivation principles, four dimensions are listed: interest, relevance, expectancy, and outcomes. 1) Interest is related to arousing curiosity and sustaining it. This is done by the use of novel, incongruous, or paradoxical events that abruptly change the status quo for the student; adolescents' interjection of the personal and emotional element into the lesson; a mix of what students already know with a dose of the unfamiliar; the use of analogies; and guiding students into a process of question generation. 2) Relevance is instruction that is related to personal needs or goals. This occurs through a combination of risk/no-risk opportunities; instruction that is responsive to choice, power, and responsibility. 3) Expectancy means a likelihood of achieving success based on personal effort and ability. 4) Outcomes which are the satisfaction of a goal accomplished provides motivation for engaging in further activities in the future.[35]

A number of suggestions from Brophy and his colleagues can be considered Deweyan in their outlook via William Heard Kilpatrick. Kilpatrick spoke of activity leading to further student activity, student interest and resulting effort (directly from Dewey), and also the "felt (learning) needs" of students. While not having a common terminology due to the decades that separate the two men, both Brophy and Kilpatrick have their similarities.[36]

The standards movement is also a major reality to be considered when teaching history. Although arguably not taken to the extent of literacy and mathematics assessments, the history curriculum increasingly in the past quarter century has become more codified and prescribed. One set of 8th grade textbooks covering just four subjects—math, science, language arts, and social studies—lists 1,500 important topics. With approximately 170 instruction days in place for most schools and the emphases on math and literacy, the fear of history being increasingly narrowed is legitimate.[37] The content of history now appears within most state standards, sometimes referred to as frameworks or curriculum maps. From organizations such as the National Council for Social Studies to the websites of state departments of education, thematic outlines and specific content within history are provided to teachers. History textbooks themselves could be viewed as a curricular map. The standardization of the history curriculum is growing.

In 2010 national attention was focused on Texas as the state board of education in that state moved to set curriculum standards in history. Viewing textbooks as having a politically liberal bias, the conservative majority of the school board asked textbook companies to make changes in order to be considered for statewide adoption. While not all of the suggestions remained in the final document, more than one hundred amendments were made to the social studies curriculum standards. They included questioning the Founding Fathers' commitment to a purely secular government, presenting Republican party philosophies in more positive light (e.g. rehabilitating Senator Joseph McCarthy), removing the 1848 Seneca Falls women's rights declaration, and requiring that the inaugural address of Confederate President Jefferson Davis be taught alongside Lincoln's. A number of changes did make it into the final document including placing a greater emphasis on the Judeo-Christian influences of the Founding Fathers and teaching that the words "separation of church and state" are not found in the Constitution. Even the philosophically market-driven U.S. Secretary of Education Arne Duncan called the process a case of politicians deciding curriculum.[38]

Bigelow has warned that it is not only Texas that has delved into textbook content. He has found that even more liberal states already have curriculum standards on the books that skew history toward a status-quo, conventional wisdom approach to the teaching of history. Examples would be downplaying the issues of social justice, poverty, and areas such as race, gender, and social class—all, admittedly, topics that liberals find pivotal in the teaching of history. Due to the quickly changing nature of the textbook industry, though, states are better able to tailor textbooks to different state standards. The fear by some that Texas, the second-largest consumer of textbooks in the country after California, will dictate curriculum is not as strong as it was even five years ago. While there has been, again, a call for national standards in lieu of state standards, two states—Texas and Alaska—have demurred. The fear has always been that the $7 billion K–12 textbook market will be overly influenced by large states.[39]

Closely aligned to the standards movement has been the rise of what has been familiarly termed "high stakes testing." Assessing what has been prescribed to learn has emerged as central to the teaching and learning process. As noted above, literacy and mathematics have been the major focus of high-stakes testing. But in a number of states, especially through the use of exit or graduation examinations, students face these tests in history. Support for high-stakes testing in history can be witnessed in the expanding list of states that utilize them. Thoughtful educators and historians have made the case both for and against their use by citing examples of how policy is impacting testing and, conversely, how testing is impacting policy.[40]

A final area that is inextricable with the learning process is classroom management. If the students are not attending to the material, the teacher, or their peers, then virtually none of the suggestions of this book will be of use to educators. While all too familiar to veteran teachers, Feinstein has listed a number of common conflicts that create classroom management problems. They include not finishing work, bullying, tardiness, lying, failure to listen, disrespect, and overreaction to interpersonal situations. She also suggests that teachers often unintentionally add to the lack of engagement by adolescents in the classroom by giving vague directions and presenting boring lessons. A common occurrence in history classes is teachers taking part in unproductive verbal exchanges often in response to the question "Why do I need to know this?" Add to the mix adolescent sleep deprivation which leads to falling asleep in class, daydreaming, and difficulty paying attention or feeling tired during class.[41] Even the most innovative lesson led by a charismatic teacher will not succeed without a well-managed classroom based on informed practice that is built on sensible structure, realistic guidelines, and mutual respect.

While this chapter will not take further time to deliberate these 21st-century school realities, the teaching of history cannot ignore learning theories, the standards movement, high-stakes testing, or classroom management. As a result direct instruction may be preferred over inquiry teaching, the repetition of a few historical topics are favored over examining a wider variety of topics, and an emphasis of learning in order to pass a test rather than what history can mean to a student on the personal or civic level may occur. These scholarly and policy debates should and will continue. It is, though, apparent that these four topics and issues have resulted in the narrowing of instructional strategies and limiting the content examined in history classrooms.

There will be no attempt in these pages to grapple with the "social studies" versus "history" debate. This book will mainly use the term history, only occasionally referring to the social studies when the literature pertaining to history is framed as "social studies." History will be examined from a wider context than the political, economic, and military. The scholarship since the 1960s and 1970s, as Whelen has noted, has even moved beyond social history to areas such as women's studies, ethnic history, and community and family history to list but a few. Whelen has also argued that history is the core of the social studies curriculum. "The nature of human existence is essentially historical," he writes. "All peoples have always studied history" because "it explains who they are."[42]

One further assumption is made in this book. The teaching of history is both a science and an art. Statistics have added a dimension to history not previously available. Ever increasing demographic data on populations gives historians more information with which to work, and econometrics assist in better explaining economic downturns and expansions. Today's computers then allow historians to manage and manipulate such data bases, providing better analyses and context. But history remains an art as well. It is a story that is told in different ways by different historians. Judgment, sequence, connections, and literary style must all come into play, especially in trade books and textbooks, when illuminating the past for adolescents.

With these assumptions and observations in mind, we proceed to a number of suggestions that can be utilized to best engage the adolescent learner with history. The following can be categorized as methods, approaches, or strategies. These areas will only be successful, or partially successful, when they occur within a positive school climate that includes supportive and involved teachers, high expectations for students' conduct and achievement, and student engagement. The ideas will obviously work better when the student is active (working individually or within a group) rather than passive (listening or watching for an extended period of time with no direction.)[43]

The World of Practice
Looking for Mr. Wright
by Caryn Ellison

One of the great things about teaching in a self-contained elementary classroom is the opportunity to make connections within units of study. When I write units, I start with our state's academic standards. No matter what the focus of the unit is, I always look at all four subject areas (math, language arts, science, and social studies) so that connections can be made. Next I consider how to incorporate the different levels of thinking; I most often use Bloom's Taxonomy as a guide. I then give consideration to the various products I want my students to produce. Some products are required while others are self-selected by the students. These products are often pieces that can be used for evaluation purposes. And finally, I locate available resources, which includes print materials, people, places, and technology.

The setting of the novel *The Wright 3* by Blue Balliett, is Chicago, and the focus is an actual house built by Frank Lloyd Wright. Those of us in the Midwest are familiar with this famous architect, as many of his uniquely designed houses and buildings are located in Indiana, Illinois, and Wisconsin. I immediately sensed an opportunity for my students to read a good mystery story as well as learn about Frank Lloyd Wright. I thought it important for them to become knowledgeable about his unique style of architecture and how he drew inspiration from the geographical features of the Midwest. My unit idea was born: *Looking for Mr. Wright.*

After doing a little research, I discovered that the Robie House, which is at the center of the story, is located in Hyde Park, Illinois. In fact, most of the buildings in the story are within just a few blocks of each other in this neighborhood. It got even better when I discovered that the Robie House offered a tour especially tailored to the book my students would be reading! I drove to Chicago to tour the house myself and found every resource I would need in the Robie House gift shop. I then went to work designing an interdisciplinary unit that would encourage the students to read, write, research, and ultimately travel to the Robie House.

I believe a good question needs to be at the heart of learning. Not only was *Looking for Mr. Wright* a clever title, it was also the question that guided our study. *The Homes of Frank Lloyd Wright* is a DVD produced by the History Channel, and it introduced the students to the three structures that all served as homes and design studios for Mr. Wright. Using a viewing guide I created, they learned how each home connected to a different period in Mr. Wright's life. At the end of our study, I challenged them to consider which home was the best reflection or representation of his life and work.

Using the Curry-Samara Matrix Model for differentiating curriculum, I created a variety of activities that connected the different parts of our study. Examples include:

- Art glass is an integral part of Wright's designs. Students could create a design for an art glass window using the Fibonacci number series and share it with the class.

- Students could analyze their own house (or another familiar building) using Frank Lloyd Wright's principles of design and share their ideas through a compare and contrast chart.

- There was an opportunity to connect the art "dilemma" in the story to Hitler's effort to define art in Germany in 1939.

- The educational resource packet provided by the Robie House contained an easy-to-read floor plan. Since the footprint of this house is very definitive, the students wrote concrete poems about the house, using the house's outlined floor plan.

I purchased several nonfiction books to aid the students in their research and their desire to learn more: a biography written for young adults, architecture basics, and the most amazing pop-up book of many homes and buildings designed by Frank Lloyd Wright. Students were given the chance to pursue individual areas of interest and study as well as complete some selected projects. One of the more notable products was a PowerPoint tour of a student's favorite Wright buildings, including everything from Google maps to admission information. Interestingly enough, about two days after the student made his presentation, NBC news did a story on the Guggenheim Museum in New York City…which was one of his choices!

The culmination of this unit *had* to be a trip to Robie House. At this point, it almost felt like a pilgrimage! I wrote a grant proposal to pay for the admission costs, and as luck would have it, the train from South Bend to Chicago had a stop at 57th Street, which was six blocks from our destination. It was a very exciting Friday as one nervous teacher supervised twenty-six students and fourteen parents to visit the Robie House and walk through the adjacent neighborhood.

Did we ever find Mr. Wright? We couldn't help but NOT find him in so many different ways. At times, we had to remind ourselves what was fact and what was fiction. Not all of my units come together in such a unique and exciting way, but this one certainly set the bar just a little bit higher.

Caryn Ellison is a 5th & 6th grade gifted and talented teacher at Twin Branch Model School in Mishawaka, Indiana. This idea was named an award-winning project by the History Channel.

Endnotes

1   Dewey, John. *Experience and Education*. New York: Collier Books,1938. 23.
2   Juel, Connie, Heather Hebard, Julie Park Haubner, and Meredith Moran. "Reading Through a Disciplinary Lens." *Educational Leadership* 67. 6 (2010): 16.
3   Cuban, Larry. *Hugging the Middle—How Teachers Teach in an Era of Testing and Accountability*. New York: Teachers College Press, 2009. 69.
4   Taken from lecture by Howard Zinn taped for C-SPAN. *BookTV* 18 Jan. 2007.

5   Downey, Matthew T. and Linda S. Levstik. "Teaching and Learning History." Ed. James B. Shaver. *Handbook of Research on Social Studies Teaching and Learning.* New York: Macmillan, 1991. 407.

6   Loewen, James W. *Lies My Teacher Told Me: Everything Your American History Book Got Wrong.* 2nd ed. New York: Touchstone Simon & Schuster, Inc., 2007. 1. 330 and 340.

7   Goodlad, John I. *A Place Called School.* New York: McGraw-Hill,1984. 212.

8   Yazzie-Mintz, E. "Voices of Students on Engagement: A Report on the 2006 High School Survey of Student Engagement." Center for Evaluation and Education Policy, Indiana University. (2007) Retrieved from ERIC.

9   Turk, Diana, Rachel Mattson, Terrie Epstein, and Robert Cohen. *Teaching U.S. History: Dialogues among Social Studies Teachers and Historians.* New York: Routledge, 2010. 191.

10   Barton, Keith C. "Research on Student's Ideas about History." Ed. Linda S. Levstik, and Cynthia A. Tyson. *Handbook of Research in Social Studies Education.* New York: Routledge, 2008. 155

11   Haudan, J. *The Art of Engagement: Bridging the Gap Between People and Possibilities.* New York: McGraw-Hill, 2008. 29.

12   High, Janet and P. Gayle Andrews. "Engaging Students and Ensuring Success." *Middle School Journal* 41. 2. (2009): 58–63.

13   Porter, Susan Eva. *Relating to Adolescents: Educator in a Teenage World.* Lanham: Rowman and Littlefield Education, 2009. 11–14, 21, and 132.

14   See Brown, Dave F. and Trudy Knowles. *What Every Middle School Teacher Should Know.* 2nd ed. Portsmouth: Heinemann, 2000.

15   Cavanaught S., M. Girod, and M. Pardales. "By Teens, for Teachers: A Descriptive Study of Adolescence." *American Secondary Education* 33. 2 (2005): 4–19.

16   Johnson, Burke and Larry Christensen. *Educational Research: Quantitative, Qualitative, and Mixed Approaches.* 3rd ed. Thousand Oaks: Sage Publications, Inc., 2008. 422. See also David Tyack. *The One Best System: A History of American Urban Education.* Cambridge: Harvard University Press, 1990.

17   Barton, 240–43.

18   Krug, Mark M. *History and the Social Sciences.* Waltham, MA: Blaisdell, 1967. 4–5.

19   Ibid. 244–45.

20   Berg, B.L. *Quantitative Research Methods for the Social Sciences.* Boston: Allyn and Bacon, 1998.

21   Furay, Conal and Michael J. Salevouris. *The Methods and Skills of History: A Practical Guide.* Wheeling: Harlan Davidson, Inc., 2000. 6–7.

22   Barton, 246.

23   Johnson, Andrew P. *Making Connections in Elementary and Middle School Social Studies.* Thousand Oaks: Sage Publications, 2010. 255.

24   Ibid. xviii–xix.

25   Wineburg, Sam. *Historical Thinking and Other Unnatural Acts: Charting the Future of Teaching the Past.* Philadelphia: Temple University Press, 2001. See chapter 2 "The Psychology of Teaching and Learning the Past" pp. 28–59.

26   Feinstein, Sheryl G. *Secrets of the Teenage Brain: Research-Based Strategies for Reaching and Teaching Today's Adolescents.* 2nd ed. Thousand Oaks: Corwin, 2009. 3, 17

27   Larson, Bruce E. and Timothy A. Keiper. *Instructional Strategies for Middle and High School.* New York: Routledge, 2007. 6–7.

28 Carnine, David. "Why Education Experts Resist Effective Practices." April 2000 at the Thomas B. Fordham website <http://www.edexcellence.net>.

29 Marzano, Robert J. *Building Background Knowledge for Academic Achievement.* Arlington: Association for Supervision and Curriculum Development, 2004. 5, 24, and 35–40.

30 Oliva, Peter F. *Developing the Curriculum.* 6th ed. Boston: Allyn and Bacon, 2005. 364, 366.

31 Ibid.

32 Ibid.

33 Johnston, Howard. "Climate: Building a Culture of Achievement." *Schools in the Middle* (November–December, 1995): 10–15.

34 Brophy, Jere. *Motivating Students to Learn.* 3rd ed. New York: Routledge, 2009. 87–89; Ames, Carol. "Motivation: What Teachers Need to Know." *Teachers College Record*. 91 (2009): 409–21; and Epstein, Joyce. "Family Structure and Student Motivation." A Developmental Perspective." Ed. Carol Ames and Russell Ames. *Research on Motivation in Education. Volume 3: Goals and Cognitions.* San Diego: Academic Press, 1989. 259–95.

35 Brophy, 313, 315; and Keller, John. "Motivational Design of Instruction." Ed. Charles Reigluth. *Instructional-Design Theories and Models: An Overview of Their Current Status.* Hillsdale: Erlbaum, 1983. 383–434.

36 Beineke, John. *And There Were Giants in the Land: The Life of William Heard Kilpatrick.* New York: Peter Lang, 1998. 287–316.

37 Brady, Marion. "Cover the Material—Or Teach Students to Think." *Educational Leadership* 65. 5 (2008): 66.

38 See Bigelow, Bill. "Those Awful Texas Social Studies Standards." *Rethinking Schools* 24. 4 (2010): 46–48 and Weber, Paul J. "Experts: Texas Textbooks are Unlikely to Spread." *The Associated Press.* Retrieved 2 June 2010 at <http://www.ap.org/ >.

39 Ibid.

40 For a strong case against both the standards movement and the attendant testing milieu see Wineburg, Sam. "What does NCATE Have to Say to Future History Teachers? Not Much." *Phi Delta Kappan* 86. 9 (2005): 658–65. For an in-depth examination of state history testing practices that opens with O.L. Davis's blunt statement, "The idea of 'measuring' history can only be ludicrous," (p.vii) See *Measuring History: Cases of State Level Testing Across the United States.* Ed. S.G. Grant. Greenwich: Information Age Publishing, 2006. And also Kohn, Alfie. *The Case Against Standardized Testing: Raising the Scores and Ruining the Schools.* Portsmouth: Heinemann, 2000.

41 Feinstein, 60, 114.

42 Whelen, Michael. "History as Core of Social Studies Education." E. Wayne Ross. *The Social Studies Curriculum: Purposes, Problems, and Possibilities.* Albany: State University of New York Press, 1997. 33, 36.

43 Rutter, Michael M. "School Effects on Pupil Progress: Research Findings and Policy Implications." *Child Development* 54. 1–29 and Sirin, Selcuk R. and Lauren Rogers-Sirin. "Components of School Engagement among African-American Adolescents." *Applied Developmental Science*, 9 (2005): 5–13 and Shernoff, David J. and Mihaly Csikszentmihalyi. "Student Engagement in High School Classrooms from the Perspective of Flow Theory." *School Psychology Quarterly*, 18 (2003): 158–76.

Two

Gaining Historical Knowledge:
Textbooks and Primary Sources

The Use and Misuse of Textbooks

"Throughout the history of education in the United States, one type of text-book or another has dominated the curriculum." So states curriculum specialist Ken Henson.[1] Marion Brady, a teacher and author, has used words even stronger than "dominate" to describe his beliefs about textbooks:

> Notwithstanding their ever-expanding size and weight, marginal notes, extravagant color, text-box gimmickry, supportive extras, and appalling cost, they're still textbooks, just glitzed-up versions of the read-and-remember, answer-the-questions-at-the-end-of-the-chapter tools they were a century ago.[2]

Data support the assertions of both Henson and Brady. In a review of the research on textbooks, Michael Apple has reported that they are in fact crucial to the curriculum for several reasons. Textbooks are constitutive (essential) parts of the curriculum in most schools. Nearly all research on textbooks documents their central location as the primary curricular artifact—and in many places, in essence, the curriculum. Research has reported that nearly 50% of student time in public schools is related to textbook use with students in history classes spending a majority of their time with a textbook. And it is estimated that 80% of teachers use textbooks in their classroom as a primary curricular device with 80–90% of classroom and homework assignments textbook-driven or textbook-centered.[3]

The textbook is indeed often the centrality of the curriculum, especially the history curriculum. While there are critics of textbooks, and their views will be explored in this chapter, Henson has suggested reasons why textbooks hold a central place in classrooms. He has pointed out that textbooks provide organization for the curriculum, that they can be a good starting point for building curriculum, and that they increasingly align with state standards, frameworks, and benchmarks. He contends that the definition of "textbook" has expanded in many districts to include non-textbook instructional materials such as primary source readers in the history classroom. Henson does warn, though, that textbooks should never become the sole source of the curriculum and strongly suggests the use of supplemental materials.[4]

Ryan and Cooper believe that textbooks have *de facto* become "the national curriculum." In their widely used introduction to education textbooks, they tell teacher education students that most of what teachers and students do in the classroom is textbook-related. Materials that accompany many of the newer editions—such as lesson plans, websites, and learning activities—make textbooks attractive to teachers. And yet the use of textbooks is not without criticism and controversy. Ryan and Cooper report that the content of textbooks and the textbook adoption process is highly political in some states, especially the South. And there is the accusation of lack of expertise in curriculum by boards of education—both state and local—in the adoption of textbooks.[5]

In terms of pedagogy, there are other critics who believe that textbooks have been "dumbed down" to meet lower reading level standards, leaving them less interesting and stilted in their narratives. Textbooks may try to "cover" too much material, thereby lacking the depth that assists students in understanding ideas, concepts, and substance. And the debate between textbooks (a secondary source in history) and primary sources (first-hand accounts such as letters, diaries, and oral histories) is ongoing.[6]

Ornstein and Levine agree that textbooks can dominate the scope, nature, and sequence of a course and have a profound impact on students' learning. They also believe, as others do, that textbooks can have limitations. They concur with other critics that textbooks tend to be bland, general, and noncontroversial, aimed at the greatest number of average students. Textbooks, in fields such as history, can also quickly become outdated. In addition, textbooks, as Loewen and others argue, can reflect the author's lack of knowledge and bias. By aiming at the greatest number of students—"the average"—textbooks may fail to meet the needs and interests of many students. Summarization, something that occurs frequently within history textbooks, often leads to superficiality that discourages conceptual thinking, critical analysis, and evaluation of the material at hand.[7]

Yet Ornstein and Levine do see advantages to textbooks such as their capacity to provide teachers with outlines for planning lessons, the gathering in one place of pertinent information, and supplying teachers with a common resource for all students in their classes. In addition, textbooks conveniently include photographs, graphs, and maps that facilitate learning for visually oriented learners. And increasingly, textbooks offer a plethora of resources especially through new web-based materials.[8]

There have been suggestions as to how to improve textbooks. One study undertaken by a group of researchers with early adolescents recommended the rewriting of history textbooks to better connect a cause to an event and an event to a consequence. In other words, textbooks just did not explain things very well. They provided an example. Textbook version: "In 1763 Britain and the colonies ended a 7-year war with the French and the Indians." Re-written version: About 250 years ago, Britain and France both claimed to own some pieces of land, here, in North America." The finding showed a slight increase in understanding for students with the re-written passage.[9] This finding may be more informative for textbook writers and publishers than teachers who do not have the time to rework, rephrase, and modify words, syntax, and passages in history texts. But it does point to the problem of clarity of the written word in our text-dominated history classrooms.

The accurate but often forgotten idea regarding textbooks is that they are a form of media—a means of mass communication. The term mass has not been lost on publishers. Selwyn and Maher make this point in their recommendation that students think of textbooks as media and analyze them as such. Some of the features and areas of history textbooks that are in need of scrutiny and evaluation by educators include:

- Does the textbook have a theme and connections or is it merely a series of episodes?

- What can be gleaned from the titles of the chapters?

- Is the fact that there is diversity of thought and point of view, even among groups such as Native Americans, evident?

- Is historical controversy among historians or even the authors present in the textbook?

- How does the textbook—not the teacher—expect students to become engaged with the material?[10]

James W. Loewen's *Lies My Teacher Told Me: Everything Your American History Textbook Got Wrong*, provocative title and all, surveys in a scholarly manner the failures and fallacies of current history textbooks. Loewen provides a number of germane points regarding history textbooks that cannot be discounted. These include breadth and depth of content, organization of material, and special features such as photographs, maps, summaries, and reference tools. He notes that textbooks can be terminology and information dense, user (student) unfriendly in terms of readability and interest, uneven in treatment of certain historical periods (especially recent times and events), and, unfortunately, factually incorrect.[11]

Novelist Sarah Shun Lien Bynum in her novel about a middle school teacher has mildly ridiculed the recent penchant for locating and pointing out errors in our textbooks. She writes about her fictional teacher Ms. Hempel's thoughts on the practice:

> Ms. Hempel realized that a small industry had sprung up, whose sole purpose was to reveal the lies and hoaxes of American history. Paul Revere did not shout 'The British are coming!' Thomas Jefferson did not seduce and impregnate Sally Hemings, his slave. The Founding Fathers were not the least bit interested in equality for all. And mad John Brown was perfectly sane. Ms. Hempel felt irritated and betrayed . . . here was a whole shelf of scholarship casting doubt on everything that she was about to teach.[12]

Irritating to Ms. Hempel or not, Loewen has on a number of occasions been right about historical accuracy and textbooks. And it appears from all the evidence that Ms. Hempel's source on Thomas Jefferson and Sally Hemings got it wrong.

In one of his other books, Loewen has written that textbooks in 70% of history classes bore students, that they do not learn much from them, and that they widen the achievement gap between genders, races, and socio-economic classes. He adds that textbooks cause students to learn meaningless "twigs" as he calls them or what might be labeled historical factoids. College professors, Loewen maintains, find these historical facts often pointless for college freshmen. And yet students spend more time with their textbooks in history classes than any other subject.[13]

One possible antidote to the disinterest in textbooks would be increased student involvement in their selection. In an unscientific survey of the textbook selection process, teachers and administrators in the author's graduate middle level curriculum courses were asked if students had a role in choosing the textbooks they would be using. Having asked hundreds of educators this question, there have been almost none that include students in the process. Reasons range from "we have never done it that way" or "we don't know why" to "sounds like a reasonable idea" and "we might try it sometime." As will be seen in the chapter on using nonfiction and fiction to support and reinforce the teaching of history, self-selected reading encourages reading. The same might very well hold true by involving students in the textbook selection process.

Providing adolescent readers with structure is critical when utilizing text-books. The International Reading Association has published an expansive number of examples of what have previously been labeled "study guides" to assist in this undertaking. *Guiding Readers Through Text: Strategy Guides for New Times* draws from research on effective reading practices and comprehension. This work includes interactive reading guides, profiler guides, inquiry guides, and listening/viewing guides to be used in conjunction with textbooks and media.[14]

There is also the issue of "coverage" within history textbooks. Loewen reports that in the 1940s the Civil War was located in the second half of most history courses.[15] It is now common in year-long American history high school courses to complete the first semester at the conclusion of Reconstruction. A similar division is found within two-semester college courses—American history before 1877 and American history after 1877. The problem is that this has been the configuration since the 1960s and we have had forty to fifty additional years of history since then. And the half-century includes a number of important topics such as the Vietnam War, Watergate, the fall of the Berlin Wall and Soviet domination of eastern Europe, multiple military actions in the Middle East, and the election of the first Black president. Either realignment or a reduction in attempting to "cover" everything needs to be considered. Yet this is more a subject matter selection issue for teachers than a problem with textbooks. Textbooks do include within their pages material on recent history.

Five randomly selected history textbooks from local school districts were examined in the preparation of this chapter.[16] This review of textbooks used in middle schools and the early high school years affirms the concern as to the large (literally) size of current adoptions. (The average weight was just shy of 5 pounds.) But as for more substantive criticisms of textbooks there are two global observations or concerns: segmentation and style. Even on a cursory inspection of text-books it is readily evident that there is a serious problem with what might be called "segmentation." The narrative, what there is of it in textbooks, is interrupted with boxes and sidebars of questions, lists, maps, terms, skill sets, charts and graphs, mini-biographies, assorted activities, and reviews. Even that list is not complete. It seems as though the authors are vying for the student's attention—"Look here. No, read this first. Now glance at this. Don't miss this picture over here."

Some editions try to reduce these "interruptions." Textbooks used in Advanced Placement (AP) courses seem to "calm" things down a bit by using longer narratives and fewer visuals. (AP history texts are often slightly revised versions of college texts. The AP textbooks, no doubt due to following collegiate publication schedules, also seem to revise their volumes more frequently than the middle and high school history texts.) Visuals are essential. But in this day and age of sound-bites and short attention spans, segmented textbooks may need to revisit their mission. Maybe, as will be explored next, narratives are deficient in style due to lack of space as they are edged out by all the other "bells and whistles" of current textbooks.

The other global observation would be the prevalent mundane writing style of textbook authors. The more engaging textbooks, again, are the AP volumes. It is not really an issue of "readability" with AP texts using longer words and sentences. In fact, the vocabulary is actually not that much different. Here are two samples, both drawn from the introductory paragraphs of textbooks introducing chapters on the 1920s. The first selection is from the non-AP Davidson, Castillo, and Stoff's *The American Nation*:

> In the decade after World War I, Presidents Harding and Coolidge encouraged business growth. The economy grew rapidly as factories churned out new consumer goods, and stock prices soared. American society also changed dramatically. Inexpensive cars and a wide variety of new products for the home became available for the first time. Manners became freer. Young people danced to a wild, new music call jazz. Not all Americans shared in the good times of the boom years. Even for those Americans who seemed fortunate, trouble loomed ahead.[17]

The second selection is from Kennedy and Cohen's *The American Pageant*, which is an AP textbook:

> The boom of the golden twenties showered genuine benefits on Americans, as incomes and living standards rose for many. But there seemed to be something incredible about it all, even as people sang,

> *My sister she works in the laundry,*
> My father sells bootlegger gin,
> My mother she takes in the washing,
> My God! How the money rolls in!

> New technologies, new consumer products, and new forms of leisure and entertainment made the twenties roar. Yet just beneath the surface lurked widespread anxieties about the future and fear that America was losing sight of its traditional ways.[18]

Kennedy and Cohen use words and phrases that are much more descriptive—golden, incredible, lurked, bootlegger. In comparison, the Davidson book uses words such as soared, wild, and freer. In addition, Kennedy and Cohen employ a catchy song of the era (a primary source) to capture the feeling of the time. As will be seen in a future chapter on the use of works of nonfiction, skillful and talented writing will engage students. Bland textbook writing that fails to bring history alive is a poor substitute in the publishing industry already under fire from many quarters.

While some textbooks are both exhaustive (and at times exhausting), a recent move in the history textbook industry has been the use of "brief" or "short" histories. Some, such as the Center for Civic Education's *We the People* and *Project Citizen*, are what could be termed "focused textbooks" that target specific issues such as constitutional democracy and public policy within the framework of an historical context.[19] Although abbreviated, they usually do not sacrifice accuracy. The downside is that they must often forego photographs and other visuals that make full-length textbook treatments more appealing to the student. They also lose the content that falls outside the political, military, and economic arenas such as the cultural and social components of our history—or at least offer them less space. Yet to counter the above criticisms of history textbooks, the use of an abbreviated history text with accompanying resources such as visuals and primary sources may be a better response to current concerns on these apparently obligatory, even compulsory, educational tools. In the final analysis textbooks need to be improved upon rather than jettisoned.

While textbooks, in some form, will be part of the history classroom in the foreseeable future, there are novel and innovative trends on the horizon. Some of these, reported by Richard Hull, Executive Director of the Text and Academic Author Association, include rental or open (free) textbooks online, smaller textbooks functioning as guidebooks to Internet-based resources, E-textbooks, and Wikipedia-type texts that allow for interactive/additive features. Another option now available is the customized history textbook that allows districts and possibly teachers to select the chapters and primary sources they wish to include in "their" textbook. It has even been suggested that student-authored textbooks will appear where students write and build a textbook as a classroom project.[20]

Kozol points out that student-written textbooks are nothing new. Two examples that he provides are textbooks created by students in the South during the Civil Rights era. Rather than "Dick and Jane-like" books they were the stories of the struggles and rebellions of Blacks. And in the labor union movement, "counter-textbooks" were also produced. This is not the history of power, privilege, and pleasure or of presidents, generals, financiers, and inventors. But rather what Kozol calls "history from the bottom up"—the exploiters and murderers of the Native Americans; steel, coal and railroad workers' unions; frontline soldiers in the nation's wars; and the staffs of clinics in the inner cities. (This is similar to Howard Zinn's approach to teaching history that will be explored later in this book.) Comic books (also examined later) and self-published newspapers and magazines with strong points of view are encouraged by Kozol.[21]

As for web-linked textbooks, Harvard history professor Niall Ferguson has helped create a World War II strategy game that will be linked to a still-in-development "web-enabled" textbook that integrates his lectures with data, images, and mini-games for students. Ferguson is best known as a "counterfactual historian"—a historian who explores the "what ifs" of history. Publishers, according to Ferguson and his software partner Dave McCool, were not interested five years ago in multimedia textbooks. Attention is being focused on Ferguson and McCool's work now, though, due to new economic realities in publishing and the low student opinion of traditional textbooks. Initial estimates are for the production of 50,000 to 100,000 copies of the game. One place the game will definitely be used is Ferguson's undergraduate history course at Harvard.[22]

Textbooks, because the written word often takes on an indisputable aura of factuality, are frequently viewed as "truth." One strategy that has enlightened students is to view historical events through the lens of textbooks from other nations. The nuances of how the story is told can help students make comparisons and analyze alternate viewpoints found in these textbooks. (French, Vietnamese, Canadian, and American comparisons of the Vietnam War in these nations' respective textbooks are examples.) *History Lessons: How Textbooks from Around the World Portray U.S. History*[23] is an excellent source for readings from these international textbooks.

DeRose has suggested that historical thinking such as bias, reliability of sources, and how historians decide and construct their narratives can be observed by examining these international texts. Questions recommended by DeRose include: How are accounts similar and how are they different? What perspectives and biases can be detected in the textbooks? What makes an account from one textbook more reliable than another? Can textbooks be relied upon to explain history? How can the historian finally decide?[24]

It should be noted that there are history teachers who teach without textbooks. And there are a growing number of advocates for teachers "winging it" when it comes to teaching history. Yohuru Rashied Williams has written a book titled *Teaching U.S. History Beyond the Textbook: Six Investigative Strategies, Grades 5–12*. Using the theme of the highly popular crime scene investigation (CSI) television series, Williams provides six examples and strategies of how to teach absent the ubiquitous textbook. Among the activities are treating historical episodes as "cold cases"—cases that have never been solved. In what would be mini-research assignments, students follow the CSI approach of identifying the person or event, establish the ESP (economic, social, or political) importance of the person, select sources to be used in the investigation, and set up a chronology of the events.

Williams also uses a criminal justice system connection by looking at SCOTUS—the Supreme Court of the United States. Of the three branches of government, students and adults alike know the least about the judicial branch. Using selected court cases (primary sources), which can be challenging for some students, the class follows the course of major decisions. SCOTUS assignments are definitely more work for the teacher. Cases often need to be located and edited, state content standards need to be connected to the cases selected, and guest speakers on legal issues often need to be located.[25] These "textbook-less" strategies do, though, get away from the limited outlines or reviews on historical material found in textbooks.

A final word on the culture of textbooks. As has been demonstrated, textbooks play a major role in the curriculum. Therefore, history teachers should be highly engaged in the process of textbook adoption. It is not outlandish to suggest that teachers prepare themselves to go through the textbook adoption process. This can take the form of professional development sessions. Teachers should also be ready to ask questions about textbooks and the process. These would include: What is the ideal role of textbooks in learning? Is diversity (beyond the "heroes and holidays" approach) present in the history textbooks being considered? What are the pivotal questions that textbook representatives should be asked about their products? How can students be involved in the textbook adoption process? And finally, who are the authors of the textbooks?

As practice and research have demonstrated, textbooks are controversial—cherished by some educators and eschewed by others. But they remain a major component of schooling that cannot be totally ignored by history teachers. Textbooks will be used in the teaching of history, although many teachers across the country are effective without them. The focus when using textbooks needs to be on the purposes for which they are employed. When used creatively they can give structure and information to students. When not, they can add to the student belief that history lacks both importance and relevance.

Primary Sources

The use of primary sources has been viewed as central to the teaching of history at all levels, but especially for adolescents. A primary source has been defined as any form of documentation that was created by a direct witness or, in some way, directly involved or related to an historical event.[26] The most recognizable primary sources that historians use are diaries, letters, memoirs, and oral histories. Additional examples include government documents, court records, birth and death records, statistical data, speeches, debates, music, literature, photographs, interviews, brochures, films and literature. Even items such as a telephone book, postcards, logos or advertisements, posters and T-shirt designs can be considered primary sources. Two outstanding locations to retrieve primary sources would be the National Archives and the National Council for the Social Studies' professional journal *Social Education*, which publishes within its pages "Teaching with Documents."[27]

The reliance on textbooks, a secondary source rather than a primary source, remains a dominant starting place and foundation in history classrooms. But it is not an "either/or"—primary or secondary source—choice for teachers; rather it is a "both." Hicks and his colleagues have found that over half of the social studies teachers surveyed did employ primary sources in their courses.[28]

Singleton and Pereira have provided what may be the most persuasive rationale for the use of primary documents:

> Primary source documents can be a key element in conversation and deliberation. They lend authenticity to student consideration of issues facing our democracy and stimulate student interests. In addition, a conversation about primary documents leads to a much deeper understanding of that document and can raise authentic questions for further exploration.[29]

A number of pivotal questions need to be asked by the teacher selecting primary sources. These include: Is the primary source one that the student will be able to relate to and/or understand in any way? Is the primary source directly related to the lesson? How can the primary source serve as motivation for the student compared to other materials that might be used in the lesson?

The use of primary sources actually allows the student to become engaged in the historical inquiry and reasoning process used in analyzing these pieces of evidence. Adolescents, especially older adolescents, are able to sift through these primary sources to create a narrative. Some have called it thinking as historians or disciplinary literacy. This disciplinary history approach provides a framework for curricular design and classroom instruction according to Ravi. Ravi has written:

> Because history has multiple meanings and definitions, learning history must include understanding the sources of these meanings and articulating them. By learning to interpret and contextualize a historical document, compare it to other documents, and extrapolate ideas from those documents, students learn how texts are understood and interpreted and how evidence is marshaled to support a historical argument.[30]

Although debated by some as to whether they are truly primary sources, newspapers and magazines provide a fairly uncomplicated way to incorporate primary sources in the teaching history. Newspapers are accessible in microfilm form or on the Internet. Original editions of magazines, such as *Time* or *Newsweek,* are often archived in university and public libraries. One primary source lesson used by the author asks students to find an article from the World War II era (1939–1945.) They make a copy of the article they select from the microfilm, if a newspaper, or the actual magazine if available. Students then provide an overview of the article followed by an evaluation of their thoughts on the article in the context of today. Two frequent observations that students make in doing this assignment are that newspapers of the prior era are more text-dense per page than their counterparts today and that the reading level of the newspapers and magazines is markedly higher.

While not new in the teaching of history, transcribed or recorded interviews—oral histories—are still valuable to students studying the past. The approach can teach the need for preliminary research before undertaking an interview, the framing of questions within the interview, and then sorting or analyzing the material that emerges from the interview. The last step calls for evaluation, authentication, and judgment as to what was important in the interview and whether the interviewee was a reliable and helpful source to the project.

Primary sources can be challenging for the adolescent learner. Direction and assistance from the teacher are critical for students to successfully draw on and make use of primary sources. Multiple avenues, such as guiding questions, are available for teachers in this arena. Questions to be used when working with primary sources, such as photographs, might include: What title would you give this picture? List three to five words that describe what you see in the photograph. What does the photograph tell you about the period of history when it was taken? A photograph, for example, of a young Civil War soldier—clearly too young to be fighting and looking none too happy about being in uniform—can lead to hypotheses and creative writing activities by students.

Other considerations when using primary sources in the adolescent history classroom are the need to edit or abbreviate the primary sources, the readability levels of the documents, and providing concepts and background for the primary source. An example of the readability issue would be the possible variance in language and vocabulary used in a primary source of a century or more ago compared to today. One may not need to go back that far to potentially baffle 21st-century adolescents. "Groovy," "neat," and "cool" from the 1960s would be alien and probably seem silly to most students today.

One aspect of primary sources that must be kept in mind is the issue of reliability. Just because it is in a primary source does not mean it is accurate, real, or dependable. But this too can be a potentially useful characteristic of primary sources. Having students question, evaluate, and judge a primary source can be a constructive learning strategy. An often-used example of this point is the conflicting accounts of the "Boston Massacre" by both British and colonial soldiers present at the scene. Another example would be examining the documents of secession drawn up by states such as South Carolina and Virginia that provided their justifications for leaving the Union.

As noted above, working with primary sources, especially in the area of oral history, can be challenging to students and demands a certain amount of discipline and maturity. But some projects have been successful. Projects in the field of military history are popular, but must be addressed with sophistication and sensitivity. A middle level student or older adolescent's simple question to a veteran may bring back to the interviewee memories that the person may not wish to revisit. Guidance in this arena can be found within four exemplary projects. The Veterans History Project of the Library of Congress, the U.S. Army Military History Institute, the Army Heritage and Education Center, and U.S. Army Center of Military History are all resources and have readily accessible websites. Support materials include background and contextual information and surveys and questionnaires for student use. In addition, examples of primary sources are available at these sites. The following organizations all have websites that will prove useful to students studying military-related content: Veterans of Foreign Wars of the United States, American Legion, American Veterans, Disabled American Veterans, American Ex-Prisoners of War, and the Military Officers Association of America.[31]

One additional military primary source is the World War II Army Enlistment Records. They contain approximately nine million women and men who enlisted in the United States Army between 1939 and 1946, including the Women's Army Auxiliary Corp. Data include name, state, county, place of enlistment, date of enlistment, grade, Army branch, term of enlistment, place of birth, age, education, civilian occupation, and marital status. The records of the Japanese Americans relocated during World War II are also available.[32]

An additional unique rationale for the use of primary sources has been to promote "empathy." Research has suggested that the use of primary sources allows students to gain an understanding of a particular historical period not readily available by traditional secondary sources. Primary sources have the potential to provide an avenue for students to empathize with the ideas, values, and beliefs of women and men from the past.[33] An example would be photographs from the Great Depression of the 1930s or the Mississippi Delta in the 1960s that display egregious documentation of poverty and malnutrition.

There are, as has been seen, multiple locations and venues for primary sources. Many textbooks have primary source documents that accompany the text. An outstanding source that has been updated and revised over the years by historians such as Henry Steele Commager, Alan Nevins, and Stephen Ambrose is *Witness to America: A Documentary History of the United States from the Revolution to Today*. Popular historian Douglas Brinkley has edited the most recent edition. The strength of this particular resource is the selection of "voices" that include the unknown as well as the famous. For example, one entry is by Connie Dvorkin, a high school student writing in 1970. Titled "A Teenage Girl Contemplates Feminism in Suburbia,"[34] Dvorkin describes her campaign to enroll in a shop class rather than home economics. The volleys between her and the school administration are highly enlightening as to how America worked and did not work for an adolescent unwilling to accept the status quo due to her gender.

Other entries in *Witness to America* include sports writer Roger Kahn telling of Jackie Robinson breaking the color line when he joined the Brooklyn Dodgers in 1947. Broadcast pioneer and icon Edward R. Murrow in 1959 gives his opinion on what television can and cannot do for the American public. ("It is a limited medium; it can amuse, entertain, and it can sell goods. It can also arouse curiosity, stimulate interest, cause the viewer to read and argue. It can stretch the horizon of his interest. But it can't reason—and is no substitute for reading."[35]) There is also the World War II correspondent Ernie Pyle telling the folks back in the United States what war is really like for the G.I.s on the frontline. And an immigrant who crossed the U.S. and Mexican border as a child tells her story. The entries in *Witness to America* are diverse and powerful.

Not all primary sources are to be found in print. Teachers can employ artifacts which are also primary sources. Schramm suggests how an Edison cylinder record produced in 1908 and secured for five dollars at an antique store can be used to teach about technology. Technology, as Schramm observes, is not always the "electronic devices, whose origins and inner workings are largely masked from the human eye." Students can see and handle the Edison record and its cardboard sleeve. The licensing agreement on that sleeve is similar to what is seen in the fine print of modern CDs. The artifact "resonates deeply with students raised in an age of pirated music downloads."

In addition to smaller artifacts that can be held in the student's hand, Schramm recommends military museums that often house a variety of larger artifacts from jeeps to tanks to airplanes. (The role of the public history will be explored in a later chapter.) Ft. Leonard Wood in Missouri has a World War II-era barracks and mess hall. Finally, technology can be observed at the ever-growing railroad museums. It is not just the usual locomotives and cabooses. Some museums have passenger cars (also known as Pullmans) that still display the divided "white" and "colored" sections. Such an example demonstrates how "artifacts that fill our material world are expressions of the broader society."[36]

For all the advocacy of primary sources, Keith Barton has challenged history teachers to be critical users of these materials. While labeling original sources as a "centerpiece of the history classroom," Barton points out that primary sources must be used selectively. As an example he observes that having students read the Northwest Ordinance solely to find out that slaves had to be returned to their owners may not be as effective as just telling students this fact. In contrast, Barton has found that showing a photograph of coal miners in the 1920s is much more valuable in students' understanding of miners' strikes than laboriously describing or even reading about the event. Another example of the selective use of primary sources is having students read or view Martin Luther King, Jr.'s "I Have a Dream" speech rather than the teacher attempting to describe the importance of the March on Washington in 1963.[37]

Barton has a point on the use of primary sources. The author once observed a lesson in a girls' high school in the midlands of England on Woodrow Wilson's Fourteen Points. While the term "torment" would be an exaggeration, the word "anguish" would not. The teacher slogged through each point, most of which would be little remembered or even needed by the students to gain an adequate understanding of the World War I peace process. With the teacher literally sweating his way through the lesson, the young women with glazed eyes endured the lesson for an hour. It was painful to witness.

An excellent use of primary sources that crosses over into both diversity and controversial topics is the case study of Abraham Lincoln's words on the issues of Blacks and slavery. The primary source documents of the 1858 Lincoln-Douglas Debates are replete with quotes that most Americans today would find repugnant. And they come from the Great Emancipator. Wineburg has provided the original documents and an outline approach to teaching from these primary sources.[38]

Howard Zinn, the late "people's historian," published a companion volume of primary sources to his *A People's History of the United States* titled *Voices of a People's History of the United States*.[39] It is not that there is a lack of primary sources. As noted above, *Social Education* has been publishing primary source material for history lessons for over twenty years. And textbooks increasingly include primary sources in their supplementary materials. But, as Libresco points out, Zinn's volume provides a number of critical additions not found in most primary sources collections. First, of Zinn's collection of 200 documents, almost half of them are from the modern, post-World War II era, a period often given short shrift in history courses. And second, the collection "gives voice to those left out of mainstream history books, the nonwhite, the non-wealthy, the non-powerful, the non-male."[40]

Zinn's compilation draws on excerpts from songs, poems, novels, autobiographies, speeches, eyewitness accounts, petitions, testimonies, and essays. In addition, Zinn has saved the teacher a great deal of time even if they had used the Internet. For example we find Martin Luther King's sermon given at New York City's Riverside Church on the Vietnam War and Mark Twain's condemnation of America's occupation of the Philippines in 1899. Also found in the volume are gems such as Angelina Grimke Weld's testimony in 1838 against slavery ("I have seen it—I have seen it. I know it has horrors that can never be described.") And an 1844 letter from Henry Bibb, former slave writing to his former owner from Canada "If you should ever chance to be traveling this way, and will call on me, I will use you better than you did me while you held me as a slave." In Zinn's own words, "More important than who sits in the White House is who sits outside it."[41]

Examples of primary sources are growing. Eleanor Roosevelt, in addition to her role as First Lady to her husband Franklin D. Roosevelt, was also a journalist. In the magazine *Woman's Home Companion* she solicited the views of citizens. She wrote, "I want you to write to me. I want you to tell me about the particular problems which puzzle or sadden you, but I also want you to write me about what has brought joy into your life." In the year 1933 alone she received an estimated 300,000 letters. These letters, written during the Great Depression, are a window into the lives of families in the areas of their financial needs such as food, clothing, and shelter; their health problems such as polio and tuberculosis; and their hopes for education and what the future might hold. These letters allow students to see the connection between the personal struggles of citizens at the time and the policies of the federal government in the New Deal to address these challenges.[42]

An amazing and yet simple place to discover primary sources is through the history teachers' own personal and professional readings. While usually not directly a part of formal history standards, the exploration of the lives and events surrounding gangsters and outlaws of the 1930s sheds light on the Great Depression. Many outlaws like John Dillinger, Lester Joseph Gillis (a.k.a. Baby Face Nelson), George "Machine Gun" Kelly, and Charles Arthur "Pretty Boy" Floyd gained notoriety, if not celebrity, in their often brief lives. Two popular yet scholarly biographies of the Depression-era bank robbers and killers, Clyde Barrow and Bonnie Parker, were published in 2009. One of the books contains multiple primary sources such as letters, poems, and transcripts of telephone wiretaps. Clyde Barrow, who always stole Ford V-8 automobiles, wrote a letter to Henry Ford complimenting the automaker on the quality of his cars and how effective they were in outrunning police officers. There is some controversy over whether Clyde actually wrote the letter as expert opinion is mixed. Ford actually responded to the letter, but of course the Postal Service had no more luck tracking Barrow down than law officials had at the time. Bonnie Parker wrote a poem that she gave to her mother shortly before her death. (She and Clyde were apparently resigned to the fact they would be killed.) Titled "The End of the Line" and later known as "The Story of Bonnie and Clyde" it had sixteen stanzas from which two of the following are taken:

> You've read the Story of Jesse James—
> Of how he lived and died;
> If you're still in need
> Of something to read
> Here's the story of Bonnie and Clyde.
>
> Some day they'll go down together;
> And they'll bury them side by side
> To a few it'll be grief—
> To the law a relief—
> But it's death for Bonnie and Clyde

There were also in the last days of their lives wiretaps placed on the phones of their relatives in West Dallas, Texas. As a primary source they provide insight into the topics of conversation and manner of speech of people in the 1930s and how a code was used on the telephone by the families to set up meetings with their outlaw relatives. These primary sources, taken from the last days before their violent death, only added to their legend at the time as they did again for a new generation in Warren Beatty's and Faye Dunaway's 1967 film *Bonnie and Clyde*.[43]

Possibly the best supply of primary sources (and increasing all the time) can be mined from the Library of Congress (LC), the largest library in the world. In addition to books, the LC collects maps, audio and video recordings, photographs, and other printed materials. Not all material, of course, is available on the LC website http://www.loc.gov. The American Memory collection is available at the website in the LC's Digital Collections and Exhibits. On the LC website there is a section called "Tools for Teachers" with teaching information, activity sheets, and lesson plans.[44]

A prime example of how the American Memory LC primary sources can be used is found in Bobbi Ireland's *Abraham Lincoln and His Era: Using the American Memory Project to Teach with Primary Sources*. (Some items in the American Memory Collection LC website do have copyright restrictions.) Two lessons that demonstrate the range of the collection are an "Eyewitness Account of President Lincoln's Assassination" and a "Letter from Ulysses S. Grant about the First African American Troops." The former is an account written by James S. Knox on April 15, 1865—the day Lincoln was shot. The second is a letter to Lincoln from Grant written on August 23, 1863, in connection with raising Black regiments to deploy in the Union army in the South. The lessons are for middle level students and Ireland includes objectives, timeframes, standards, ideas for implementation, and rubrics.[45]

Wyman has adapted from the Library of Congress a series of questions that can be used with students when they are working with primary sources.[46] The objective of the questions is to engage the student in judging the reliability and quality of the primary sources. The student may not be able to respond to all or any of these questions, but it allows for questioning the motive, authenticity, and status of the primary source under review. Samples of these questions include:

- Who created the source and why?

- Did the author have first-hand knowledge of the event or did the author report what others saw and heard?

- Was the author a neutral party or did the creator have opinions or interests that might have influenced what was recorded?

• Can the information in the narrative be corroborated by another source?

Shirley Engle in his classic look at using primary sources—and secondary as well—provides a comprehensive template for exploring all primary sources. He has suggested five questions students and teachers should pursue. First, when and why was it written? Second, whose viewpoint is presented? Third, is the account believable? Fourth, is the account supported by other sources? And fifth, after reading the document or viewing the image, how is one supposed to feel about the America that has been presented?[47] Using these questions, along with the other suggestions in this chapter, can make the use of primary sources an indispensable source to adolescents to gain historical knowledge.

The World of Practice
The Power of Primary Sources
by Don Maness

Primary sources can play an important role in the overall learning process in teaching history or social studies in the K–12 setting or college and university levels. Primary sources allow students and teachers, alike, the opportunity to share, discuss and learn directly from the words of a person or an historical document. So often in the K–12 environment, students are assigned worksheets to complete. These assignments may or may not assist with the learning process. However, worksheets usually do not provide students with information or understanding regarding how specific individuals in history interrelated and interconnected to make us the people and country we are today. I strongly believe and advocate that using primary sources may engage students within history or social studies classes and provide them with active learning opportunities.

Primary sources abound with a multitude of information about the history of the United States. Teachers will have many choices as they prepare to use primary sources for a class or unit assignment. However, some teachers may want to select their own primary source materials. Looking at 19th-century U.S. history/social studies, for example, a teacher may want to compare and/or contrast the Missouri Compromise with the Compromise of 1850. How did the country change socially, politically, and economically during that 30 years? Works that could be included are Henry David Thoreau's "Civil Disobedience" and Frederick Douglass's article "*What to a Slave is the Fourth of July?*" July 5, 1852. Other noteworthy sources for teaching events in history include Lincoln's Gettysburg Address, Washington's Farewell Address, and Martin Luther King's "I Have a Dream" speech. Another example would be to compare/contrast the Supreme Court's cases from the 1950s such as *Dennis v. United States* with *Yates v. United States* in order to grasp the difference a few years made in regard to freedom of expression.

Recently I had the opportunity to work with the Civil War letters of William McKnight. In 2002 I was allowed to see a letter dated September 14, 1863. It was from McKnight, an Ohioan blacksmith, to his wife Samaria. It described General Ambrose Burnside's operations in eastern Tennessee and the Union action around the Cumberland Gap. Reading the letter I was intrigued about the possibility of additional letters. Further inquiry elicited that there were well over one hundred letters in the McKnight collection. Most of the letters were written on fibrous paper and folded in the original envelopes, approximately three by five inches in size. These letters, almost a century and a half old, are the primary sources from which historians research and write history.

During the research project and eventual publication of his letters it became apparent that selected portions of his letters could be incorporated into lessons or units that could be taught in grades 7–12 and at the university level. The importance of using letters has multifaceted implications for the inter-connectedness of various issues. The letters provide learning opportunities in history, geography, social and political issues, and English usage and grammar to mention a few areas of classroom application.

For example, a teacher could take a small portion of a letter and ask students to rewrite the letter using 21st-century grammar usage. From the William McKnight letter collection students could correct the following passage using correct rules of spelling and grammar: "I have not received a letter from you for nearly 2 weeks. I am allmost sick to hear from home but I hope you are all wel. The Lord has been very kind to us I have not been sick a day nor have I had any serious Colds as I used to have at home. I pened you a few lines from Nickolisville teling you to direct to Danvill but I believe you had better direct to Lex to be forwarded to the Regmt. Nomore. In haste yours truly and until Death. Dearest good by love to you al" (Maness and Combs 2010, 65). This brief excerpt provides a simple yet powerful tool or opportunity to connect students with 21st-century language skills with a 19th-century writer.

U.S. students tend to lack knowledge and application of geography. Again the McKnight letters may assist students in their understanding of, "Where are we?" "Why are we at this location?" "How did we get here?" "Where do we go from here?" Many of McKnight's letters provide material for geography, history, language arts and social history lessons. The quotation below is a description of the Union army taking control of the Cumberland Gap. A host of questions could be developed around this brief passage. "The 7th OVC had the Honor of being the first Regmt from the South side of the mt to enter the Gap. Thursday Sep 10th might have seen me at 8 1/2 ock at the very top of the C"mt viewing the Giberalter of the Rebels. Here one can look into Tennessee to the south Virginia to the North East & Ky to the North West with seven ranges of mountains in sight. It is one of the strongest fortifications naturealy that one can conceive of. It is no use for me to attempt a discription. It cant be described nor imagined it is the Grandest sight that I ever expect to witness" (Maness and Combs 2010, 126).

The Civil War provided the literate soldiers the opportunity to communicate with their families. Today the Internet, social networking and other instant communication technologies provide U.S. military personnel the opportunity for direct communication with family and friends. The common theme of the Civil War soldier was loneliness and homesickness. Civil War letters are rampant with this theme; teachers could use Civil War letters and compare them with reactions of the soldiers that are currently serving in Iraq and Afghanistan. Students at various grade levels could correspond with U.S. soldiers stationed overseas and analyze, compare/contrast these letters or emails with selected letters from the Civil War, WWI and WWII. These activities may bring a humanizing element or relevance to history and current events. Primary sources abound from the colonial period to today's events. I would recommend that more teachers take advantage of the opportunity to use primary sources to enhance their teaching and make their classes more vibrant and memorable for their students. There is power in reading from an original source.

Maness, Donald C. and Combs, H. Jason. *Do They Miss Me At Home: The Civil War Letters of William McKnight, Seventh Ohio Volunteer Cavalry*, Ohio University Press. 2010.

Don Maness is the Dean of the College of Education and Professor of Teacher Education at Arkansas State University. He is an avid Civil War enthusiast and author, with Jason Combs, of *Do They Miss Me At Home: The Civil War Letters of William McKnight, Seventh Ohio Volunteer Cavalry*, published by the Ohio University Press.

Endnotes

1   Henson, Kenneth T. *Constructivist Teaching Strategies for Diverse Middle-level Classrooms*. Boston: Allyn and Bacon, 2004. 95.
2   Brady, Marion. "Cover the Material—Or Teach Students to Think." *Educational Leadership* 65.5 (2008): 66.
3   Apple, Michael W. "Curriculum Planning: Content, Form, and the Politics of Accountability." *The Sage Handbook of Curriculum and Instruction*. Ed. Michael F. Connelly. Thousand Oaks: Sage Publications, Inc., 2008. 25–26.
4   Henson, 95–96.
5   Ryan, Kevin, and James M. Cooper. *Those Who Can, Teach*. 12th ed. Boston: Wadsworth Cengage Learning, 2007. 143.
6   Ibid.
7   Ornstein, Allan C., and Daniel U. Levine. *Foundations of Education*. Boston: Houghton Mifflin, 2008. 427–28.

8   Ibid.

9   Beck, Isabel L., et al. "Revising Social Studies Text from a Text-processing Perspective: Evidence of Improved Comprehensibility." *Reading Research Quarterly* 26.3 (1991): 257. *Education Research Complete*. EBSCO. Web. 16 Aug. 2010.

10   Selwyn, Douglas, and Jan Maher. *History in Present Tense: Engaging Students Through Inquiry and Action*. Portsmouth: Heinemann, 2003. 100–2.

11   Wintner, Gene. *Texterpts: Mastering College Textbook Reading*. 2nd ed. New York: Pearson Education Inc., 2007. 3. See also Loewen, James W. *Lies My Teacher Told Me: Everything Your American History Textbook Got Wrong*. New York: Touchstone, 1996. i–ix.

12   Bynum, Sarah S.L. *Ms. Hempel's Chronicles*. New York: Harcourt, Inc., 2008. 119.

13   Loewen, James W. *Teaching What Really Happened: How to Avoid the Tyranny of Textbooks and Get Students Excited About Doing History*. New York: Teachers College Press, 2010. 30–31.

14   Wood, Karen D., et al. *Guiding Readers Through Text: Strategy Guides for New Times*. 2nd ed. Newark: International Reading Association, 2008.

15   Loewen, 20.

16   Texts examined included: Garcia, Jesus, et al. *Creating America: A History of the United States*. Evanston: McDougal Littell, 2002; Appleby, Joyce, et al. *The American Journey*. 6th ed. New York: Glencoe/McGraw-Hill, 2008; Davidson, James West, et al. *The American Nation*. Upper Saddle River: Prentice Hall, 2002. Two Advanced Placement texts examined were Boyer, Paul S., et al. *The Enduring Vision: A History of the American People*. 6th ed. Boston: Houghton Mifflin Company, 2008; and Kennedy, David M., and Lizabeth Cohen. *The American Pageant*. 13th ed. Boston: Houghton Mifflin Company, 2005.

17   Davidson et al., 672.

18   Kennedy and Cohen, 720.

19   For good examples of this type of textbook see Remini, Robert V. *A Short History of the United States*. New York: HarperCollins Publishers, 2008, and *We the People: The Citizen and the Constitution* and *Project Citizen* from the Center for Civic Education <http://www.civiced.org>—both designed for middle level students.

20   See <http://www.onlineschools.org/2009/12/20/10–predictions-for-the-future-of-the-textbook>.

21   Kozol, Jonathan. *On Being a Teacher*. Oxford: Oneworld Books, 1981, 2009. 57–60, 64.

22   Restuccia, Paul. "Company, Harvard Prof Work on Web-Linked Textbook, WWII Game." *Boston Herald*. 24 May 2010. <http://www.bostonherald.com>.

23   Lindaman, Dana and Kyle Ward. *History Lessons: How Textbooks from Around the World Portray U.S. History*. New York: The New Press, 2004.

24   DeRose, John J. "Comparing International Textbooks to Develop Historical Thinking." *Social Education* 71. 1 (2007): 36–40.

25   Williams, Yohuru R. *Teaching U.S. History Beyond the Textbook: Six Investigative Strategies, Grades 5–12*. Thousand Oaks: Corwin Press, 2009. 29–30, 89–107. For Supreme Court cases, two useful websites are <http://www.landmarkcases.org/> and <http://www.oyez.org/tour/> .

26   Johnson and Christensen, 429.

27   For the National Archives see <http://nara.gov.education> and for the National Council for the Social Studies (NCSS) see <http://socialstudies.org/resources/twd>.

NCSS's journal *Social Education* published a theme issue, "Teaching U.S. History with Primary Sources" 67. 7 (2003). The example of the Civil War photograph is taken from King, Daniel C. "Drummer Boys: Creating Historical Fiction and Studying Historical Documents." *Middle Level Learning* 35 (2009): M10–12 published by the National Council for the Social Studies.

28   Hicks, D., P. Doolittle, and J. Lee. "Social Studies Teachers' Use of Classroom-based and Web-based Historical Primary Sources." *Theory and Research in Social Education* 32 (2004): 213–247.

29   Singleton, Laurel, and Carolyn Pereira. "Civil Conversations Using Primary Documents." *Social Education* 69.7 (2005): 405.

30   Ravi, Anita K. "Disciplinary Literacy in the History Classroom." *Content Matters: A Disciplinary Literacy Approach to Improving Student Learning.* Ed. Stephanie M. McConachie and Anthony R. Petrosky. San Francisco: Jossey-Bass, 2010. 59, 37.

31   Lynch, Michael. "Every Soldier Has a Story: Creating a Veterans Oral History Project." *Magazine of History*, Oct. 2008: 27–40.

32   Potter, Lee Ann. "Documents in the Digital Age: Electronic Records May Alter the Way We and Our Students Think about Primary Sources." *Social Education* 69. 3 (2005): 118–123. Web.<www.aad.archives.gov/aad/topic_search_reaulra.jsp?filter=ALL>.

33   Lee, P., and R. Ashby. "Empathy, Perspective Taking and Rational Understanding." *Historical Empathy and Perspective Taking in the Social Studies.* Ed. O.L. Davis, S. Foster, and E. Yeager. Boulder: Rowman and Littlefield, 2001. 21–50.

34   Brinkley, Douglas, ed. *Witness to America: A Documentary History of the United States from the Revolution to Today.* New York: HarperCollins, 2010. 464–67. For one of the most comprehensive resources on primary sources in history in terms of sources and methodology in locating them see Presnell, Jenny L. "The Thrill of Discovery: Primary Sources." *The Information-Literate Historian: A Guide to Research for History Students.* New York: Oxford University Press, 2007. 92–135.

35   Brinkley, 425–26.

36   Schramm, Jeff. "Holding History: Teaching with Technological Artifacts." *Magazine of History* July 2010: 49–52. See also virtual tour of the Edison Historical Site at <http://www.nps.gov/edis/>.

37   Barton, Keith, C. "Primary Sources in History: Breaking Through the Myths." *Phi Delta Kappan* 86.10 (2005): 745–53.

38   Wineburg, Sam. *Historical Thinking and Other Unnatural Acts.* Philadelphia: Temple University Press, 2001. 9–112.

39   Zinn, Howard, and Anthony Arnove. *Voices of a People's History of the United States.* New York: Seven Stories Press, 2004.

40   Libresco, Andrea S. Rev. of *Voices of a People's History of the United States* by Howard Zinn and Anthony Arnove. *Social Education* 69. 5 (2005): 287.

41   Libresco, 288–89.

42   Royal, Mary Mason. " 'Maybe You Could Help?': Letters to Eleanor Roosevelt, 1934–1942." *Social Education* 69.1 (2005): S2–9. Copies of letters to Mrs. Roosevelt may be purchased from the Franklin Delano Roosevelt Presidential Library and Museum. See <http://www.fdrlibrary.marist.edu>. Additional letters can be found in Cohen, Robert. *Dear Mrs.Roosevelt: Letters from Children of the Great Depression.* Chapel Hill: University of North Carolina Press, 2002.

43   Guinn, Jeff. *Go Down Together: The True, Untold Story of Bonnie and Clyde.* New York: Simon and Schuster, 2009. 298–9, 304–305, 311–313.

44   Ireland, Bobbi. *Abraham Lincoln and His Era: Using the American Memory Project to Teach with Primary Sources.* Santa Barbara: Teacher Ideas Press Book, ABC-CLIO, 2010. 1.

45   Ibid. 57, 65–67.

46   Wyman, Richard M., Jr. *America's History Through Young Voices: Using Primary Sources in the K–12 Social Studies Classroom.* Boston: Pearson Education, 2005. 3.

47   Engle, Shirley. "Late Night Thoughts About the New Social Studies." *Social Education* 50.1 (1986): 21.

THREE

Using Young Adult Books to Teach History

"I taught English at a boarding school after the army and I can tell you it's pretty much a lost cause, getting boys over ten to read. Most of them don't own a single book you know." So states the central character, Ernest Pettigrew, in Helen Simonson's novel *Major Pettigrew's Last Stand*. But it is not just figures from works of fiction that grapple with encouraging adolescents to read. Teachers today compete with media that in turn compete with the traditional printed word for students' time and attention. Employing teacher-selected and student-selected works of non-fiction can be one response to this current educational conundrum which is especially problematic in the teaching of history.[1]

The use of nonfiction books for the adolescent reader is critical in supplementing and augmenting the teaching of history. First, some definitions. Author and publishing advisor Aaron Shepard labels middle school nonfiction trade books as including grades four to six, usually 60 to 100 pages in length, and published in most cases in a slightly oversized paperback format. Young adult nonfiction trade books are written for grades seven and up, are usually 100 to 150 pages long, and published in standard paperback or hardback format. Young adult literature is often a sub-heading of children's books and found within that professional literature.[2]

In three research studies, young adult book author Denise Johnson found that when children and young adults were given a choice of books to read, nonfiction was their preference.[3] (The National Endowment for the Arts reported in 2007 that fiction reading had declined sharply among younger readers.) Yet studies have shown limited nonfiction books for young readers due to inadequate exposure by teachers to these books, the dominance in schools of basal readers, the narrow selection and availability of these books, and a lack of teacher knowledge on how to teach from nonfiction trade books. *Writer's Digest* (special issue "Writer's Yearbook 2010") has reported "The young adult (YA) book sector remained strong (in a challenging economic year), partly because more adults were starting to read YA titles. Children's/YA hardcover sales were up 30.7% the first half of 2009 compared to adult hardcover decrease of 17.8%."[4]

There are a number of important reasons why adolescent nonfiction books need to be given greater attention and priority by teachers. One of these reasons is diversity, and it is not just race that needs to be considered. Gender is also an issue. There appears, for example, to be a lack of books for young male readers. Whitmire has written that the young adolescent section of bookstores contains books aimed mainly at young females. The reason, he suggests, may simply be marketing. Girls read books and boys do not—or not as much. The feminist movement of the 1970s produced numerous books portraying females in a positive light. (Probably a needed counter to the predominantly male-centered view of history.) Whitmire quotes Kristen McLean, executive director of the Association of Booksellers for Children: "If you walk into a bookstore and you're looking for a book for a fourteen-year-old boy you might be able to get some good recommendations, but very few booksellers pull a section together just for boys."[5]

Whitmire suggests two potential sources of bias by publishers against nonfiction for young males. First, most children's publishing firms are run by women. Being careful not to suggest prejudice on the part of these female publishers, they may just feel more knowledgeable and comfortable with books about young women. A second form of bias, according to Whitmire, is the view by teachers and librarians that nonfiction is really not literature. What could be considered an almost opposite form of bias is the idea that young males are not interested in feelings, relationships, and personalities. Steve Hill, a Boston-based publisher, holds that boys are more interested in books about adventure, history, and travel.[6] The dearth of non-fiction books for adolescents is real, but it does not mean that topics, themes, and subjects are gender-specific.

One source to meet the need for bona fide and readable history books for adolescents might be found within the realm of academia. Without berating textbooks any further in this volume, it does seem to be true that few if any adolescents, except those who are highly academically oriented, will pick up a textbook to read for pleasure. But nonfiction books for adolescents stand in stark contrast to textbooks. The authors of young adult nonfiction books have as their major purpose to bring interest (an overused word, but we will use it here) and hopefully pleasure to the adolescent reader. It is understood, and hoped, that the authors of these books have done their historical homework. The idea is to tell a story and to share it with the young adult reader. With most academic books, though, the aim seems to be to demonstrate the intelligence of the author. Bestselling author and historian Jeff Guinn has said, "You don't want to write what is a lecture, but a conversation."[7] Such nonfiction literature for young adults usually concentrates on people and seeks to include overlooked "nuggets" of history that are out of the ordinary.

The connection and comparison with academic books (and at times textbooks) is marked. Academic writers often do not write with style. It is a misfortune that academics, with few exceptions, have divorced themselves from working with the young adult genre. The unprepared students that the academy often complains about receiving from K–12 schools might be better equipped if historians in higher education lent their considerable knowledge and insight to writing for youth rather than writing for each other. Why don't academics write young adult books? First and foremost, such books may not count toward tenure or be viewed as scholarly. Others may not be familiar with the genre and know how to go about shifting their writing style to meet the needs of younger readers. For some academics young adult books may seem like mere "popularizing," not a respectable term for the rising or even established professor. And there may plainly just be no interest or time to devote to such a project.

But what can academics add? Why should historians or professional educators write young adult books? First, they have expertise in their field and know how to go about research. David McCullough, historian and bestselling author, has written that "In the writing of history and biography, one has to call on imagination—in the sense of transporting oneself into that other time and the lives of those people, all but vanished, distant, and different. That takes research and analysis to be sure."[8] In one young adult book, in a short bibliographic essay, an author indicated how a primary source (a set of letters) started her on her way to writing the book.[9] To her it seemed a moment of discovery. For historians primary sources are familiar tools of the trade.

Joseph Ribar, former high school history teacher and consultant to the Bradley Commission on History in the Schools, has written in support of moving beyond the textbook and incorporating literature through stories into the history classroom:

> The stories of history, like the stories in literature, are made up of basic elements: characters, setting, and plot or action. All three elements are needed to tell a successful story. For this reason, if you "stick with the story," you must necessarily become a better historian than if you merely relied on a single textbook to provide the story. You may need to search through several sources to find clear and lively information on all three elements.[10]

Good history is indeed about stories and most adolescents will connect to a story well told. It has been said that good history reads like fiction and good fiction reads like history. Historian and Advanced Placement textbook author David Kennedy has written of the power of stories to tell about history: "There is something in the human mind that makes the narrative form an especially attractive medium in which to contain, transmit, and remember important information."[11]

Andrew Johnson has extended this line of thinking by providing four reasons why trade books should be used in the teaching of history. First, trade books use stories, myths, and legends which the human mind seems better able to absorb and remember. They elicit emotions, experiences, and associations in the lives of young readers. Second, they make contact vicariously with the thoughts of others in terms of their dreams, thoughts, and ideas. Third, a trade book has the potential to expose students to the values and moral reasoning of others. And fourth, reading about the actions of others, without actually experiencing the consequences, has the potential to avoid possible problems in their own lives.[12] All of these reasons have direct application to the teaching of history. Emotions, vicarious experiences, values, and learning from the successes and mistakes of others are essential features in the study of history.

Gay Ivey, in the journal *Educational Leadership*, addresses the need for youth and books to bond. She writes, "You can't learn much from books that don't matter to you. The right books can help students care about content." Ivey recommends, "Instead of focusing on how to get students to remember what they read, our best bet is to provide texts that are more memorable." She believes that nonfiction books can do for students what a single textbook cannot—provide the potential for connection. "You can learn from books that matter to you and you can't learn much from just one book," she adds.[13]

One of the most powerful tools in the use of nonfiction literature to support the teaching of history is to encourage student choice in the selection of their independent reading. Atwell put it succinctly when she wrote, "If we want our students to grow up to appreciate literature, we need to give them a say in decisions about the literature they will read."[14] Stairs and Burgos have provided multiple studies that support the efficacy of independent, self-selected reading for adolescents. Examples include the correlation between leisure reading and reading achievement, independent reading as a motivator to increase reading by boys, and the amount of high-quality books in a classroom correlated to overall reading comprehension. These two researchers even include a study that found 93% of graduate students allowed to select their own reading found it more meaningful than what was assigned to them in class by the instructor.[15]

Asking students a series of questions is one suggestion to increase independent, self-selected reading. Examples include asking students what is the best book they have ever read, what book had an influence on them, and what books they would recommend to other students. While not all books mentioned might be historical, there is a good chance that some might be. Listing these student selections on index cards, bulletin boards, and classroom or school websites will supply an excellent list from which students can draw for their own reading selections. One additional idea is to simply allow students to have more free reading time in school.[16]

The number and quality of choices of nonfiction works for young adults is growing. Three exemplary recent works that are emblematic of this emerging genre are recommended here. *Claudette Colvin: Twice Toward Justice* tells the compelling story of the Black high school student who did not give up her seat on a bus for a White person. The amazing part of the story is that she did this in Montgomery, Alabama, nine months before Rosa Parks' famous stand for justice for the same reason in the same city. Using the alluring "lost" heroines of history mode, author Phillip Hoose moves beyond biography, although biography this is. The visuals that are employed make the book appealing. Actual newspaper clippings are reproduced. Episodes that other Civil Rights leaders experienced as youths are included in sidebars. (In one vignette Martin Luther King, Jr., (Mike) traveling to take part in a school debate in another Georgia city, refused to give his seat up on a bus to a White man until his teacher convinced him to do so. Years later he recalled it as the "angriest I have been in my life.") Colvin's story was never fully told due in part to her own reticence and modesty. But Hoose tells her story well. "Claudette Colvin's life story," he writes, "shows how history is made up of objective facts and personal truths braided together."[17] This National Book Award winner is most appropriate for middle school students.

FDR's Alphabet Soup: New Deal America, 1932–1939 is by veteran young adult book author Tonya Bolden, who started writing the book before the major United States economic recession began in 2008. Enmeshed in the New Deal, she could not help but see the parallels between the two periods in our history. Although the writing is outstanding, what will make this book most attractive to adolescents is again its format and design. The book contains just the right amount of information to enlighten the reader as to what is going on at the time and why (e.g. seven brief reasons, beyond the stock market crash, are listed to the question, "What Caused the Great Depression?" Just the right number.) Also included are editorial cartoons that adolescents will readily understand, a letter from a fifteen-year-old telling President Roosevelt about the challenges she is facing every day, and references to movies and gangsters of the period. Bolden's prose every once in a while slips into the idiom of youth. For example, in describing the unsuccessful attempt to assassinate then president-elect Franklin Roosevelt, she writes that Giuseppe Zangara "tried to *off* the president-elect."

Bolden also gives her opinions. In telling of the attempts to paint Roosevelt as a socialist, Bolden writes, "He was nobody's puppet. The notion that he could be hoodwinked into socialism was ludicrous, but it was an effective scare tactic by people furious over the federal government getting so big." (One who follows current events will not fail to see the comparison between 1933 and today.) And almost three dozen actors, writers, and artists, probably not familiar to youth but very much so to adults, are listed as recipients of paychecks from one of those "alphabet soup" agencies—the Works Progress (Projects) Administration.

Some writers are aiming at the older adolescents with history books that are denser in text with fewer photographs, yet are written with the young adult reader in mind. One is the 294-page *The Rise and Fall of Senator Joe McCarthy* by James Cross Giblin. The essence of McCarthyism (a term coined by editorial cartoonist Herblock) can be defined as guilt of disloyalty by association, false accusations, and the questioning of a citizen's patriotism. The details of how all this came about can become quite complicated. Giblin is able, by his writing style, to keep the material understandable. At the same time he does not shy away from some of the more controversial aspects of the communist witch hunts of the 1950s such as the issue of an alleged homosexual relationship between two of McCarthy's aides. (Giblin's use of "Joe" throughout the book when referring to McCarthy is perplexing. The young adult reader may not know if the shortening of the name is the author's preference to be more reader friendly or reduce the use of the senator's full first or last name.) On the surface, as Giblin tells the story of McCarthy, he seems almost neutral toward his subject. In the end, though, he is not. McCarthy's pattern of dishonesty is evident from the beginning of the book. And his epilogue makes clear that "McCarthyism" is permanently within our language for a good reason. Political labels are still parlayed around in the media to damn candidates and office holders. Integrating more of the epilogue throughout the book would have made his concerns about and connections to the present much clearer.[18]

There are many other outstanding authors producing solid works in history and social studies for the adolescent reader. Russell Freedman, for example, has written stellar works in both history and biography. In Freedman's view "the best way to introduce yourself to a new subject is pick up a children's book."[19] His works on Babe Didrikson Zaharias, Eleanor Roosevelt, and Abraham Lincoln are models for any one writing in the biographical arena.

History is about people and biography is the story of individuals. It has even been said that there is no proper history, only biography. Adolescents connect with people. The lives of women and men in American history can resonate with adolescents. Several studies cited by Barton indicate that students are interested in the lives of ordinary people when studying history and also the impact that events have on individuals. And, they seem to prefer trade books because they find them "more entertaining . . . [and] have a greater sense of voice" for the reader.[20] Denise Johnson has given four categories of biographical subjects: 1) Discovery and

Exploration, 2) Political Leaders and Social Activists, 3) Artists and Authors, and 4) People Who Have Persevered.[21]

Biographies are indeed an excellent genre for young adult books. Veteran biographer Robert Ferrell has exuberantly written, "How wonderful is biography? For we teachers it is the queen of historical writing." Not all adolescents, though, will follow Ferrell's notion and begin to enjoy biographies by merely visiting a library or bookstore and start picking books off of a shelf. But he does make a good case for teachers to use biography with both their students and for their own professional development.[22] In a society that can be considered a cult of personality and celebrity (magazines that meet the public's seemingly endless interest in the lives of others such as *People* and *Us*) there could indeed be the occasional life of a woman or man from the past that a student will find appealing.

Writing about how the biographer's work is to evoke the personality of the subject so that "a living being walks off the page,"[23] biographer Kim Nielsen has written:

> When [students] read good biography they often mistakenly feel as if they are avoiding more difficult academic work. In fact, analyzing biographical sources is important historical work. Teachers can take advantage of biography's interplay between individuals and structural forces in history. Through biography, they discover how individuals both shape and are shaped by the world around them.[24]

Nonfiction youth author Tracey Dils has written that biographies are one of the most popular nonfiction categories.[25] Most of the winners of the Carter G. Woodson Book Award[26]—a prize given to social studies trade books—are biographies. While biographies can be about famous individuals, young adults like to read about young adults—and if the book covers the subject's life, then material on the subject's childhood and young adult period should always be prominently included.

While biographies of historical figures for adults have long been prize-winners and bestsellers—Jon Meacham's *American Lion: Andrew Jackson in the White House* and David McCulloch's *John Adams* have been recent Pulitzer Prize winners—young adult biographies for adolescents is a developing niche. The subjects run the gamut from the famous to the obscure, the national to the local. *No Easy Answers: Bayard Rustin and the Civil Rights Movement* examines how a black leader on the national stage battled for social justice. At a community level, *Going Over All the Hurdles: A Life of Oatess Archey*, explores how an African American from Indiana in the last half of the 20th century overcame and prevailed against discrimination in the fields of education, teaching, coaching, law enforcement, and politics.[27]

Examples of effective biographies are indeed growing. Shirley Leckie has recommended several compelling titles including *Incidents in the Life of a Slave Girl* (1861). This nineteenth-century book brings into focus the sexual vulnerability of slave women as well as the relationship between enslaved females and their mistresses. Another choice from Leckie is Lois Scharf's *Eleanor Roosevelt: First Lady of American Liberalism* (1987), which surprises students who discover that the subject of the biography had an unhappy childhood in spite of her wealth and social status. A third biography that Leckie suggests is *Reagan's America* (1988) by Garry Wills, who compares passages from his book with Reagan's own autobiography *Where's the Rest of Me* (1965). The comparison shows that Great Depression era federal government projects kept the Reagan family financially afloat, yet years later he demonized big government when a candidate for president.[28]

Times Books has continued The American Presidents Series that was being edited by historian Arthur Schlesinger, Jr. at the time of his death. These biographies, while written for a general audience, make excellent choices for adolescents reading about the presidents. First, they are fairly short—fewer than 200 pages in length. Second, the volumes published thus far are by not only historians but also journalists and are, therefore, quite well written. Third, they examine the "big" issues of the subject's presidency, not getting bogged down in minutiae and details that often turn away adolescent readers.

Teachers need to constantly be seeking new titles in biography for their students and for their own professional development. Two recent titles, both from the state of Indiana and both about women in World War II, are exceptional examples. Hoosier historian James Madison, while walking in the American military cemetery in Normandy, France, came across a grave marker etched with the name "Elizabeth A. Richardson" and the words "American Red Cross, Indiana, July 25, 1945." Madison contacted the library in Richardson's hometown of Mishawaka, Indiana, and received copies of her obituary. He then came into contact with Liz Richardson's brother who had boxes filled with her letters, photographs, paintings, and a diary. From these primary sources emerged *Slinging Doughnuts for the Boys: An American Woman in World War II*.[29] Since women were not permitted in direct combat roles in World War II, how Liz Richardson came to be buried in Normandy will be left to the curious reader to discover.

Another Indiana woman from the World War II era has told her own story. Frances DeBra was one of over 150,000 American women who served in the Women's Army Corps (WAC's). She became one of the very few women who worked in technical jobs such as mechanics, interpreters, and weather observers. DeBra was a draftsman—or rather draftswoman. *An Army in Skirts: The World War II Letters of Frances DeBra*, is one WAC's autobiography following her from basic training in the States to the buzz bombs of London and the liberation of Paris. DeBra's story has a more favorable ending than Liz Richardson's as she marries and goes on to a career in teaching and art. And then, six decades later, writing of her wartime experiences serving in the European theater of the war.[30]

Collected biographies are also valuable sources for students and teachers. One distinctive contribution to this field is *How Lincoln Learned to Read: Twelve Great Americans and the Educations that Made Them* by Daniel Wolff. These interconnected essays—a chapter long each—examine how a highly diverse dozen Americans went about learning both inside and outside the classroom. The patrician Henry Adams, in his book *The Education of Henry Adams*, asked the question "what part of education has . . . turned out to be useful and what not?" And Wolff bases his book on that question. He focuses on ages five to eighteen, and lets the twelve women and men answer in their own words. What a splendid idea. The chapters are mainly titled with their childhood names. Wolff's selections include Abigail Adams ("Nabby"), Elvis Presley, Sojourner Truth, John Kennedy ("Jack"), W.E.B. Du Bois (Willie), and Abraham Lincoln ("Abe"). One chilling conclusion from this book is that formal education does not rank very high to Wolff's group. "The man of sixty can generally see what he needed in life," wrote Adams, and for him it was not school.[31]

A creative book that is a variation of the collected biography is Phillip Hoose's *We Were There, Too!: Young People in U.S. History.* As noted, since students enjoy reading about individuals their own age, this book matches that need well. Hoose has identified many youth, who like Blacks were "lost, stolen, or strayed" from the pages of the history books. Over half the crew members on Columbus's voyage were under the age of eighteen. Fifteen-year-old Joe Nuxhall pitched for the Cincinnati Reds during World War II when many players were off to war. And Hoose tells of the valiant struggle of teenager Ryan White, who battled AIDS when little was known about the disease.[32]

Locating appropriate history books to reinforce regular classroom materials is not always easy, but lists can be helpful. *Recommended Literature: Kindergarten Through Grade Twelve*, produced by the California Department of Education, is a very strong resource for teachers. It provides recommendations that reflect the quality and complexity of outstanding literature for adolescents. The online data bases parse the suggestions of books by specific categories such as genres, awards, disciplines, standards, cultural designations, and selection policies in addition to the traditional areas of author and titles.[33] Another source is the American Library Association's Young Adult Library Services Association that provides numerous lists of books for the reluctant reader as well as books by prize-winning authors. The Margaret A. Edwards Award, for example, was won by Jim Murphy, who has written books on the Civil War, the Revolutionary War, and a trilogy on famous fires, plagues, and blizzards.[34] One final place for excellent reviews of children's and young adult books is the *New York Times Book Review*, although it tends to focus in its pages on younger children rather than adolescents.

Sometimes older standard works can still be of value to today's students. In the 1950s and 1960s, Random House published a series of nonfiction young adult books under the Landmark series imprint. Long out of print, but still available in some university and school collections, these historical and biographical works were often written by major authors, were lightly illustrated, and ran fewer than 200 pages in length. Thomas B. Costain, a popular historical novelist, produced two books in the series—*William the Conqueror* and *The Mississippi Bubble*. The latter takes place in 17th-century North America and France and includes colorful individuals, realistic imagery of the times, and even a not-too-painful lesson in economics.[35] A current publisher should take a look at this catalog and either re-issue them or look to add to the collection.

While this chapter focuses on nonfiction, there is outstanding historical fiction available for students as well. Again, young adult novels that are about young adults will appeal to young adults. One example is the young adolescent fictionalized memoir *The Watsons Go to Birmingham 1963* by Christopher Paul Curtis. While it is a book about race and drawn from real events, the connection to youth is its autobiographical perspective. Edinger and Fins, who recommend this book, suggest that teachers consider having their own students write a brief memoir themselves. The rationale is that the role of memory is closely linked to historical knowledge and its creation.[36] There are resources for teachers that can assist them with this suggestion. The book *Inventing the Truth: The Art and Craft of Memoir*, while aimed at older students, has ideas that can also be used with younger students. These include dealing with painful memories; the use of family mementoes, photos, and artifacts to trigger memories; and employing authentic voices to reflect diverse cultures.[37] Another work of fiction for younger adolescents that connects to the topic of King Philip's War is *Thunder from the Clear Sky* by Marcia Sewall. This fictionalized version of the events between the Pilgrims and the Wampanoag tells the seventeenth-century episode from distinctly differing points of view.[38]

History education and social studies journals often provide lists of historical fiction aimed at adolescents. The literature-based approach to engaging students in history has been shown in two pieces of research (doctoral dissertations) to be effective. One study found that using literature in conjunction with history courses enhanced higher-order thinking skills and changed their perceptions and attitudes about history.[39] Another dissertation found that while there was no statistical increase in the rate of achievement, student interest with a class that used literature to accompany a history textbook was higher than for those students who just used a textbook.[40]

One additional way to connect adolescents to reading is to involve the author. For most young adults an author has little meaning to them—at best they are a name on the cover of a book or a photograph on the back page. Forging a link between authors and students is possible. Surprisingly, authors are more available to their readers than one would think. Authors live all over the country, and so there just may be one near you. With Web cams, teleconferencing, and email, visits do not necessarily have to be in person. A well-known young adult author visited our local public library for an evening presentation, and to everyone's surprise she lived less than 100 miles away.

David Polochanin, a middle level educator and writer himself, has found that students, when properly prepared for an author visit, are capable of asking productive questions. These might include: Why did you decide to write a book? How do you select a topic? Where do you get the ideas for plot and characters? Authors will often give suggestions on other books students should read. And authors can gain much from the experience also. Feedback from the readers of their works is essential.[41] All authors, whether they admit it or not, read what reviewers and critics say. And students are both frontline consumers and frank critics of an author's work.

Whether the self-selected adolescent trade book is nonfiction or fiction, these works can be an effective motivator for most students, even reluctant readers. As they are an increasingly popular genre, the teacher will need to seek out these books by reading reviews or the books themselves. Teachers reading themselves, and allowing for free reading in their classrooms, will be a model for students. Oral renditions of good literature also have the capacity to draw students into a historical time or setting. Although viewed as a literary tool to use only with younger children, teachers reading brief passages or stories to adolescents can be a welcome strategy for the learner. It is acceptable to read to middle school students, and even those in high school. If books are worth the teacher's time to read themselves or to the class, then students may well find books worth their time as well.

The World of Practice
"A Good Story": Writing Biography
by Ray E. Boomhower

In her book *Biography: The Craft and the Calling*, Catherine Drinker Bowen, who in her eclectic career examined the lives of such figures as Tchaikovsky, Oliver Wendell Holmes Jr., John Adams, and Francis Bacon, states that the biographer's aim is to "bring to life, persons and times long vanished. He [the biographer] has a conception of his hero which he desires to share; he cannot bear that this man should be forgotten or exist only in dry eulogy or brief paragraphs of the history textbooks." David McCullough, the author of best-selling biographies of such American notables as Theodore Roosevelt, Harry Truman, and John Adams, agrees with Bowen's assessment, but adds that a biographer "must genuinely care about his subject."

Both of these legendary writers offer sound advice for the budding biographer. But what is it that inspires someone to partake in the long, painstaking process of digging into a person's life? In my case, I have to take you back to the year 1967. At that time, I was in the third grade at Mary Phillips Elementary School in Mishawaka, Indiana. That year I had as my teacher a young woman named Patricia Swarm. For some reason, perhaps because of my gap-toothed grin or bizarre haircut inflicted on me by a barber new to his trade, Miss Swarm took an interest in me, particularly my growing love of reading. Although other teachers might have scolded me for reading ahead in the text during a classroom assignment, Miss Swarm noticed my enthusiasm for the printed word and encouraged me to read whatever interested me. In my case, this happened to be any book on history or biography.

My favorite room in the school quickly became the small library located on the ground floor. The room featured such state-of-the-art equipment for the time as a record player with earphones, which I used extensively to listen to a National Aeronautics and Space Administration album filled with the sounds of the American space program. I became entranced at the exploits of those early space pioneers, and vowed to become an astronaut myself—a dream killed by my fear of heights and low scores in mathematics. My favorite spot in the library, however, occupied a space just off the room's entrance: a row of shelves filled with biographies on the childhoods of famous Americans, a series of books released by the Bobbs-Merrill publishing firm in Indianapolis. Today, more years later than I would like to admit, I can still recall details from those charming tomes, including Lou Gehrig hunting eels with his mother in New York City, a young Andrew Jackson standing up to a British officer during the Revolutionary War, and Babe Ruth pitching for his baseball team from the Saint Mary's Industrial School for Boys in Baltimore, Maryland.

The Bobbs-Merrill series sparked my lifelong interest in history, which in turn led me to where I am today—an author who has published eleven books, the majority of which have been biographies. None of this would have been possible, however, without the encouragement of a dedicated teacher. In some way, I think, I write about history in order to pay back Miss Swarm's kindness to her young pupil.

In their book *After the Fact*, historians James West Davidson and Mark Hamilton Lytle advise their readers that when historians neglect the literary aspect of their discipline, when they "forget that good history begins with a good story," they risk losing the wider audience that all "great historians have addressed." In my twenty-four years working at the Indiana Historical Society, I have been able to indulge my love of biography by writing "good stories" for the popular history magazine, *Traces of Indiana and Midwestern History*, and also turning some of those articles into book-length manuscripts. My position as senior editor at the

IHS Press has also granted me the opportunity to work with other authors on a variety of book projects, including one—the Youth Biography Series—targeted at readers in middle and high schools. Since the series began in 2005, it has examined the lives of a wide swath of Hoosier notables, including World War II correspondent Ernie Pyle, religious leader and saint Mother Theodora Guérin, and teacher and lawman Oatess Archey. Future books in the series will detail the life and work of such diverse people as nature writer Gene Stratton-Porter, artist T. C. Steele, labor leader Eugene Debs, and AIDS pioneer Ryan White.

The series came about in an unexpected way. In 2003 the IHS, with the support of a grant from the Lilly Endowment Inc., was able to purchase for its William Henry Smith Memorial Library an extensive collection of images and documents of President Abraham Lincoln, including material on the sixteenth president's assassination and the hunt for the conspirators responsible for his death. In addition, the IHS Press worked with the library staff to prepare and issue a coffee-table publication on the collection, titled *Abraham Lincoln Portrayed in the Collections of the Indiana Historical Society*. Taking advantage of some unexpended funds from the Lilly grant, the Press was also able to supplement the volume with a book that became the first in the Youth Biography Series, a look at the life of Hoosier politician, general, and writer Lew Wallace. Wallace seemed the perfect choice as a subject, as he had some connection with Lincoln early on in his law career, had served as a major general for the Union cause during the Civil War, and had served on the military court that tried the conspirators behind Lincoln's assassination.

In this first book in the series the Press set the stage for the volumes to come in terms of its style of writing and design. In examining other examples of biographies for our target audience, I, as editor of the series, was impressed by the work of the Newberry Award-winning author Russell Freedman, especially his book *Lincoln: A Photobiography*. Freedman's work featured the style of writing—clear, concise, and engaging—I attempted to have each author in the series follow when writing about their subjects. If any author happened to stumble and call for help, I would advise him or her to imagine trying to make a subject understandable for the average newspaper reader, and tell them to remember William Strunk's most helpful rule: "Omit needless words!" Freedman's book also included another feature we try to highlight in our series—a heavy use of illustrations. The Press is fortunate to be able to draw upon the vast photographic collection of our library, as well as its many maps, postcards, and drawings from the days of the Old Northwest to contemporary times.

I have been lucky enough to write a number of books in the series and have discovered I relish writing for a younger audience (although we have discovered that the biographies appeal to a wide range of readers, especially older adults looking for a concise, but comprehensive examination of a subject's life and times).

What is challenging is providing the proper historical context for younger readers, getting them to realize, as President Harry S. Truman once observed, "the only thing new in the world is the history you don't know." Sometimes this involves beginning the tale not with the birth, but with the final few moments of your subject's life, as I did with Pyle and his death from Japanese gunfire during the battle of Okinawa. The worldwide sorrow and grief expressed by soldiers showed just how much respect and admiration the average GI had for the reporter from Indiana.

There always remains, however, the difficulty of connecting today's generation with the past, as the issues seem too wide in scope to be relevant to their lives. One way to establish ties between a reader and a subject is to show that even worldwide events affect young individuals in dramatic ways. It is a technique I used in our latest volume in the series, which looks at the life of Alex Vraciu of East Chicago, Indiana, who served as a navy fighter pilot in the Pacific. To draw the reader into the story I began the book with the recollection of a young girl who witnessed the Japanese attack on the American fleet at Pearl Harbor, plunging the United States into World War II. I ended the book by telling how a Japanese teenager living in Hiroshima had begun what he thought was a normal morning only to have to deal with the awful destruction unleashed on his city by the dropping by an American B-29 bomber of the first atomic weapon—a development that helped to finally end the war.

As with other smaller publishers, the IHS Press will face immense challenges in the years to come, as the book industry perhaps moves from hard-copy tomes to electronic versions readable on a variety of handheld devices. Although I believe there will always be a market for "real" books—nothing can match the tactile pleasure of holding a book in your hands—I am intrigued by the promise of electronic publishing. The ability to imbed links to websites, interviews with those who knew the subject, and even perhaps video of their exploits will only enhance our abilities to be storytellers, bringing the past into focus for our readers.

For Further Reading

Bowen, Catherine Drinker. *Biography: The Craft and the Calling*. Boston: Little, Brown, 1969.

Davidson, James West, and Mark Hamilton Lytle. *After the Fact: The Art of Historical Detection*. New York: McGraw-Hill, 1992.

Freedman, Russell. *Lincoln: A Photobiography*. New York: Clarion Books, 1987.

Pachter, Marc, ed. *Telling Lives: The Biographer's Art*. Washington, DC: New Republic Books, 1979.

Ray E. Boomhower is senior editor at the Indiana Historical Society Press, where he is responsible for the quarterly popular history magazine *Traces of Indiana and Midwestern History*. He is the author of numerous books, including *Fighter Pilot: The World War II Career of Alex Vraciu* (2010), *Robert F. Kennedy and the 1968 Indiana Primary* (2008), and *Fighting for Equality: The Life of May Wright Sewall* (2007).

Endnotes

1   Simonson, Helen. *Major Pettigrew's Last Stand*. New York: Random House, 2010. 62.
2   Shepard, Aaron. *The Business of Writing for Children*. Los Angeles: Shepard Publications, 2000. 22.
3   Johnson, Denise. *The Joy of Children's Literature*. Boston: Houghton Mifflin Harcourt Publishing Company, 2009. 278.
4   Ohi, Debbie Ridpath "2009: The Year in Review" *Writer's Digest: Writer's Yearbook 2010*, 7–8.
5   Whitmire, Richard. *Why Boys Fail: Saving our Sons from an Educational System That's Leaving Them Behind*. New York: American Management Association, 2010. 49–51.
6   Whitmire, 52–53.
7   Jeff Guinn on *C-SPAN BookTV*. 14 March 2010.
8   Silvey, Anita, ed. *Everything I Need to Know I Learned from a Children's Book: Life Lessons from Notable People from All Walks of Life*. New York: Roaring Book Press, 2009. 129.
9   Wells, Rosemary and P.J. Lynch. *Lincoln and His Boys*. Sommerville, MA: Candlewick Press, 2009. 95–96.
10   Ribar, Joseph P. "For Better Secondary Teaching: Stories Old and New." *Historical Literacy: The Case for History in American Education*. Ed. Paul Gagon. New York: Macmillan Publishing Company, 1989. 292.
11   Kennedy, David M. "The Art of the Table: Story-Telling and History Teaching." *The History Teacher* 31 (1998): 318.
12   Johnson, Andrew P. *Making Connections in Elementary and Middle School Social Studies*. Los Angeles: Sage Publishing, 2010. 232–33.
13   Ivey, Gay. "Texts That Matter." *Educational Leadership* 67. 6 (2010): 20–21.
14   Atwell, Nancie. *In the Middle: New Understandings About Writing, Reading, and Learning*. 2nd ed. Portsmouth: Boynton and Cook, 1998. 36.
15   Stairs, Andrea J. and Sara S. Burgos. "The Power of Independent, Self-Selected Reading in Middle Grades." *Middle School Journal* 41. 3 (2010): 41–42.
16   Ibid. 44–47.
17   Hoose, Phillip. *Claudette Colvin: Twice Toward Justice*. New York: Melanie Kroupa Books/Farrar, Straus, Giroux, 2009.
18   Giblin, James Cross. *The Rise and Fall of Senator Joe McCarthy*. Boston: Clarion Books, 2009.
19   Silvey, 187.
20   Barton, Keith C. "Research on Students' Ideas about History." *Handbook of Research in Social Studies Education*. Ed. Linda S. Levstik and Cynthia A. Tyson. New York: Routledge, 2008. 245–46.
21   Johnson, 285–86.

22   Ferrell, Robert H. "From the Stacks." *Organization of American Historians Magazine of History* 20.1 (2006): 7–8.

23   Vandiver, Frank E. "Biography as an Agent of Humanism." *The Biographer's Gift: Life Histories and Humanism.* Ed. James F. Veninga. College Station: Texas A&M University Press, 1983. 16.

24   Nielsen, Kim E. "Using Biography to Teach Disability History." *Organization of American Historians Magazine of History* 23.3 (2009): 41.

25   Dils, Tracey E. *You Can Write Children's Books.* Cincinnati: Writer's Digest Books, 2009 . 47.

26   See May–June issues of *Social Education* for the yearly *Woodson Book Awards* along with the list of Honorable Mentions.

27   Miller, Calvin C. *No Easy Answers: Bayard Rustin and the Civil Rights Movement* Greensboro: Morgan Reynolds Publishing, Inc., 2005; and Beineke, John A. *Going Over All the Hurdles: A Life of Oatess Archey.* Indianapolis: Indiana Historical Society Press, 2008.

28   Leckie, Shirley A. "Why Biographies Matter in the Classroom." *Organization of American Historians Magazine of History* 20. 1 (2006): 7–8.

29   Madison, James H. *Slinging Doughnuts for the Boys: An American Woman in World War II.* Bloomington: Indiana University Press, 2007.

30   Brown, Frances DeBra. *An Army in Skirts: The World War II Letters of Frances DeBra.* Indianapolis: Indiana Historical Society Press, 2008.

31   Wolff, Daniel. *How Lincoln Learned to Read: Twelve Great Americans and the Educations that Made Them.* New York: Bloomsbury, 2000.

32   Hoose, Phillip M. *We Were There, Too!: Young People in U.S. History.* New York: Farrar, Straus, and Giroux, 2001.

33   See <http://www.cde.ca.gov/ci/rl/11/>.

34   See American Library Association at <http://www.ala.org>.

35   Costain, Thomas B. *The Mississippi Bubble.* New York: Random House, 1955.

36   Edinger, Monica and Stephanie Fins. *Far Away and Long Ago: Young Historians in the Classroom.* York: Stenhouse Publishers, 1998. 36.

37   Zinsser, William. ed. *Inventing the Truth: The Art and Craft of Memoir.* New York: Mariner Books, 1998.

38   Sewall, Marcia. *Thunder from the Clear Sky.* New York: Aladdin Publishing, 1998.

39   Van Middendorp, Judy E. "An Eighth-Grade Literature-Based U.S. History Classroom: Reactions, Responses, Perceptions, and Participation." Diss. U of South Dakota, 1990.

40   Corbin, Denee J. "Using Literature to Teach Historical Concepts in Fifth-Grade Social Studies." Diss. U of Iowa, 1990.

41   Polochanin, David. "What Were You Thinking?: Connecting Students and Authors." *Middle Ground* 13.14 (2010): 16–17.

FOUR

Political Cartoons and Comic Books

Two of the most effective tools currently available for teaching history to adolescents are political cartoons and comic books, which also includes longer works known as graphic fiction and non-fiction. Old and yet new in terms of medium and genre, these similar, yet distinct media offer much to the teacher seeking to motivate students in a subject in which they may or may not be readily drawn. Teachers must themselves understand the history and the ideas behind these media to effectively use them. The emphases in this chapter will be on descriptions of these media and also resources that the teachers may draw on for use in their classroom. The occasional teaching strategy for utilizing these media will be included. Most importantly, the use of political cartoons and comic books provides adolescents with the opportunity to do what all history teachers wish most—to develop positive thoughts and feelings (yes, feelings) toward the study of history.

Political and Editorial Cartoons

Who doesn't enjoy a cartoon? On opening a newspaper editorial page, one's eyes often dart first to the cartoon, usually placed near the top of the page. Steinbrink and Bliss have written that "cartoons are universal because they depict diverse topics and appeal to many age groups and audiences." They add that "cartoons are especially useful for helping . . . learners recognize bias, satire, and exaggeration."[1] Writes W. Ray Heitzmann, "Name a teaching methodology that enlivens lectures, prompts classroom discussion, promotes critical thinking, develops multiple talents and learning styles, helps prepare students for standardized tests and even provides humor. The answer: interpreting political cartoons."[2]

Fortunately for history teachers, their textbooks frequently use cartoons. Assessments are using editorial cartoons within standardized tests to gauge analysis, application, and interpretation. Alan Nevins, a historian, and Frank Weitenkampf, a librarian, together in their classic work *A Century of Political Cartoons: Caricature in the United States from 1800 to 1900*, suggest three major requirements of "a really good political cartoon." First, wit and humor. The second requisite is truth or "at least one side of truth" as Nevins and Weitenkampf put it. A third requirement is moral purpose. Supplemental attributes would include distortion, satire and "a vigor almost brutal" and yet the "delicacy of a waspish sting."[3]

Offering another definition is Lucy Shelton Caswell, who has written that in a democracy the role of journalists is to inform, persuade and advocate—the perfect job description, she has said, for the editorial cartoonist. The Association of American Editorial Cartoonists is a professional organization that views their calling with a passion. Editorial cartoonist Dave Horsey has said that his job was "to poke people in the eye" in order to get a response from the reader and move them to action.[4]

Although caricatures and drawings created for humorous effects have existed for centuries, the art of political cartooning is of fairly recent vintage. While some date the first political cartoon to the time of the pharaohs, thirteen centuries before Christ, the actual application and purposeful use of drawings to make political arguments in newspapers dates from colonial days.[5] Illustrations made their way to colonial America and were imitated by Americans such as Benjamin Franklin and the engraver and silversmith Paul Revere. What is considered the first American political cartoon appeared on May 9, 1754, in Benjamin Franklin's *Pennsylvania Gazette*. It depicted a snake severed into sections, each segment representing a colony or region with the caption "Join or Die." Since these beginnings there is little doubt that the medium has been a powerful one. "Let them who will, write a nation's history. Give me the boys who draw the pictures," wrote Stewart Holbrook in 1946.[6]

The political cartoon in America came into full flower in the nineteenth century. Abraham Lincoln was the first president to receive almost non-stop attention from the cartoonists. (Andrew Jackson admittedly did have several notable portrayals during his presidency.) Cartoons from obscure and regional magazines are now surfacing that are giving editorial cartoon historians and educators a chance to reconsider traditional views of Lincoln. These recently discovered political cartoons are from 1860, the year of his election. One reason cartooning loomed so large at Lincoln's election was due to a technological breakthrough. The old method of using wood carvings to produce the cartoons was jettisoned for a more expeditious way to produce the woodcuts, thus allowing for the production of more cartoons. Some of these early Lincoln cartoons show the candidate and president put upon by events and besieged by the opposition. Publications, through their cartoons, often took their frustrations out on him concerning the Union's frequently adverse military situation. As the war improved, so did the depiction of Lincoln in the cartoons.[7]

Lincoln continued to be the subject of the cartoonist's pen well into the 21st century. Weinburg has written that Bill Mauldin's famous cartoon of Lincoln grieving, head in hands, at the assassination of President Kennedy in 1963 "secured for Lincoln a permanent place in the history of modern political cartoons." In a November 4, 2008 post-election cartoon, Lincoln is depicted jumping for joy at Barack Obama's election. Weinburg examines, as history teachers in the classroom should, the actual beliefs of Lincoln toward Blacks during his time and speculates on what he might have thought about the election of the nation's first African American president.[8]

Donald Dewey suggests that after the Civil War cartoonists, such as Thomas Nast, "developed an almost visceral intimacy with the form," going on to calling his work caustic, lecturing, and harsh. Nevertheless, Nast is credited with creating the symbol of the elephant (1874) for the Republican Party and re-popularizing the donkey (1869) to represent Democrats. Abraham Lincoln was said to have quipped that cartoonist Thomas Nast was his "best recruiting sergeant." Editorial cartoons became widespread in American newspapers after the Civil War. Thomas Nast's 1871 portrayal of Boss Tweed as "The Brains" (with his head a moneybag) has been described as the perfect cartoon: humorous, well drawn, an accurate message, and clearly symbolic.[9]

Post Civil War cartoons evolved the medium even further, once again due to the men in public office. Roscoe Conkling, James G. Blaine, Grover Cleveland, and of course Theodore Roosevelt all became favorites for cartoonists. Nevins and Weitenkampf conclude that the "political cartoon is a valuable item in the documentary outfit of the historian. The laugh-provoker of yesterday has become a serious contribution to history" as a "combination of the amusing and the instructive."[10] Theodore Roosevelt refusing to shoot a bear cub on a hunting trip in Alabama, Woodrow Wilson as the lecturing professor to an unruly classroom of Mexican revolutionaries, and references to the Teapot Dome Scandal are examples of early-twentieth-century cartoons. In 1940, Nevins and Weitenkampf wrote that political cartoons of the last fifty years were guilty of "too many thoughts and too little thought."[11]

Before he was Dr. Seuss, Theodore Seuss Geisel was an extraordinarily gifted political and editorial cartoonist. His work from the World War II era for the New York daily newspaper *PM* will immediately connect with adolescent students. The World War II related caricatures of people (Hitler and Tojo) and bizarre animals, drawn in the style of his children's literature books that began in the 1950s, are easily recognizable to today's students. This "early Seuss" made his political analysis in the 1940s as clearly as any of today's editorial cartoonists.[12]

If there is an exemplar of the political cartoonist it is Herbert Block, who adopted the signature Herblock and became one of the most influential editorial page cartoonists of the twentieth century. Over the span of his career he won the Pulitzer Prize four times. In 1942 and 1954 he was the recipient of the award for his individual work on political cartoons that dealt, respectively, with World War II and the death of Joseph Stalin. He later shared a Pulitzer Prize with his colleagues at the *Washington Post* for their collected coverage of the Watergate scandal. A fourth Pulitzer was awarded in 1979 honoring his lifetime body of work. Speaking of his own profession he once said, "The political cartoon has always served as a special prod—a reminder to public servants that they are public servants." An editorial cartoonist for the *Washington Post* for 50 years, and before that a nationally syndicated cartoonist, Block covered the presidencies of Herbert Hoover to George W. Bush. His autobiography is replete with a trove of cartoons excellent for classroom use.[13]

It would not be a president that first drew the ire of Herblock, it was the junior senator from Wisconsin, Joseph McCarthy. The unprincipled, communist-hunting legislator, however, at the height of his influence, was a formable force and adversary to those who opposed him. His unscrupulous tactics were touted as "McCarthyism," an appellation coined by Block himself in a March 29, 1950 cartoon. Block drew McCarthy as an unshaven bully emblazoning the term McCarthyism on the side of a tar barrel. The junior senator from Wisconsin's fellow communist hunter ("witch-hunter" to some critics), Richard Nixon, was also drawn by Block with a five o'clock shadow. In one 1954 cartoon he drew Vice President Nixon coming out of a sewer as a campaign band played. McCarthy, himself, was finally censured by the Senate, and history, dying in disgrace of alcoholism in 1957 at the age of 48.

CBS broadcast journalist Eric Sevareid called Block "The most powerful and effective political commentator in the United States." Poet Carl Sandburg viewed him as "a wit and philosopher, one of the brightest figures in the American scene" and also "one of the supreme all-time American cartoonists, a great craftsman and, rather distinctly, a pictorial historian of current events." To the end of his life, Block remained an unreconstructed liberal. He supported gun control, expanding federal spending for education, campaign finance reform, greater representation for the District of Columbia, and, of course, civil rights. Block, early in his career addressed the issue of racism and said that his feelings to treat all citizens equally emerged from his parents who modeled the idea of looking out for all people.[14]

While copyright issues, as always, must be kept in mind when using published works, the technology of today has made the use of cartoons, such as those by Herblock, readily accessible. Johnson and Katz have published a book that examines the life and work of Block in broad brushstrokes. What is most helpful to teachers is that the book contains a DVD with the entire corpus of Block's work—18,000 cartoons—from his high school newspaper days to his final panels just before he retired at age 92 in the year 2001.[15]

There remain a number of highly talented editorial or political cartoonists at work today. Although he works in the medium of four panels as is found in the comics pages of newspapers, Gary Trudeau's *Doonesbury* has been a mainstay of political and social commentary since his days at Yale in the 1960s. (Newspapers often place him on the editorial page rather than the comics pages.) Usually following a weekly storyline, Trudeau has exclusively used symbolism and off panel narrative when dealing with political figures, showing the White House, for example, with words coming from it rather than depicting the president in caricature. Trudeau's work has covered wars (Vietnam to the Middle East), political events and elections, cultural trends, and other assorted topics including education, environmental policy, and the media itself. Trudeau on occasion even self-references his own field of cartoons.

Other high-profile and prize-winning editorial cartoonists now working include Mike Luckovich of the *Atlanta Journal-Constitution*, Stephen Breen at the *San Diego Union-Tribune*, *David Horsey* from the *Seattle Post-Intelligencer*, and Jim Borgman who is with *The Cincinnati Enquirer*. Some, like Luckovich, are openly political (he is a Democrat) and are often irreverent toward their subjects. In an interview, Luckovich, who is a Pulitzer prize winner, has called cartooning "a negative art form, so we kind of enjoy that."[16]

Cartoons have represented an important component of American newspapers and magazines for much of our history. The only major American newspaper that has not utilized cartoons on their editorial pages has been *The New York Times*. (Not only political journals but education journals have employed cartoons to great effect. The best example is *Phi Delta Kappan*, the monthly publication that is considered by many to be the premier journal in education.)[17] While political or editorial cartoons are still very much in evidence in newspapers and some journals of opinion (there is even a monthly newspaper publication titled *Funny Times* that prints a compilation of recent political cartoons[18]), the overall number of cartoonists has decreased dramatically since the 1950s.

It has been noted that at one time in the 1920s every self-respecting newspaper in the United States had its own political cartoonist who was often the most highly paid and prized member of the paper's editorial staff. The decline in the mid-twentieth century coincided with the reduction of the competitive press, reflected by fewer competing dailies in most large cities, along with the "toning down" of cartoon controversial content. When a newspaper had an in-town rival there was usually a need to stake out an identity with strong and controversial material in both print and graphics on the editorial page. As cities and towns were reduced to only one newspaper, temperance and compromise in the name of community consensus became paramount. As Henry Ladd Smith has noted, "The cartoon is strictly an offensive weapon. Asking a cartoonist to attack delicately is like arguing with a cannon to do its work without so much noise."[19]

The number of editorial cartoons and cartoonists has been depleted even further since Smith wrote about the phenomena over a half century ago. The rise of newspaper conglomerates like Gannett and Knight-Ridder has consolidated many papers. If there were few political cartoonists in the 1950s there are even fewer now. The new competition from online outlets for newspaper content is here and will continue to grow in the future. Even newspapers themselves are either publishing online editions of their own product along with their print version or going totally online.

As the 21st century dawned and September 11, 2001 became a monumental benchmark in the affairs of the United States and the world, cartooning also changed. A series of Danish cartoons in 2006 caused chaos and violent backlashes from the Muslim world toward cartoonists. Mohammed, according to Islam, is not to be visually depicted or placed in narratives beyond the accepted confines of their beliefs. The Danish cartoons generated a response from Iran which created a contest for cartoons aimed at ridiculing Israel. The connection between the Danish cartoons and the role of Israel was never made clear. Cartooning had indeed become a serious business, even in a realm as large as international politics.

While there exists a plethora of cartoons available to teachers, the implementation and pedagogical approaches to teaching with these cartoons must be undertaken with both caution and skill on the part of the teacher. Heitzmann indicates that judging whether a student "really gets the artist's message" is often in doubt. He quotes a 1930 study that concluded that those who read and view editorial cartoons must bring a great deal of information to the interpretation process.[20] The same would hold today. Students also must have a knowledge base to interpret political cartoons, especially those from the past.

Heitzmann has recommended a strategy for teaching skills that is tied to higher and lower order thinking through the use of what he terms sub-skills. Lower order sub-skills would include students recognizing the use of caricature and symbolism and explaining the use of historical references and images. Higher-order sub-skills would be judging the cartoonist's bias and interpreting the message or viewpoint. The latter sub-skills build on the former. An example of caricature would be the use of exaggeration to aid in the recognition of the person or object. Questions to determine understanding of caricatures would include: Who knows who this is? How did you know? Is the caricature positive, negative or neutral? Teddy Roosevelt is probably the best personification of caricature. His grin or grimace with the full set of teeth, the glasses, and the energy he exuded were all a cartoonist's dream. Symbolism constitutes a type of visual shorthand—the elephant, the donkey, a dove, or Uncle Sam.[21]

Additional suggestions for questions to employ when working with political and editorial cartoons include: Describe the objects and people that you see in the drawing. Which of the objects on your list might be used as symbols? What do you think each symbol means? List adjectives that describe the emotions portrayed in this political cartoon. Describe the action taking place in the cartoon. What do you think is the message of the cartoon? What interest groups might agree or disagree with the cartoon's message and why?[22]

More than once in this chapter the quandary of definition has or will emerge. Before shifting from cartoons to comic books, some works can be placed in both camps. An example of this dilemma in definitional nomenclature is Gonick's *The Cartoon History of the United States*. This particular work can be seen as caricatures or a "sound-bite" approach that delivers up an entertaining story of American history through brief, often comedic portrayals. The history is quite accurate, revisionist (read critical), and irreverent to the icons of U.S. history. As with editorial cartoons, background knowledge in history is necessary for the learner to "get" the full impact of the messages being delivered. But Gonick's cartoons could also be seen as a comic book. The style of the pages is to show a single panel, General Grant for example, with ten to twenty words of narrative. For Grant, the script reads, "A hard drinker, a failure as a civilian, an anti-Semite . . . but he won battles." The next two panels show Lincoln directing Grant to "finish 'em off" but then notes that Lee was much more imaginative, while Grant's tactic was attrition.[23] Leaving Grant in the book as the hard-drinking, bigoted, and unimaginative general who won wars by disregarding the life of his own soldiers is not exactly complimentary.

Comic Books and Graphic Non-Fiction

Comic books and graphic non-fiction may very well be one of the most promising vehicles to teach history to adolescents. When educators think of utilizing comic books in the teaching of history they must set aside any preconceived notions they may have concerning the medium. One common and erroneous belief is that comics are merely simplistic images with script in balloons over the characters' heads. The complexity of comics will be documented in the remainder of this chapter. The medium is, according to one scholar, "burgeoning." Evidence of this includes the impressive new literature in the field and the "construction of a scholarly infrastructure" that includes archives, conferences, journals, and university courses. Previously viewed as an offshoot of other art medium, usually literature or film, the contemporary study of comics is providing "a fresh appreciation for the distinctive properties that set comics apart from other mediums."[24]

Another misconception is that comics are a tool to entice students to read "serious" material. Thompson in *Adventures in Graphica: Using Comics and Graphic Novels to Teach Comprehension* states, "Reading comics can serve as a conduit to heavier reading and even greater instances of reading traditional texts."[25] Such a quote would be disputed among authors and scholars of comics in addition to being highly offensive to them. While comic books can engage learners to seek out additional information in other media, graphic narratives are not solely stepping stones to lure students to read other material. In short, it is reading, a type of reading that requires its own specialized skills and knowledge. Witek in his "Seven Ways I Don't Teach Comics" supports the contention that comics are frequently seen as a low prestige area of study, which is why he never apologizes for them. (One of his seven points.) He also does not try to position comics as cultural victims.[26]

Yet a scholar in the field of English (a common home for comic studies) has found that:

> One of the very pleasant discoveries that new teachers of graphic novels will make is that students usually do not have to be urged to read them. Students enjoy them not only because of their largely—although by no means exclusively—contemporary content but also because graphic novels fit students' sensibilities at a deep cognitive level. In sequential art, the experience of reading text is combined with the experience of, omnipresent today on the electronic screen, of viewing . . . While the reading of text unaccompanied by images will continue to be important, sequential art seems a perfect fit with modern reading habits.[27]

A definition of comic books is needed for teachers to better understand this powerful learning tool. A standard work defining comics is Scott McCloud's comic book *Understanding Comics: The Invisible Art*. Albeit at times controversial in the literature on comics, for McCloud comics are "juxtaposed pictorial and other images in deliberate sequence intended to convey information and/or to produce an aesthetic response in the viewer."[28] Charles Hatfield has argued that McCloud's definition brackets comics too rigidly rather than indicating that comics both resemble and differ from other textual forms.[29] Another scholar has wisely suggested that in teaching comics it is best not to get bogged down in definitions.[30]

Comics can run the gamut in terms of art work from the realistic to the abstract, from the simplistic to the complex. McCloud notes that the more simplistic or universal the artwork the more iconic it becomes for the reader. There is also a range of subject matter in comics to reflect the age of the readers. For example, when Marvel Comics readership shifted from pre-adolescent to adolescent, the content began to mirror the anxieties and moods of that age group.[31] The adolescent will eventually move from reading material aimed at their age level to adult literature. Comics are also to be found today across all age groups. Modernistic "underground" comics have been labeled "comix," reflecting more adult and counter-culture themes and issues. Examples are civil rights, anti-war, and women's rights. Representative comics' authors and illustrators from the 1960s and 1970s include Robert Crumb, Art Spiegelman, and Harvey Pekar.

The term graphic novel is often used when referring to a longer version of a comic book. (The word graphic itself in this context usually means a pictorial depiction of some kind.) The term graphic non-fiction better fits these longer renderings when applied to history. Graphic non-fiction also has different manifestations not only in subject matter but in the pictorial design. Some graphica (another term also used) can be a mixed-media with more script than visuals. Graphica can, of course, include fiction. One scholar has stated that youth who read graphic novels frequently seek out other types of books for pleasure reading at a rate higher than those youth who do not read graphic novels. In contrast to the idea that comic books represent only one-dimensional villains and heroes, practitioners observe graphic novels offering complex plots that address relevant cultural themes and current political issues. This is especially true in that comics often address personal and social issues pertaining to adolescents.[32]

Bucher and Manning have endorsed the graphic novel, especially for use with older adolescents, due to the genre's ability to address history requirements such as the National Council for the Social Studies (NCSS) Standards. The NCSS Standards speak to concepts such as individual development and identity, power, authority, and governance—all areas that are often dealt with in graphic novels.[33] A historical graphic novel that Bucher and Manning highly recommend is *Stuck Rubber Baby* by Howard Cruse. This work pursues in tandem the issues of civil rights and sexual orientation and is set in the South of the 1960s.[34]

There is also a crossover genre that mixes non-fiction and fictional graphica labeled the "graphic novel non-fiction." Monnin, although writing about graphica for English Language Learners, has attempted to clarify the distinction between the two by placing the graphic novel nonfiction into two categories: 1) Informational Non-Fiction Graphic Novel, which is an expository attempt to strictly convey or explain only factual information. An example of this would be Butzer's *Gettysburg: The Graphic Novel*[35] and 2) Creative Nonfiction Graphic Novel, which focuses on factual events, people, places, and times, but the author uses creative license or storytelling. Spiegelman's *Maus I* and Maus *II* (see further discussion of Spiegelman's works in this chapter) would be examples.[36]

The veritable question that has been asked of historical fiction—comics or otherwise—is how does one know when the event, people, time, place, and/or artifact are factual? Again, good history should be good storytelling (well-written and for comics well-drawn) and good fiction should be rooted in solid historical research. But can adolescent history learners discern the difference? Or does it matter? The two standards for assessing this question should be: 1) Did the student learn something new about history from the work? and 2) Did the work lead the student to further pursue the investigation of history?

Comic books have a rich history in and of themselves.[37] The medium of comics is older than the medium of film, though the latter has received more scholarly attention. Comic themes and characters have incorporated elements from historical events such as the Great Depression, World War II, and the Cold War. In fact, they are reflections of the time period they come from thereby making them primary source documents in history. Three major comic book heroes/heroines emerged from these eras. Captain America appeared punching Adolf Hitler in the nose on the first issue's cover in March of 1941. Wonder Woman also appeared in 1941. Spider Man arrived on the scene in 1963. Aiken has tracked the histories of these three superheroes and how the comic books in which they appear can be used to teach American history. She suggests a number of ways to incorporate comics into history courses from using them as representations of propaganda to mirroring their times, especially politically.

Captain America reflected his time by fighting Nazis in World War II to battling communists in the 1950s and then shifting to social issues represented during the 1960s. In the latter time period, Captain America was joined by an African American partner, Falcon. Together they worked to reduce poverty, racism, pollution, and political corruption. Aiken notes that Captain America and Falcon remained uncharacteristically silent on Vietnam, but at the height of the Watergate scandal, an evidently embarrassed patriot, Captain America changes his name to "Nomad, the man without a country."[38]

Wonder Woman is viewed by Aiken as more a role model for young women due to the changing role of females during World War II. What women needed was proper training to assume their rightful place in society, not the "super power" of many comic figures. As with Captain America, patriotism was pivotal in the Wonder Woman series. Spider Man is the last of the superhero troika analyzed by Aiken. A product of the Cold War, he is much more closely connected to adolescents and their place in American society. Although a teenager, Spider Man (Peter Parker) is not a sidekick like Robin in the Batman series or Superboy is to Superman. He is his own person with "foibles that make him very accessible to students." Aiken views these "low-tech" comics as an effective teaching tool even in the current high-tech world of youth.[39]

There can be added a final point as to the social and political currency of comics. In a 2010 Captain America issue, the superhero observes a Tea Party-type movement event in Idaho where signs read "No New Taxes" and "Stop the Socialists." With him in Idaho is Falcon who must deal with "angry white folks." When in real life a conservative cable network aired the issue, Marvel Comics apologized and promised to pull obvious references to the Tea Party in subsequent Captain America comic book revisions.[40] Other current issues, such as environmentalism, have also been found by scholars within comic book characters such as Swamp Thing, who is often viewed as an ecological protector.

A major attack on comics was Fredric Wertham's *Seduction of the Innocent,* written in 1954 at the height of McCarthyism and the attacks on the liberal ideas of progressive education. *Seduction of the Innocent* warns the public of the dangers of comic books on American youth. Charges included their content being entertaining rather than educational and keeping students from reading the classics or even reading substitutes for the classics via the comics.[41] Wertham's crusade resulted in comic book burnings and the passing of a self-imposed comic book code—Comics Code Authority. Ironically, as seen above, some of the first comic book superheroes were closely aligned to patriotism and fighting fascism and communism.

Cord Scott has directly addressed the use of comics to teach history. A pivotal question that Scott asks is whether comics, as other forms of visual media like movies or television, can be used to teach actual events—history. Multiple examples demonstrate that comics can indeed support and inform the teaching of history. They have been used as auxiliary material in classrooms under three general forms: factual comics, historical fiction, and superhero comics with historical overtones. *Classics Illustrated* from the 1940s dealt with historical events, classic literature, and famous individuals. Scott notes a number of authors who have written comics on Lewis and Clark, crime, the Alamo, dictators of the twentieth century, Pearl Harbor, and the dropping of the atomic bomb on Japan. More recent comic titles have depicted, as will be seen below, the terrorist attacks on the United States on 9/11 and the wars in the Middle East. Many of these works added to their scholarly status by including bibliographies and sections on further reading for the students.[42]

In his analysis of using comic books to teach history, Scott provides endorsements, warnings, and questions. While indicating that comics have been used in classrooms with the approval of two states—New York and Maryland—questions include whether comics can really be used for more than teaching art, the history of graphic arts, or popular culture. Scott thinks they can. Using them in an undergraduate class, he found that they elicited more conversation and fostered increased reading in other sources. Scott ascribes much of this to the ideas of Howard Gardner and his theories of Multiple Intelligences. Due to the reliance today in many classrooms on visuals, the use of comics appears to offer a match for learners who are drawn to this format.

For all his positive views, Scott also notes that using comics as a tool to enhance reading comprehension (and the study of history is strongly dependent on reading) may be merely using a visual media with limited words which could be like teaching students to read by using subtitles on a television.[43] This is an oversimplification in that comics are more complex and television and film are a different media. Then there is John Nichols who has written on the intersection of print and visual culture. He has turned conventional thought on its head by ingeniously suggesting that film can be used to attract students to read comic books.[44]

The best-known historical comic book is Art Spiegelman's *Maus,* which won a special Pulitzer Prize. (See Richard Graham's discussion of this work in this chapter's "The World of Practice" section.) Told in the first person as the son of a Holocaust survivor, Spiegelman received accolades and harsh criticisms regarding the work. Much of the controversy swirled around his portrayal of the main characters as animals. The Jews were mice, the Nazis were cats, and the Poles were pigs. While mature in theme, *Maus* could be used in history and literature classes for older adolescents or gifted and talented students.

Spiegelman would later write about 9/11 in his book *In the Shadow of No Towers.* He was again non-conventional in use of comics as a medium depicting history from format to characterization to format in this work.[45] This pivotal episode in American history also received treatment in the comic book *The 9/11 Report: A Graphic Adaptation,* based on the 2004 *The 9/11 Report: The National Commission on Terrorist Attacks upon the United States.* At 15% the size of the 800-page original report, the graphic non-fiction book has received glowing endorsements from the *School Library Journal* suggesting it be used as a text with older adolescents and that no library be without a copy of it.[46] *The 9/11 Report: A Graphic Adaptation* is more than the medium it is presented in—the point is that few if any students would pick up the 800-page original book in any format. This rendition they will. Another highly recommended comic book for adolescents (this one from early American history) is George O'Connor's *Journey Into Mohawk Country.* In it the author adds graphics to the actual diary of a Dutch trader in the seventeenth century. This comic book addresses diversity and place in authentic ways. There is a single frame of nudity and a bloodless depiction of a scalping.[47] Such diaries and other primary sources will serve as rich models and sources for future historically based comic works.

Again, biographies play a central role in history and have also become increasingly popular in the area of both comic books and graphic non-fiction. Rosen Publishing has released a series of biographies for younger adolescents profiling six women and men from American history: Christopher Columbus, Hernan Cortez, George Washington, Abraham Lincoln, Harriet Tubman, and Sitting Bull. The work on Lincoln, *Abraham Lincoln: The Life of the Sixteenth President* by Gary Jeffrey, Kate Petty, and Mike Lacey, demonstrates the variety of forms that graphic books can take.[48] Fifty-plus pages long, a mix of narrative and illustrations, and a brief "further reading" section, this book and the others in the series are more illustrated narratives than comic books or graphic non-fiction.

Another series of biographies appearing in comic book format for young adolescents has been produced by The Center for Cartoon Studies. Historical personages in this series, representing a diverse selection of individuals from the past, include Harry Houdini, Satchel Paige, Henry David Thoreau, and Amelia Earhart. The volume on Earhart, *Amelia Earhart: This Broad Ocean* by Sarah Stewart Taylor and Ben Towle, focuses on the aviatrix's 1928 flight from Canada across the Atlantic as witnessed through the eyes of a young girl. Aimed at younger adolescents, this comic book is more visual than narrative, although it does have an extensive selected panel discussion section at the end of the book. The added historical information, also in the back of the book and aimed at adult readers, demonstrates that the research on the book was taken seriously by the author.[49] Stone, in reviewing the book for *The New York Times Book Review*, commented that while "engaging and appealing," it may not be, strictly speaking, a work of non-fiction. Calling it a "sort of graphic-novel-style biography" in that the narrator of the book is a fictional adolescent, Stone positively reports that one reluctant reader "devoured it."[50]

One exemplary work of nonfiction is *Malcolm X: A Graphic Biography* written by Andrew Helfer with art by Randy DuBurke. This biography is historically accurate and comprehensive in its treatment of Malcolm's life. The black and white panels are finely illustrated, starkly depicting the dramatic and shocking events in the life of this Black American leader. This book is appropriate for students in middle school through college.[51]

Howard Zinn provided much fodder for many movements in both education and history and it is no surprise that his *A People's History of the United States* has been a rich source for comics. Taking one chapter from Zinn, Paul Buhle and Mike Konopacki have used the late historian's perspectives on colonialism and the United States in their *A People's History of American Empire*. Steve Darnall and Alex Ross have also drawn heavily on Zinn in their book *Uncle Sam*.[52] While not necessarily conservative in content, the traditional Great Books Foundation has included three graphic stories in their *The Great Books Foundation Short Story Syllabus*, an anthology with 39 entries.[53]

Although subtitled "For Beginners," a series of books on topics ranging from philosophy to literature to science has several titles that are highly appropriate for older adolescents. Historian Paul Buhle with illustrator Sabrina Jones collaborated to create *FDR and the New Deal for Beginners*, a work of narrative and cartoons with an afterword by comic book icon the late Harvey Pekar. Each of the five chapters begins with comics interspersed with other comics throughout the work. Additional drawings and editorial cartoons are included. It provides a most appropriate mix of visual and narrative presentation of this critical period in our history and its strong leader, FDR. It is a model for further works of history in the comic book medium.[54] Other historical figures in this particular series include Barack Obama and Malcolm X.

Professional development for teachers via comic books can be acquired through *To Teach: The Journey, in Comics* by controversial educator and notorious (the journal *Rethinking Schools* has called him a "troublemaker"[55]) 1960s anti-war activist William Ayers. The illustrator is Ryan Alexander-Tanner.[56] Drawn from his book *To Teach: The Journey of Teacher*, this comic book covers, not surprisingly, similar topics from his original book such as creative insubordination, finding allies, dealing with criticism, and learning from your own experience. The format demonstrates, as suggested above, that comic books as a medium are not only for children and adolescents.

The World of Practice
Picturing History: Using Comics and Cartoons to Explore Our Past by Richard Graham

When it comes to reading, we want to give students something to capture their attention and appeal to a wide level of literacy and tastes. In a time of iPods, laptops, and cell phones, technology is further complicating strategies to develop students' deep reading skills. For history teachers seeking to incorporate new approaches for engaging students, comics and cartoons can provide a new lens for examining various concepts, scaffold and encourage further reading, and establish common ground.

Suitable for the Classroom?

In the past, teachers, parents, and even librarians have expressed concerns about comics acting as a distraction from the learning process. The sparse use of text and the accompanying images used in comic books were traditionally viewed as perpetuating low literacy practices, while the "formulaic" content was decried as morally harmful. Frederic Wertham and his acolytes in the 1950s declared the comic book a cultural threat to the United States, capable of turning helpless children into illiterate criminals. David Hajdu's portrayal of the history of the North American comic book, *The Ten Cent Plague*, is an excellent retelling of the inquisition wrought from this concern. This movement had the lasting effect of reducing a once thriving medium primarily to superhero stories. Yet the influence of many "underground comix" in the '60s, coupled with the marketing changes in the 1990s, led to an explosion of more complex themes and genres. Today, the graphic novel (book-length comic) has attained some level of legitimacy, beginning when Art Spiegelman's *Maus II* won the Pulitzer Prize in 1992. This revived the interest of educators, who began exploring the positive benefits of using comics in the classroom. Many teachers discovered that comics did not diminish reading confidence—rather they boosted it. Comic readers graduated to more complex reading materials after using comics as a scaffold.

In a media-rich world, the extensive use of images in comics fits the reading style of today's learners. Because of the cognitive processes required to successfully interpret the time and space captured in panels, instructors can connect reading comics with Bloom's Taxonomy and Howard Gardner's Multiple Intelligences. For teachers of history, the comics medium can be used in a variety of ways in the classroom: as narratives that introduce world or local history by means of biography or autobiography, as primary popular culture artifacts that act as windows into contemporary attitudes and perspectives, and to provide an appropriate and beneficial opportunity to bring youth culture into the classroom.

Comics as Historical Literature

Maus, mentioned above, tells the story of the author's father, a survivor of Auschwitz. Famous for its depictions of Jews as mice and Nazis as cats, *Maus* is an excellent example of presenting complex and powerful material as a readable text and giving a strong personal view of history. In her memoir, *Persepolis*, Marjane Satrapi provides a funny and heartbreaking story about growing up in Iran during the 1979 Iranian Revolution and later fleeing as a teenager to Austria. Using powerful black-and-white images, she recounts the dethroning of the Shah, the rise of Islamic fundamentalism, and Iran's war with Iraq. She also describes her exile in Austria and her dealing with many social issues of young adulthood, providing an account of a shared or common experience for many readers. The illustrations of issues such as war and revolution, being an outsider, and complex relationships with parents, make Satrapi's and Spiegelman's work accessible. By being based on factual occurrences and personal experiences, these works display thematic and narrative maturity worthy of inclusion in the history classroom. Of course, like other media, comics can provide a diverse range of styles and content matter that require you to evaluate whether a given text aligns your classroom objectives. Local librarians may also be a resource in helping choose appropriate materials.

Comics as Primary Sources

Comics also can be seen as representing the cultural beliefs and practices of the time in which they were produced. As popular culture artifacts, they often convey a shared or common meaning and can provide insight into shifting historical contexts and themes. Their use of stereotypes as part of the visual grammar also displays the many attitudes and beliefs of the intended market audience. Katherine Aiken, a professor of history at the University of Idaho, incorporates Captain America comic books from the 1940s in her class discussions of World War II. The visual depictions of the "bad guys" provide an opportunity to introduce issues of race and ethnicity, as well as to discuss propaganda and the concept of the "enemy."

The diversity of political or editorial cartoons, long the staple of opinion and editorial pages of newspapers, also has appeal as teaching devices. While cartoons differ from comics in that they are not necessarily stories told in sequence (using more than one panel, etc.), they share many of the same devices, such as caricature, symbolism, and exaggeration. These tools were often used as biting satire and commentary of contemporary issues and popular leaders and figures. The tradition of the editorial cartoon is one of criticism of hypocrisy, injustice, corruption, and social ills and can be used to introduce discussions of any popular personality, era, or aspect of American or world history.

Motivating Student Readers

We have long known that it doesn't require much effort to get a student to read a comic. The appeal of images is too great to pass up. Couple that inclination with the success of popular films and television shows based on comic characters, and there is potential to grow enthusiasm for reading.

Beyond selecting comics as primary texts, another objective to consider is having students *create* comic books. This is another potential strategy to harness the delight students take in comics, while allowing them to analyze their appeal and collaborate in incorporating or synthesizing the course content. George Chilcoat describes the process of having his students create a comic book in his history class as a way for them to "crystallize complex issues into logical and orderly patterns of understanding." This provides students another way of communicating what they have learned.

Conclusion

Using comics and cartoons in the classroom is a creative way to make history a more interesting and meaningful subject to students. We must realize the influence of popular culture has grown exponentially and cannot be underestimated or scorned. Having comics or cartoons present in an educational setting is not an embarrassing attempt to appear "cool" or co-opt youth culture. Rather, it is an acknowledgment that recognizes that the interests of our students can contribute value to the classroom. Comics as history texts can stimulate curiosity about the past and allow students to make meaningful associations and relationships from historical facts. As print culture gives way to a brave new media-saturated world, comics can act as a bridge to instilling sustained or deep reading habits in our students.

References, Further Reading

Of course, the comics and graphic novels I specifically mentioned above are North-American or English-language based. There are many distinct comics traditions around the world, and I urge you to investigate: *manga* from Japan, *bandes dessinées* from France and Belgium, and *foto novellas* from Mexico and Central America. For further reading on using comics specifically in a history classroom:

Aiken, Katherine G. "Superhero History: Using Comic Books to Teach U.S. History." *OAH Magazine of History* April 2010: 41–47.

Chilcoat, George W. "How to Use the Comic Book as a Creative Idea to Teach History." *Southern Social Studies Quarterly* 13.3 (1988): 18–32.

Witek, Joseph. *Comic Books as History: The Narrative Art of Jack Jackson, Art Spiegelman, and Harvey Pekar.* University Press of Mississippi. 1989.

Richard Graham is the Media Services Librarian and Associate Professor at the University Of Nebraska-Lincoln. His specialty is the use of comics in education.

Endnotes

1   Steinbrink, John E., and Donna Bliss. "Using Political Cartoons to Teach Thinking Skills." *The Social Studies* September/October 1988: 217.
2   Heitzmann, William Ray. "Looking at Elections Through the Cartoonist's Eye." *Social Education* 64. 5 (2000): 314.
3   Nevins, Allan and Frank A. Weitenkampf. *Century of Political Cartoons: Caricature in the United States from 1800 to 1900.* New York: Scribner's and Sons,1944. 11–18, 134.
4   Caswell, Lucy Shelton. "A Short History of the American Political Cartoon." *Attack of the Political Cartoonists: Insights and Insults from Today's Editorial Pages.* Ed. J.P. Trostle. Madison: Dark Storm Press, 2004. 6–8.
5   Hess, Stephen. *The Ungentlemanly Art: A History of American Political Cartoons.* New York: The Macmillan Company, 1968. 15.
6   Holbrook, Stewart H. *Lost Men of American History.* New York: The Macmillan Company, 1946. 36.
7   Bunker, Gary L. " 'Old Abe' in Political Caricature: Revisiting the Drawn Lincoln." *Magazine of History* 23.1 (2009): 37–41. See also Bunker, Gary L. *From Railsplitter to Icon: Lincoln's Image in Illustrated Periodicals, 1869–1865.* Kent: Kent State University Press, 2001.
8   Weinburg, Carl R. " 'Abarack Lincoln' and Lincoln's Legacy through Political Cartooning." *Magazine of History* 23.1 (2009): 49–50.
9   Dewey, Donald. *The Art of Ill Will: The Story of American Political Cartoons.* New York: New York University Press, 2007.
10 Nevins and Weitenkampf, 16–18.
11 Ibid. 134.
12 Minear, Richard H. *Dr. Seuss Goes to War: The World War II Editorial Cartoons of Theodor Seuss Geisel.* New York: The New Press, 1999; Schriffrin, Andre. *Dr. Seuss & Co. Go to War.* New York: The New Press, 2009.

13   Block, Herbert, and Katherine Graham. *Herblock: A Cartoonist's Life.* New York: Crown Publishing Group, 1998.

14   For more on Herblock see Hess, Stephen, and Milton Kaplan. *The Ungentlemanly Art: A History of American Political Cartoons.* New York: The Macmillan Company, 1968; Graham, Katherine. "Herblock's Half-Century: A Tiger by the Tail." 31 Dec. 1995. Web. <http://www.washingtonpost.com/wp-srv/politics/herblock/graham.htm>; and Katz, Harry L. "About Herblock: Herblock's History: Political Cartoons from the Crash to the Millennium." Web. < http://www.loc.gov/rr/print/swann/herblock/about.html>.

15   Johnson, Haynes and Harry Katz. *Herblock: The Life and Work of the Great Political Cartoonist.* New York: W.W. Norton and Company with the Herblock Foundation and the Library of Congress, 2009.

16   Mummolo, Jonathan. "Tooned in to Politics." *Newsweek* 11 September 2006: 9.

17   Provenzo, Eugene F., and Anthon Beonde. "Educational Cartoons as Popular Culture." Eds. Paul Farber, Eugene F. Provenzo, and Gunilla Holm. *Schooling in the Spotlight of Popular Culture.* Albany: State University of New York Press, 1994. 231.

18   See <http://www.funnytimes.com> or contact Funny Times at P.O. Box 18530, Cleveland Heights, OH, 44118.

19   Smith, Henry Ladd. "The Rise and Fall of the Political Cartoon." *The Saturday Review* 29 May 1954: 7–9, 28–29.

20   Heitzmann, 314. See also Shafer, L. *Children's Interpretations of Political Cartoons.* New York: Teachers College Press, 1930.

21   Heitzmann, 314–315.

22   Johnson, Haynes, and Harry Katz. *Herblock: The Life and Work of the Great Political Cartoonist.* New York: W.W. Norton and Company with the Herblock Foundation and the Library of Congress, 2009. "An Abolitionist Cartoon, 1830." *Social Education* 69. 5 (2005): S16.

23   Gonick, Larry. *The Cartoon History of the United States.* New York: HarperCollins Publishers, 1991. 176–177.

24   Heer, Jeet and Kent Worcester, Eds. Introduction. *A Comics Reader.* Jackson: University Press of Mississippi, 2009. xi, xiv.

25   Thompson, Terry. *Adventures in Graphica: Using Comics and Graphic Novels to Teach Comprehension* . Portland, ME: Stenhouse Publishers, 2008, quote taken from *Graphica.* <http://www.rosenclassrooms.com>. Web.

26   Witek, Joseph. "Seven Ways I Don't Teach Comics." *Teaching the Graphic Novel.* Ed. Stephen E. Tabachnick. New York: The Modern Language Association, 2009. 218–19.

27   Tabachnick, 3–4.

28   McCloud, Scott. *Understanding Comics: The Invisible Art.* New York: HarperCollins, 1993. 9.

29   Tabachnick, 23.

30   Witek, 219.

31   McCloud, 46, 52, 53, 126.

32   *Using the Graphic Novels in the Classroom, Grades 4–8.* Westminster: Teacher Creative Resources, 2010. 3.

33   Bucher, Katherine T. and M. Lee Manning. "Bringing Graphic Novels into a School's Curriculum." *The Clearing House* 78.2 (2004): 71.

34   Cruse, Howard. *Stuck Rubber Baby.* Boulder: Vertigo, 2010.

35 Butzer, C.M. *Gettysburg: The Graphic Novel.* New York: HarperCollins, 2009.

36 Monnin, Katie. *Teaching Graphic Novels: Practical Strategies for the Secondary ELA Classroom.* Gainesville: Maupin House Publishing, Inc., 2010. 67, 74, and 80.

37 See Wright, Bradford. *Comic Gook Nation.* Washington, D.C.: Johns Hopkins University Press, 2001, and Sabin, Roger. *Comics, Comix, and Graphic Novels.* London: Phaidon Press,1997.

38 Aiken, Katherine G. "Superhero History: Using Comic Books to Teach U.S. History." *Magazine of History* 24. 2 (2010): 41–47.

39 Ibid. 47.

40 Ibid. 41.

41 Wertham, Fredric. *Seduction of the Innocent.* Port Washington: Kennikat Publishing,1954.

42 Scott, Cord. "The 'Good' Comics: Using Comic Books to Teach History." *International Journal of Comic Art* 8. 1 (2006): 546–61.

43 Ibid. 558–59.

44 Nichols, John G. "Violent Encounters: Graphic Novels and Film in the Classroom." *Teaching the Graphic Novel.* New York: The Modern Language Association, 2009. 230–37.

45 Ibid. 552. See Spiegelman, Art. *In the Shadow of No Towers.* New York, NY: Viking, 2004.

46 Jacobson, Sid and Ernie Colon. *The 9/11 Report: A Graphic Adaptation.* New York: Hill and Wang, 2006.

47 O'Connor, George. *Journey Into Mohawk Country.* New York: First Second Publishers, 2006.

48 Jeffrey, Gary, Kate Petty, and Mike Lacey. *Abraham Lincoln: The Life of the Sixteenth President.* New York: The Rosen Publishing Group, 2005. For other titles in the series see <http://www.rosenclassrooms.com>.

49 Taylor, Sarah Stewart and Ben Towle. *Amelia Earhart: This Broad Ocean.* New York: Disney-Hyperion, 2010.

50 Stone, Tanya Lee. "Full Throttle." Rev. of *Amelia Earhart: This Broad Ocean* by Sarah Stewart Taylor and Ben Towle. *The New York Times Book Review.* 14 March 2010. 15.

51 Helfer, Andrew and Randy DuBurke. *Malcolm X: A Graphic Biography.* New York: Hill and Wang, 2006.

52 Vizzini, Bryan E. "Hero and Holocaust: Graphic Novels in the Undergraduate Classroom." *Teaching the Graphic Novel.* New York: The Modern Language Association, 2009. 238–44; Buhle, Paul, and Mike Konopacki. *A People's History of American Empire.* New York: Metropolitan Books, 2008; and Darnall, Steve, and Alex Ross. *Uncle Sam.* New York: DC Comics, 1998.

53 *The Great Books Foundation Short Story Omnibus.* Chicago: The Great Books Foundation, 2009.

54 Buhle, Paul. *FDR and the New Deal for Beginners.* Hanover: Steerforth Press, 2010.

55 Review of *To Teach: The Journey, in Comics,* in *Rethinking Schools* 24. 4: 58–59.

56 Ayers, William and Ryan Alexander-Tanner. *To Teach: The Journey, in Comics.* New York: Teachers College Press, 2010.

FIVE

Critical Thinking and Controversial Topics in History

Critical Thinking

Examining critical thinking in a chapter that includes a discussion of controversial topics in history may seem anomalous—or an unlikely match at best. But both critical thinking and controversial topics are forms of active learning. Critical thinking is an imminent part of all aspects of the study of history, especially in dealing with controversial issues. Critical thinking is both a major goal and vital strategy for students working in the discipline of history. Some in the public continue to view schooling as the process of "covering the material." Most educators, though, firmly maintain that the purpose of education is to support and guide students in learning how to be independent thinkers. And nowhere is independent thinking called upon more than in exploring controversial issues.

As mentioned in the introduction to this book, ideas and issues may not always be an "either/or" proposition. Learning history and undertaking the work of critical thinking are not mutually exclusive. This is not to say that there is not a debate. Brady has written that there are indeed barriers. Some individuals outside the schools are not truly convinced that the teaching of thinking is even doable. As segments of the business community wish to push for more academic rigor, politicians seek higher test scores, and the troika of the publishing, testing, and consulting industries each has reservations about moving too far away from "covering the material."[1] With such competing agendas and practices, critical thinking must defend its legitimacy in the classroom.

There is little argument in the professional educational literature of the past three decades that critical thinking, though, through the art and science of questioning is central for students to successfully learn history.[2] This includes questions asked by teachers and questions asked by students. The National Middle School Association affirmed this consensus in their document *This We Believe* by stating: "An effective middle level curriculum is distinguished by learning activities that appeal to young adolescents and create opportunities to pose and answer questions that are important to them."[3] Ciadiello has written that the use of questions is a "pathway to wandering and wondering."[4]

Creating and guiding student discussion, while maintaining a climate that supports student contributions, are essential elements in teaching critical thinking. The art of asking questions and classroom questioning strategies, on the part of students and teachers, is an integral component in achieving higher-order thinking. As Neil Postman and Charles Weingartner wrote in their classic 1960s book *Teaching as a Subversive Activity*, "Once you have learned how to ask questions—relevant and appropriate and substantial questions—you have learned how to learn and no one can ever stop you."[5]

John Dewey said in 1933: "The mind is not a piece of blotting paper that retains and absorbs automatically. It is rather a living organism that has to stretch for its food, that selects and rejects according to its present conditions and needs, and retains only what it digests and transmutes into part of energy of its own being."[6] Dewey's physiology may not hold up completely with 21st-century brain research, but the essence of his idea remains valid in terms of our thinking processes.

Teaching that incorporates higher-order thinking questions based on Bloom's Taxonomy remains a solid model for learning theorists of most persuasions. Bloom's six levels of higher-order thinking—knowledge, comprehension, application, analysis, synthesis, and evaluation—have been used effectively to permit students and teachers to reach understandings of material beyond recall and memorization of facts represented by the first two or three levels of his taxonomy. Bloom's 1956 work *The Taxonomy of Educational Objectives* has been modified and updated a number of times over the past fifty years—over twenty times in total with two revisions of note in the last decade. Brady has written that Bloom's work provides a "useful tool for thinking and talking about what is happening and not happening inside students' heads. Having words for different thinking skills make it easy to get a fix on the kinds of thought processes that students are using." Brady believes the best way to achieve higher-order thinking skills is to emphasize "first-hand thinking," not "second-hand thinking." First-hand thinking would be students making sense of their own day-to-day experiences. Conversely, second-hand thinking consists of internalizing the thoughts and views of others and then repeating them—the recall level of thinking.[7]

Anderson and his colleagues published in 2001 *A Taxonomy for Learning, Teaching, and Assessing: A Revision of Bloom's Taxonomy of Educational Objectives.* That work updated Bloom's original framework vis-à-vis cognitive psychology, used a different terminology based on a new taxonomy of categories, updated domains, and provided practical examples.[8]

The most recent and most comprehensive refashioning of Bloom has been undertaken by Robert Marzano and John Kendall in the second edition of their 2007 *The New Taxonomy of Educational Objectives.* As with Anderson's work there is a new taxonomy, with six levels of processing: 1) retrieval—recognizing and recalling, 2) comprehension—integrating and symbolizing, 3) analysis—comparing, contrasting, and generalizing 4) knowledge utilization—decision making and problem solving, 5) metacognition—specifying and monitoring goals, and 6) self-system thinking—examining important emotional responses and motivation. In tandem with the six levels of processing or mental operations are three domains of knowledge (information, mental procedures, and psychomotor procedures.) The originators of the New Taxonomy prefer to view their creation as a model or theory rather than a framework. This allows for the prediction of phenomena or behavior, rather than the description of characteristics of phenomena.

Differing from the work of Anderson and his team, the New Taxonomy's goal is applicability. This is accomplished in several ways. First, while it remains, as with Bloom's original work, a structure for classifying educational objectives, Marzano and Kendall use their adaptation to address assessment, standards, curricular design, and thinking skills. The creators of the New Taxonomy claim that it improves the design of assessment by better articulated objectives and thereby render it "more interpretable and useful for students. They jettison the term "higher-order" thinking skills, suggesting that only exceptional students can master such material. "Self-system thinking" is at the "top of the hierarchy due to the fact that it controls whether or not a learner engages in a new task" with energy, motivation, and choice. This is the result of a more explicitly stated taxonomy. Finally, the New Taxonomy addresses not only the cognitive domain, but also the affective and psychomotor.[9]

An example from history using the New Taxonomy is drawn from the essay form of assessment. After reading excerpts from the Lincoln-Douglas Debates, the following scenario and question are employed: The student imagines that she lives in 1858 Illinois; after hearing one of the debates, the student returns home and is asked by her cousin to explain what of importance was discussed during the debate. Also, what should the cousin understand about the problems facing the nation? The essay is to explain which ideas and issues the cousin should understand. Marzano and Kendall see such essays as effectively providing assessment data for almost all types of knowledge across almost every level of the New Taxonomy.[10]

An entirely dissimilar component of critical thinking is having students think like a historian. Stanford University professor Connie Juel and three of her doctoral students have explored this idea. "Understanding how . . . to think like a historian can provide students with direction as they read particular texts," they have written. Critical thinking can be "messy, long, difficult, but the act of shifting through puzzling, conflicting, and biased texts should constitute at least part of a student's experience." A distinctive trait of the discipline, they conclude, "is the ability to synthesize vast amounts of text into a cohesive narrative . . . the kind of critical thinking we want our students to do."[11]

For all the advocacy for higher-order thinking strategies, the literature reports that teachers continue to use lower level questions in their classrooms. A recent study by Bintz and Williams of middle level classrooms confirmed this finding. A majority of teacher-asked questions called only for basic recall of the information on the part of the students. Teachers were indeed asking a large number of questions, they were just the wrong kind. They give the example of a lesson on the Boston Tea Party. When asked after the lesson what they knew about the event, students provided an almost uniform response that "tea was dumped into Boston Harbor." No deeper meaning seemed to have been taken from the lesson and the researchers indicated a lack of higher-level thinking the reason.[12]

One way to counter the practice of teachers asking lower level questions is to encourage more questions on the part of students. To quote from *This We Believe* again, "Student generated questions may lead to more demanding study, particularly when the prescribed curriculum is too often preoccupied with answers to questions young adolescents never ask."[13] Three ways that Bintz and Williams view as helpful to encouraging more and higher quality student questions are: 1) teaching students about higher-level questions by beginning with closed (single-answer, low level) questions and open (more complex, high level) questions and "thick" (big) questions and "thin" (little) questions; 2) having students create and use their own questions in a lesson; and 3) teachers modeling questioning techniques in their classrooms and constantly incorporating questions into their lessons in advance.[14]

Henning has developed a critical thinking approach he calls the "bow tie." The teacher frames the discussion—one wider end of the bow tie—narrows the discussion by shifting to a conceptual discussion and then widening the other side of the bow tie with applications generated by students.[15] Creating and testing hypotheses around the causes of the Civil War presents a workable opportunity. For example, slavery was the major cause of the war with most other causes considered secondary. A hypothesis that the students could pursue would be whether the war was inevitable and were there any possible alternatives? Such activities move students into the area of higher level thinking. The thoughtful selection of questions for inclusion in classroom discussions and assessments may be the most important act on the part of history teachers in their daily decision-making.

Taxonomies are central in creating questions to be used in the history classroom. But strategies are needed to bring about effective implementation of questions. Teachers need to try questions out on themselves, suggests Johnson—a mix of questions—from low level to high level.[16] Feinstein, extrapolating from some of Marzano's earlier work, has suggested a number of strategies. Although traditional, they have been shown to aid adolescents in thinking abstractly, especially about history. These include asking students to write a summary of a lesson, identifying similarities and differences, learning to write metaphors and analogies, creating and testing hypotheses, and reinforcing lessons with cues, questions, and advanced organizers.[17]

The topics of critical thinking and questioning have become, as was seen with Marzano's work, increasingly complex. One of the more intricate and multifaceted approaches to questioning are Questioning as Thinking (QAT), a metacognitive framework that helps students and teachers focus on performance. QAT combines three widely used strategies: Think-Aloud, Question Answer Relationships (QAR), and Self-Questioning. Think Aloud is a practice where teachers model question-asking (and thereby comprehension of reading material) by reading a section of material and then stopping and asking questions that the teacher views as critical.[18] An example would be reading selections of the speeches of Martin Luther King, Jr. and Malcolm X and pausing to ask questions: What did King mean by judging people by "the content of the character, not the color of their skin"? What did he mean by character? Was King too passive in his approach in what at times were intractable situations? What did Malcolm X mean by Blacks receiving their rights by "any means necessary"? Or when he said, "We need to stop singing 'We Shall Overcome' and come out swinging" was he advocating violence as the only path to progress in race relations?

The other two strategies in QAT are Question Answer Relationships (QAR) and Self-Questioning. QAR is built on research that provides students with categories by which to locate information by asking question such as "Are these questions in the book or in my head?" If in the book are they "right there" or are they "think and search questions?" Another aspect of QAR is to assure that students are comfortable with the language, vocabulary, and key words of the material in the textbook. An example would be the need to use appropriate categories and terminology in web searches like finding a history movie on civil rights. The third piece of QAT is self-questioning. These would be questions students ask themselves such as: "Does what I just read make sense to me? How can I relate this information to what I already know? What do I need to do to remember about the ideas presented?"[19]

Wyman has listed five types of historical thinking that he connects directly to critical thinking.[20] These are:

- Chronological Thinking—the ability to develop a sense of historical time—past, present, and future—the sequencing of events and the use of time lines.

- Historical Comprehension—the ability to listen to and read historical stories and narratives with understanding and to develop the ability to describe the past through the eyes and experiences of those who were there.

- Historical Analysis and Interpretation—the ability to compare and contrast different experiences and analyze how differing motives influenced people's behavior.

- Historical Research Capabilities—the ability to formulate historical questions, acquire information concerning historical times, and to construct a historical narrative or story.

- Historical Issues-Analysis and Decision-Making—the ability to identify problems that people confronted in historical times and to evaluate alternative proposals for dealing with the problem, and make judgments about those problems.

Historiography is a historical tool that connects the discipline directly to critical thinking. Historiography is the analysis by historians of varying opinions and points of view about particular topics, issues, and episodes. Whether employed in connection with textbooks or primary sources, introducing students to historiography provides data and narrative by which to engage in the practice of critical and higher-order thinking. The depth to which teachers take their students in working in historiography is flexible. Critical thinking is involved in historiography in that it demonstrates that historians disagree and therefore supply multiple versions of history. (Two prime examples are the causes of slavery and the motivations for the Progressive Movement.) Historiography also informs students of a major part of a historian's work.

Hoefferle maintains that historiography and critical thinking skills "lay at the heart" of the National Center for History in the Schools Standards in Historical Thinking. With the vast amount of historical information available, being aware of historiography can assist the student in determining the validity of this material. Hoefferle has suggested a six-step process in teaching historiography and critical thinking:

- Author—What should students know about an author's background, such as race, gender, class, and political affiliation?

- Topic—Does topic selection reveal subjectivity or bias by the historian?

- Thesis—Identification of the historian's major thesis.

- Evidence—Seeking supporting arguments and evidence to defend the historian's thesis and conclusions.

- Theory—This step focuses on what the resultant historical conclusion says about theory and philosophy. (Possibly too complex for younger adolescents, but appropriate for gifted and talented students.)

- Critical Analysis—What is the result of the historiographical process in terms of proven, unproven, irrelevant, weak or well-documented arguments?[21]

While historiography is often deemed an activity for older students, even considered the domain of history majors in college, the process involves debate, controversy, and finding flaws in the arguments of historians. These are all potential motivators to challenge adolescents in the history classroom. Again, the methodology of historiography is one where teachers may need additional professional development and resources.

Kyle Ward in his book *Not Written in Stone: Learning and Unlearning American History Through 200 Years of Textbooks* provides history teachers with an excellent array of the "raw data" of history needed to employ the strategy of historiography in the classroom. Ward accomplishes this by using comparative versions of the same historical event drawn from textbooks written at different times in our history. These selections (from Colonization to the Philippine-American War) allow, as Ward calls them, "junior historians" (students) to see how historians are affected by personal bias, perspective, and interpretation. Ward calls the historiography process "layering." He begins, on the first layer, by reminding students that actual historical events involve real people with all their complexities and differences of opinion. In the next layer he points out that several generations have researched, written about, and analyzed these same historical events. The final layer is when students discover that historians have been influenced by their own society, culture, and time.

The example of slavery in historiography that Ward provides in his introductory remarks to his book is an instructive one. A textbook writer in the 1850s may not have mentioned slavery at all, even as an economic institution. Looking back on slavery from the 1890s, the institution may have been viewed as a "good thing"—slaves had supposedly been "happy," racial inferiority went mainly unchallenged, and the overall historical picture portrayed was a positive one. In the 1960s, historians from the Civil Rights movement took a more critical look at slavery as seen through the lenses of racial and social justice. History, as Ward notes, has a history of its own.

One of the most enlightening chapters in Ward's book is on the Alamo. The textbooks he draws from begin in 1888. There are two representative texts from the 1920s, three from the 1955 to 1970 era, and then one written in 1999. Shifting perceptions of the Mexican people, those that moved into Texas from the U.S. (then part of Mexico), and the resultant clashes change before our eyes as seen from generation to generation of historians. While Ward does not use introductory comments with his selections, he does list questions for students at the end of each section. Again, this allows students to arrive at their own conclusions about what they are reading.[22]

Two recommended works in historiography to increase teacher knowledge are Mark Gilderhus's *History and Historians: A Historiographical Introduction* and Beverley Southgate's *History: What and Why?*[23] One additional suggestion comes from Drake and Nelson—the use of photographs of famous Americans. Historiography emerges when students are asked to find four or five paintings, pictures, photographs, or caricatures of women and men over the span of their lives. How do figures like Thomas Jefferson, Abraham Lincoln, Jack Johnson, Eleanor Roosevelt, Marilyn Monroe, or Cassius Clay/Muhammed Ali change over time? Changing perceptions, even in photographs, is a form of historiography with which students can easily connect.[24]

In conclusion, students, schools, and teachers may not be the only ones in need of being queried on performance—and critical thinking. Paul S. George suggests that in a time of constant criticism of schools, maybe students should ask adults a few questions about their behavior and decision-making. In his opinion these questions should include:

- Why were there intelligence failures that led to the inability to prevent 9/11?

- Why was the war in Iraq so poorly planned and executed?

- Why was the federal government's response to Hurricane Katrina so disastrous?

- What went wrong with the ethical and technical aspects that caused the major financial collapse of 2008?

- Why is unemployment such a difficult issue to deal with?

These are not inappropriate history questions that can be applied with variations to any period in American history.

Controversial and Problematic Topics in History

Diana Hess in her book *Controversy in the Classroom: The Democratic Power of Discussion* boldly states that "democratic education demands controversial issues discussions."[25] The examination of controversial or problematic topics can be a highly motivational strategy in the teaching of history, although it could be argued that little stimulus is needed. Outside the classroom parents will quickly agree that adolescents seem genetically pre-determined to enjoy debate. It can also be one of the most treacherous and precarious approaches in teaching. Much in tune with the turbulent decade of the 1960s, two social studies educators, Maurice Hunt and Lawrence Metcalf, wrote about "problematic" or "closed" areas of study. For them, a controversial topic needed to contain some element of divisiveness, elicit strong opinions, possibly make students intellectually uncomfortable, and most critical—be boundary-pushing or considered taboo in some manner.[26] One study has indicated that approximately 90% of teachers do not relish initiating controversial subjects or engaging in a class discussion when students raise them in class. Topics included the Vietnam War, politics, race relations, religion, or family problems.[27] One wonders how to teach history to students in the 21st century without touching on any of these topics and themes.

Jonathan Kozol again reminds us that conflict and controversy are good for students and that ideas like "conflict resolution" and "values clarification," where consensus is sought, are in his opinion "bogus classroom ethics." Never one to dodge controversy, Kozol maintains that it is both healthy and intelligent to confront issues head-on. He firmly believes, however, that students have the control and dignity to handle controversy, even when it means disagreeing with the teacher. In his book *On Being a Teacher*, Kozol cites a number of American radicals. Thomas Jefferson spoke about refreshing the tree of liberty with the blood of patriots and tyrants. Abolitionist William Lloyd Garrison, when asked about his rage, replied, "I have need to be on fire, for I have mountains of ice about me to melt." Henry David Thoreau, no mere idler on Walden Pond, once said, "I fear chiefly lest my expression be not extravagant enough . . . I desire to speak somewhere without bounds." And most eloquent, Kozol quotes Martin Luther King, Jr. from his Birmingham jail cell:

Was not Jesus a an extremist for love? The question is not whether we will be an extremist, but what kind of extremist we will be. Will we be extremists for hate or will we be extremists for love? Will we be extremists for preservation of injustice or will we be extremists for the cause of justice?[28]

These are historical examples, but controversial issues remain with us in the 21st century. The court case *Morse v. Frederick* in 2007 brought the issue of student controversy and student free speech to the forefront once again in no less lofty a forum than the United States Supreme Court. A student sign reading "Bong hits for Jesus" was viewed by school officials as advocating drug use. In a classic split decision, the court ruled that school speech could be limited. Justice Clarence Thomas wrote that freedom of speech did not cover a student's right to speak in public schools. The history of American education, he said, had shown teachers to be in total control of the students. Although in the minority on the decision, Justice John Paul Stevens called for open expression. Unpopular views, by even high school students, needed to be protected and even encouraged. Clearly this is a recent and relevant case in point demonstrating how a student-related controversy eventually reached the highest level of our government.[29]

Returning to Hess, the inclusion of controversial or problematic (difficult) issues within the history curriculum should be seen as a benefit and additional resource, not a detriment. Hess has posited several reasons why a discussion of controversial issues is essential. They include discussion itself as a key aspect of democratic education. Discussions are authentic because they mirror the debates taking place outside the classroom. And discussion is a means to an end—that end being students learning how to become active citizens in a democracy.[30]

A distinction that Hess also makes is distinguishing between topics and issues. Hess advocates history classrooms to seek issues, not topics. An example is healthcare reform, a topic according to Hess. But looking at the problem of lack of access to healthcare focuses the topic on an issue that can be discussed with greater opportunity for success. Hess also adds that the classroom history teacher needs to differentiate between current events and current issues. Many current events are not important, let alone controversial. There is a difference between being aware of the news and keeping abreast of critical issues that face society. This is not to denigrate the need for history teachers to seize the well-known "teachable moment." Hess relates that during the attacks of 9/11, a number of teachers spent limited time on the event due to the need to "cover" the required curriculum. In one case this was the War of 1812 for which two days of class time had been allotted.[31] It would be analogous to students in 1941 classrooms returning to a lesson on the tariffs of the 1820s the day after the surprise attack on Pearl Harbor. Such opportunities are thankfully rare, but they should not be lost.

Hess provides three categories for controversial issues. They are labeled open, closed, and tipping. An open controversial issue is one that is alive and well in the public domain. Capital punishment is an example. A closed issue is one that is for all intents and purposes settled. Women's suffrage or child-labor are examples. And then there are the tipping controversial issues. These would include same sex marriage and global warming. Such issues are moving toward a resolution either through laws or an overwhelming public consensus. Some issues in history, Hess points out, have shifted between categories. The internment of Japanese Americans during World War II would be an example. It was first thought to be needed for wartime security (closed). It was then debated in classrooms, courtrooms, and the public in general (open). Finally, an act of Congress and a president stipulated that it had been an illegal and damaging act against American citizens (closed again).[32]

There are a number of conventional topics that have been considered controversial within history. They have included: Should Thomas Jefferson have purchased the Louisiana Territory from France even though there was no direct Constitutional authority to do so? Did Franklin Roosevelt have prior knowledge of the attack on Pearl Harbor? Or, should Harry Truman have dropped the atomic bombs on Japan? Whether any or all of these "controversial issues" are really that controversial or even of interest to adolescents is debatable. And teachers themselves may have no rationale for including them in the history curriculum.

Hesitancy on the part of teachers to engage in controversial topics in a history classroom can emerge from a variety of sources. Terrie Epstein has pointed out that teaching history as an "uncontested narrative of progress and inclusion" has been the dominant path taken by teachers. Teaching American history from such a unifying theme is less contentious. Teaching from a perspective that progress has come to the American people at the expense of others can be troubling to many. The fact that there has been as much exclusion in our history as inclusion can be uncomfortable for even teachers. Teachers who maintain a more orthodox view of American history are also less likely to draw the ire of parents, administrators, and even students. Hesitancy may also simply arise because teachers feel uninformed about some controversial topics in history.[33]

It has been said that sex, religion, and social class are the troika of verboten classroom topics. The prime example is probably sex. Recently, though, the occasional history textbook will place a sidebar within its pages providing a brief sketch of the research pioneer in human sexuality, Alfred Kinsey. Wise educators will tread carefully, but a deeper examination by older adolescents of this troubled and controversial man can lead to productive lines of inquiry. Kinsey, a biologist at Indiana University from the 1920s to the 1950s, undertook scientific interviews on sexual behavior, founding what is now the Kinsey Institute for Research in Sex, Gender, and Reproduction. He and his small research group produced two works on human sexuality, one on males in 1948 and one on females in 1953. The first book on male sexuality was surprisingly well received, although it contained for its time novel and controversial data on male sexual behavior. However, Kinsey's publication on female sexuality brought harsh criticism toward both him and his work. Although supported by the university, his institute lost its Rockefeller Foundation funding and he died prematurely a broken man. Some biographers have considered his work a precursor to what became known as the "radical sixties" in the area of social mores and sexual practices.[34] The novel *The Inner Circle* by T.C. Boyle, and the films suggested in this book's movie chapter all suggest that the boundaries on previously closed topics, such as sex in history, may become more open.

The Stonewall Riot in New York City's Greenwich Village in 1969 brought the gay liberation movement to the forefront in American history. Yet while the discussion of gender and race eventually found space in high school U.S. history textbooks, homosexuality, for the most part, has not. The issues surrounding the population identified as lesbian/gay/bisexual/transgendered (LGBT) are absent except in some Advanced Placement American history textbooks. Considering that gays serving in the military consumed the first several months of Bill Clinton's presidency (eventually creating the "Don't Ask, Don't Tell" policy) one would assume some mention of it would be made in textbooks. The Stonewall Riot or "Don't Ask, Don't Tell" are rarely referenced. LGBT certainly meets the Hunt and Metcalf test for a "closed area" of study in the social studies. Apparently the period between high school graduation and entering college is sufficient maturation time for students to handle the issue of sex.

Addressing the LGBT issue at an age even earlier than adolescence is a book simultaneously published in Great Britain and the United States. The book is titled *Undoing Homophobia in Primary Schools* and is a part of the No Outsiders Project Team.[35] (Young adult fiction through the works of authors like Judy Blume began addressing the issue of homosexuality a number of years ago.)   LGBT issues, according to *Undoing Homophobia in Primary Schools,* is to be considered analogous to any other minority group being discriminated against either now or in the past. For example, the book speaks to those who oppose LGBT and say, "I have nothing against homosexuals; I just don't want my children to hear any mention of them at their age." A recommended response to this statement might be, "Let's substitute Black for homosexual: I have nothing against Black people, but it's just that I think children need to be older before they hear about them." The point is that eventually the issue of sexual preference is going to appear in history textbooks and teachers will need to make decisions on how to pedagogically handle them. Age appropriateness when discussing any controversial topic is, of course, a serious question that needs to be handled responsibly.

The two major professional historical organizations—the American Historical Association and the Organization of American Historians—have viewed the sub-field of sexuality in history as worthy of attention. In their publications they are proposing that a variety of topics on sexuality be addressed in the history classroom. But it has also been noted that K–12 teachers are the most vulnerable group of educators in connection with this topic.[36] A teacher today teaching about sexuality could find themselves in a similar situation to that of John Scopes in 1920s Tennessee when he tested the boundaries of community acceptance to new ideas by teaching evolution in his science classroom.

One response to community concerns on the controversial topic of sexuality is to again turn to trade books. One award-winning title referenced in a previous chapter is the young adult biography of civil rights activist Bayard Rustin in *No Easy Answers: Bayard Rustin and the Civil Rights Movement* by Calvin C. Miller.[37] Black, a pacifist, at one time a communist, and also gay, Rustin embodies multiple controversial areas within one person. Leisa Meyer believes that Rustin just may be too "non-normative" to be placed in the conventional American history narrative.[38] But again, providing students choices within their own self-selected reading is a reasonable option.

Admittedly, one of the more complicated and challenging topics any history teacher faces is genocide in general and the Holocaust in particular. Chapla has written that, "Teaching young adolescents about the horrors of the Holocaust and other examples of genocide can be a challenge for middle grades teachers. The subject matter is intense and the content available may not be suitable for all students."[39] The rationale for including this material in the adolescent history class includes helping students understand why they need to know about the Holocaust and helping students make meaning from that event to their own lives. The approaches to teaching such material are fundamental. They could include preparatory readings and the use of primary sources like the testimonies of Holocaust survivors or World War II veterans who freed the camps. While the U.S. Holocaust Museum in Washington, D.C. is a premier public history teaching center, there are also Holocaust museums available in smaller communities. These are often associated with Jewish synagogues and temples.[40]

A companion issue to genocide is that of terrorism. It is readily evident to all that the issue of terrorism is not only a part of our history since America was attacked on 9/11, but will be with us as a nation in the foreseeable future. Both genocide and terrorism are difficult, but important topics, as Chapla says, and "should not be shied away from."[41] Teaching about recent events in and of itself can be controversial. The events of 9/11 fall into this category in addition to being due to differing views of Islam.

A *Time* magazine cover in the summer of 2010 asked the question, "Is America Islamaphobic?" Placing the question in historic context, a number of examples of nativism and intolerance toward religious and ethnic groups were cited. These abound from colonial attempts to expel or ban Jews and Catholics, laws aimed at curbing Native American rituals and Ku Klux Klan activity in the 20th century. Portraying Islam as a religion of hate and terrorism has resulted in attempts to ban the building of mosques in places as diverse as New York City and Wisconsin to advocating the burning of the Koran on the anniversary of 9/11.[42]

The public perception of Islam and Arab Americans is mirrored in the classroom. A study undertaken by a middle school teacher with adolescents ventured into this area with an exploration of stereotypes by students toward African Americans, Native Americans, Asian Americans, and Whites. An additional group included in the study was Arab Americans. A researcher found that many of the middle school students he was working with immediately identified Arab Americans as a group that were terrorists, wore turbans, were evil and came from the Middle East. Some students from the study used the name Osama to refer to Arab Americans and believed Arab Americans wanted to kill them. The question clearly asked for thoughts on Arab *Americans*, not people from the Middle East in general.[43]

For all the apparent conversation about diversity, race remains a topic of controversy that has never been fully dealt with by many in our society. More than one president of the United States has called for a national discussion about race. A school example is the ongoing debate as to whether *The Adventures of Huckleberry Finn* is appropriate for adolescents in terms of its language (its use of the "n" word). It is viewed by some as unrepresentative of modern day African Americans, especially after the results of the 2008 election. Allison Samuels in a *Newsweek* article titled "Rethinking Race in the Classroom" has argued its necessity and quotes Duke University professor Mark Anthony Neal: "These stories let kids know just how amazing it is that this man (Barack Obama) is president right now."[44] And yet it is problematic for some students where the discussion of race is not a welcome topic in their homes.

While topics can be controversial in teaching history, so too can how we interpret history. The "red/blue" political divide in our nation is represented not only on the presidential election maps and right-wing/left-wing talk radio programs, but in our history trade books. The title of Larry Schweikart's *48 Liberal Lies About American History: (That You Probably Learned in School)* is self-evident as to its point of view. Howard Zinn has had his *People's History of the United States* adapted for middle level students by Rebecca Stefoff with the title *A Young People's History of the United States: Class Struggle to the War on Terror*. Zinn serves up a number of varying interpretations of events in American history from the opposite end of the political spectrum as Schweikart. These include emphases on race relations, economic disparity among classes, questionable justifications for military involvements, and the venality of many politicians often viewed with great admiration by the public as a whole.[45]

Controversial issues, that may or may not take on historical importance, seem to appear on a regular basis—even controversial issues that most citizens would think are no longer controversial. A prime example is Prohibition. Prohibition as enshrined in the Eighteenth Amendment to the Constitution—and a little over a decade later "dis-enshrined"—has again, in some circles, become controversial. Some have maintained that Prohibition succeeded if considering the positive results on family life, productivity, and even crime. While not making all those claims Daniel Okrent, in his *Last Call: The Rise and Fall of Prohibition*,[46] covers the gamut of the dual trajectories of this social and Constitutional experiment in American history. Even if it were not controversial today, the issue was highly controversial at the time. In addition, it raises the question of whether unenforceable laws can be maintained in a free society.

A few conventional steps and approaches when undertaking controversial issues in the classroom are clear. First, students must be helped to understand why classroom time is being spent on controversial issues. It may be obvious to most, but not all. There must be preparation time devoted by both teacher and student to the process. And a few straightforward ground rules should be put in place to assure that all voices are heard. The classroom is indeed an ideal place to discuss controversial issues—it may even be the safest place for students, more so than at home, with friends, or in church.

A frequently asked question in the area of teaching controversial issues in the history classroom is what role the teacher should assume in the discussion. How much should the teacher divulge of his or her own personal points of view? Does the teacher's involvement, even as the "devil's advocate," add or detract from the discussion? While some students want disclosure on their teacher's point of view, it is widely believed that doing so has the potential of shutting down dialogue. But there are vital roles the teacher needs to play. To some extent the teacher, at appropriate times, needs to be a provocateur. Classroom discussions usually do not occur on automatic pilot. The teacher's role does need to be an active one. Preparation, as indicated above, is essential. Production of relevant materials, developing key questions for the discussion, and even "refereeing" are minimal obligations for teachers. And if the question is asked, "Where do you stand on this issue, Mr. Beineke?," it may need to be answered at the appropriate time. But not always, and certainly not during the first ten minutes of the discussion.

Here are two additional observations in connection with teaching controversial issues in history. The possibly apocryphal story of Woodrow Wilson who was told by a friend that there are two sides to every issue: "Yes," replied the often headstrong president, "the right side and the wrong side." It needs to be explained that in true controversial issues there is often no closure at the end of a class period. Some issues have two sides to them while others have three, four, or more sides. Finally, indicate to the students that the end of a controversial discussion is not really the end. Controversial issues are controversial because they continue on and will occasionally take years or decades to resolve. For example, some may think that the prohibition of alcohol was settled by the passage of the 21ˢᵗ Amendment to the Constitution, which repealed the 18ᵗʰ Amendment. However, there are still "dry" counties in the United States today.

A final word on controversial issues in history. In the movie *Jurassic Park* the character played by actor Jeff Goldblum says, "Just because we can do it, doesn't mean we should do it." There the reference was to reproducing dinosaurs from dormant DNA material. The same can be said of incorporating controversial issues into the classroom. Some issues, like the evolution/creationist debate, have been placed at the schoolhouse door. Others, such as abortion in the 1973 Roe v. Wade Supreme Court decision, continue to be hotly contested as both history and current issues. The point is that controversial issues may not stay within the four walls of the history classroom. America today is deeply divided as seen through the constant split decisions in the Supreme Court, a Congress that shows no signs of bipartisanship on any major issues, and presidencies shredded nightly on cable television. In this environment, history teachers will need to use sensitivity, knowledge, and wisdom when they decide to wade into the murky waters of controversial issues.

The World of Practice
Teaching Controversial Topics in the Social Studies
by Prentice Chandler

Controversial issues must be studied in the classroom without the assumption that they are settled in advance or there is only one right answer in matters of dispute. The social studies teacher must approach such issues in a spirit of critical inquiry exposing the students to a variety of ideas, even if they are different from their own.
—NCSS statement on "Academic Freedom and the Social Studies Teacher"

Teaching history or social studies is inherently controversial. Whether you choose to explicitly teach topics that you consider controversial or not, there is an aspect of nearly every topic in the social studies curricula that is considered to be controversial by some in your community. As the debates over national history standards can attest, every aspect of our national narrative is subject to debate. Whether you are teaching about Christopher Columbus, using primary documents, race and class in America, religion, the original intent of the U.S. Constitution, immigration, or any other topic, the potential for controversy is omnipresent in the history classroom. Given that history and social studies are the most inclusive and most political subjects that we teach in our schools, this is not surprising. The teaching of controversial issues is supported by teachers (Byford, Lennon, & Russell, 2009) and the NCSS, and finds its most basic justification in the argument that it helps to create democratic dispositions in our students (Hess, 2008) through the discussion and debate of persistent public issues.

Whether or not an issue becomes a controversy in your classroom depends on several intersecting factors: the politics of the community, the students in your class, your own personal biases, and the *ways in which you teach* the topics. Having said this, it is impossible to predict which topics will be considered controversial and which ones will not. There are, however, several actions you can take to avoid the perception that you are being controversial for controversy's sake. First, make sure that you are teaching the formal curriculum in your state or locale. Many states (as well as NCSS) have statements that support the teaching of controversial issues as a part of the formal curriculum. Secondly, give an *honest* account of the topic under consideration. One of the reasons that a topic is considered controversial in the first place is that there are fundamental disagreements on the meaning of this topic. This should be reflected in your classroom teaching methods (i.e. discussion models). Third, let your administrator know if you think that potential problems may arise with a particular lesson. Being transparent with your work is one of the best ways to prevent community reprisals.

In thinking about your own teaching practice, perhaps the most important aspect of teaching controversial topics in the classroom pertains to *balance*. Balance refers to how you perform your function as curriculum gatekeeper. What information are you using to teach this lesson? Do your materials reflect the ambiguity and conflict that are a part of this topic? Are you allowing your students access to all sides of an issue? Failure to not allow balance in matters of controversial topics is not only bad teaching; it neglects and ignores the complexity that is a part of social life and the historical process. You must never forget that the political leanings of your students and your own political leanings are always operating in the classroom. I am not suggesting that teaching history be free from politics; I am suggesting that political thought on the part of your students is a potent force in teaching controversial topics—how you navigate this potential minefield is of utmost importance. Many times, the success or failure of teaching controversial topics depends on teacher balance.

Another problem that teachers have with teaching controversial topics comes from the student side of the equation. Many times students are not used to being asked to deal with and debate controversial questions in the history classroom. Many students have experienced years of pedagogy that consisted of drill and routine, filling out worksheets, and memorizing dates. In teaching controversial topics to adolescent students, there is a learning curve they must overcome. There needs to be explicit instruction on "how" to have classroom discussions and explore controversial topics. We as teachers get frustrated with our students who cannot effectively discuss or debate a controversial topic, but we often forget that it is possible that you are their first exposure to controversial issues in a classroom setting. As Diana Hess points out in her article *Discussion in Social Studies: Is it Worth the Trouble?*, there are 3 basic ground rules in trying to implement controversial issues in the classroom: 1) remember that practice makes perfect, 2) explicitly teach your expectations and ground rules for discussing topics, and 3) focusing on a single idea or concept. Walking into a classroom and asking your students, "So, what does everyone think of *Roe v. Wade* and abortion" without having a structure in place for that discussion, is sure to fail.

In teaching controversial topics, many students lack the background knowledge to wrestle with the complexity of the issue under consideration. It is your responsibility as the teacher to give them the knowledge and tools as a foundation on which to delve into discussions, debates, and other methods. Attempting group methods without students having adequate background knowledge is a recipe for failure. Below you will find several methods that can be used to teach controversial topics once your students possess adequate background knowledge on a topic:

1. Classroom Discussions: In using discussion in your classroom, make sure that your discussion has a format or structure, guidelines/rules, and good content. Jeff Passe & Ronald Evans' chapter in *The Handbook on Teaching Social Issues*, "Discussion Methods in an Issues-Centered Curriculum," is great for structuring your discussions. In your organized discussions, it is helpful, as Diana Hess points out, to focus in on an aspect of the controversy that is open to multiple points of view.

2. Pro-Con: In this method, you divide the class into groups of 4; then divide the groups of 4 into 2 pairs. One pair represents the "pro" position of an issue and the other represents the "con" position. The pairings assume and argue the perspective position. After a period of time (usually 15–20 minutes), have the pairings switch perspectives and argue the opposite point of view. If your students have trouble arguing their point of view, you can direct and prompt them to a class text or by asking pointed questions. A more detailed discussion of Pro-Con can be found in Robert Stahl's book, *Cooperative Learning in the Social Studies: A Handbook for Teachers.*

3. Documentary Film: Using documentary film is an excellent way to explore controversial topics. *Teaching History with Film: Strategies for Secondary Social Studies* by Marcus, Metzger, Paxton, & Stoddard is an ex-

cellent resource to guide the use of documentary films in your classroom. Since documentary films are purposefully ideological (i.e. trying to persuade you to their point of view), they can serve as excellent segues into looking at notions of objectivity/subjectivity and competing claims that groups make against one another.

4. Primary Documents: The use of primary documents should be a constant in your classroom. The use of rich primary documents to show different perspectives in history is one of the most powerful pedagogical tools you can use. Allowing students to see the conflict of opinion across history is one of the surest ways to ensure they are able to see its use in the present. This is a hallmark of effective citizenship.

Perhaps Keith Barton & Alan McCully said it best when they wrote, "If modern democratic societies depend on the ability of citizens to take part in reasoned discussions with those whose opinions differ from their own, then surely it is our job as educators to develop this ability in our students." With this in mind, we have a profound responsibility to our students in preparing them for citizenship. With a little patience and some courage, you are doing your part to fulfill the mission of training effective citizens when you teach controversial topics in your classroom.

References

Byford, J., Lennon, S. & Russell, W. (2009). Teaching controversial issues in the social studies: A research study of high school teachers. *Clearinghouse, 82*(4), 165–170.

Hess, D. (2008). Controversial issues and democratic discourse. In L. Levstik & C. Tyson (Eds.), *Handbook of research in social studies education* (pp. 124–136). New York: Routledge.

Prentice T. Chandler is an assistant professor of secondary education/social studies at Athens State University. He teaches courses in social studies methods, foundations, and classroom management. His research and writing interests are in the areas of social studies education, critical race theory, academic freedom, and teacher agency. Before joining the professoriate, Dr. Chandler taught secondary social studies and history for 6 years in north Alabama.

Endnotes

1   Brady, Marion. "Cover the Material—Or Teach Students to Think." *Educational Leadership* 65. 5 (2008): 65.

2   See Wassermann, S. *Asking the Right Question: The Essence of Teaching.* Bloomington: Phi Delta Kappan, 1992.

3   *This We Believe: Successful Schools for Young Adolescents.* Westerville: National Middle School Association, 2003. 19.

4   Ciadiello, A. "To Wander and Wonder: Pathways to Literacy and Inquiry Through Question-Finding." *Journal of Adolescent and Adult Literacy* 47 (2003): 228–39.

5   Postman, Neil and Charles Weingartner. *Teaching as a Subversive Activity.* New York: Delacorte, 1969. 23.

6   Dewey, John. *How We Think.* Lexington: D.C. Heath and Company, 1933. 261–62.

7   Brady, 66.

8   Anderson, L.W. et al, eds. *A Taxonomy for Learning, Teaching, and Assessing: A Revision of Bloom's Taxonomy of Educational Objectives.* New York: Longman, 2001. xxii.

9   Marzano, Robert J. and John S. Kendall. *The New Taxonomy of Educational Objectives.* 2nd ed. Thousand Oaks: Corwin Press, 2007. xi, 13–16, 18, 62.

10   Marzano and Kendall, 133.

11   Juel, Connie, Heather Hebard, Julie Park Haubner, and Meredith Moran. "Reading Through a Disciplinary Lens." *Educational Leadership* 67. 6 (2010): 15, 17.

12   Bintz, William P., and Lynne Williams. "Questioning Techniques of Fifth and Sixth Grade Reading Teachers." *Middle School Journal* 37. 1 (2005): 45–52.

13   *This We Believe*, 20.

14   Bintz and Williams, 46, 50.

15   Henning, John E. *The Art of Discussion-Based Teaching: Opening Up Conversation in the Classroom.* New York: Routledge, 2008. 14–31, 153–57.

16   Johnson, Andrew P. *Making Connections in Elementary and Middle School Social Studies.* Los Angeles: Sage Publishing, 2010. 202.

17   Feinstein, Sheryl G. *Secrets of the Teenage Brain: Research-Based Strategies for Reaching and Teaching Today's Adolescents.* 2nd ed. Thousand Oaks, CA: Corwin, 2009. 26–28. See also Marzano, Robert, Debra J. Pickering, and Jane E. Pollock. *Classroom Instruction That Works: Research-Based Strategies for Increasing Student Achievement.* Alexandria: Association for Supervision and Curriculum Development, 2001.

18   Wilson, Nance S. and Linda Smetana. "Questioning as Thinking: A Megacognitive Framework?" *Middle School Journal* 41. 2 (2009): 20–28.

19   Ibid.

20   Wyman, Richard M., Jr. *America's History Through Young Voices: Using Primary Sources in the K–12 Social Studies Classroom.* Boston: Pearson Education, 2005. 8.

21   Hoefferle, Caroline. "Teaching Historiography to High School and Undergraduate Students." *Magazine of History* 21. 2 (2007): 40–44.

22   Ward, Kyle. *Not Written in Stone: Learning and Unlearning American History Through 200 Years of Textbooks.* New York: New Press, 2010. xiii–xiv, 65–172.

23   Gilderhus, Mark. *History and Historians: A Historiographical Introduction* (New York: Prentice Hall, 2007; and Southgate, Beverley. *History: What and Why?* New York: Routledge, 2001.

24   Drake, Frederick D. and Lynn R. Nelson. *Engagement in Teaching History: Theory and Practices for Middle and Secondary Teachers.* 2nd ed. Upper Saddle River: Merrill/ Pearson, 2009. 30.

25   Hess, Diana E. *Controversy in the Classroom: The Democratic Power of Discussion.* New York: Routledge, 2009. 162.

26 Hunt, Maurice P. and Lawrence Metcalf. *Teaching High School Social Studies.* New York: Harper and Row Publishers, 1968. 292–94.

27 Samuels, Allison. "Rethinking Race in the Classroom." *Newsweek* 9 Mar. 2009. 52–3.

28 Kozol, Jonathan. *On Being a Teacher.* Oxford, England: Oneworld Book, 1981, 2009. 15–19, 26.

29 See Hess, 11–12 for an extended discussion of this case.

30 Hess, 29–30.

31 Hess, 41–42.

32 Hess, 113–18.

33 Epstein, Terrie. "Research on Teaching and Learning History: Teacher Professionalization and Student Cognition and Culture." Ed. Turk, Diana, Rachel Mattson, Terrie Epstein, and Robert Cohen. *Teaching U.S. History: Dialogues among Social Studies Teachers and Historians.* New York: Routledge, 2010. 199–200.

34 See Jones, James H. *Alfred C. Kinsey: A Public/Private Life.* New York: W.W. Norton and Company, 1997; and Gathorne-Hardy, Jonathan. *Alfred C. Kinsey: Sex the Measure of All Things.* London: Chatto and Windus, 1998.

35 Atkinson, Elizabeth and Renee DePalma. *Undoing Homophobia in Primary Schools.* Sterling: Trentham Books, 2010.

36 See Eaklor, "Pamphlet Proposal from The Committee on Lesbian and Gay History" in "Teaching U.S. Lesbian and Gay History" for the American Historical Association's *Teaching Concerns Series* 2001 and Meyer, Leisa D. "Sexual Revolutions." Foreward. *Magazine of History* 20. 2 (2006): 5–6 that introduces the journal's themed issue of teaching about sexuality in historical contexts and Rupp, Leila J. "Everyone's Queer." *Magazine of History* 20. 2 (2006): 8–11.

37 Miller, Calvin C. *No Easy Answers: Bayard Rustin and the Civil Rights Movement.* Greensboro: Morgan Reynolds Publishing, Inc., 2005.

38 Meyer, 6.

39 Chapla, Peter D. "Teaching Young Adolescents About Genocide." *Middle Ground* 13. 4 (2010) 26.

40 Ibid. 26–27.

41 Ibid. 26.

42 Ghosh, Bobby. "Islam in America." *Time* 176. 8, 30 Aug. 2010. 20–26.

43 Verma, Rita. "Dialogues About 9/11, the Media, and Race: Lessons from a Secondary Classroom." *Controversies in the Classroom: A Radical Teacher Reader.* New York: Teachers College Press, 2008. 34.

44 Loewen, 327.

45 Schweikart, Larry. *48 Liberal Lies About American History: (That You Probably Learned in School).* New York, NY: Sentinel, 2008. and Zinn, Howard (adapted by Rebecca Stefoff). *A Young People's History of the United States: Class Struggle to the War on Terror.* New York: Seven Stories Press, 2007. See also Welchel, Ed. *Reading, Learning, Teaching Howard Zinn.* New York: Peter Lang, 2009.

46 Okrent, Daniel. *Last Call: The Rise and Fall of Prohibition.* New York: Scribners, 2010.

Six

Diversity:
An Indispensable Component in Teaching History

The concept of diversity when used in the educational setting can be categorized, even defined, in a number of ways. These include gender, race, ethnicity, religion, language, disabilities, and sexual identity. From these categories emerges the fundamental meaning of diversity. And from the meaning emerges learning. It must first be understood that diversity is a topic where we are all learning—as individuals, groups, and a nation. Most citizens of the United States of America like to believe that they understand diversity. They view themselves as not really prejudiced, they certainly do not discriminate against anyone, and believe the whole issue is becoming less important than it was for previous generations. While each of us may have these thoughts (and many are indeed further along on their diversity journey than others), there remains much for all of us to learn.

That does not mean that the inclusion of diversity into the classroom is popular, even with non-majority students. Studies have shown that some groups distrust history textbooks and are more willing to listen to their parents' stories and interpretations of the past. Some African Americans may view Martin Luther King, Jr. as overemphasized in the schools, and Latino students find the history taught in their classrooms irrelevant to their own experiences. One study found that some students of color even resent the inclusion in the curriculum of other marginalized groups, victims of the Holocaust for example, due to the perception of "competition" between non-majority or oppressed groups.[1]

A good starting point in exploring diversity for teachers and students alike is terminology. Barbara Gross Davis in her book *Tools for Teaching* references extensive research on this aspect of diversity.[2] Basic racial and ethnic terms in relation to identity, history, and relationships frequently evolve and shift with time. For example, the term minority has become outdated for some in favor of persons of color. Black and African American are often used interchangeably by some and not by others. The same with Latino and Hispanic. Native American, American Indian, or indigenous peoples are all used in various contexts. Oriental, long out of favor, gave way to Asian and now individuals often prefer to be identified by nationality than by continent. The point is to learn about other groups and be sensitive to how language can be both a positive and negative aspect of the classroom environment.

Gross has added a number of global recommendations when it comes to diversity in the classroom. Suggestions include not trying to "protect" any group of students, learn to correctly pronounce the names of students, be inclusive in the selection of classroom textbooks and materials, and do not assume that students will understand all cultural, literary, or historical references made by either the teacher or other students. Another practice, and this is often difficult so as not to ostracize or make students feel uncomfortable, is to speak up when distasteful and hurtful terms are used or insensitive remarks are made. This is not an attempt to censor speech, but rather make students aware that words have an impact. For the adolescent learner, the terminology they are using may be the result of words they have heard and are uninformed as to their meaning. A common example in the schools today is derogatory and offensive names and terms for gays and lesbians. Some students are oblivious to the harm done to peers who are members of these groups. Gross suggests that a positive way to counteract such incidents—whether intentional or unintentional—is to meet with students informally to explain the problem. A more formal instructional approach for students is to undertake research on race, gender, ethnicity, and sexual identity. In addition, school professionals such as guidance counselors should be available to meet with classes for discussions of diversity.

Sonia Nieto and Patty Bode in their book *Affirming Diversity: The Sociopolitical Context of Multicultural Education* make the case that multicultural education has both a unique and appropriate place in the study of history. They have written:

> U.S. history is steeped in slavery and conquest. Millions of descendents of Africans, American Indians, Mexicans, Puerto Ricans, and others colonized within and beyond U.S. borders have experienced political and economic oppression and, in schools, disparagement of their native cultures and languages. But the history of racism and exploitation experienced by so many of our people, including their children, is rarely taught. Instead, conventional curricula and pedagogy

have been based on the myth of a painless and smooth assimilation of immigrants.[3]

Nieto and Bode affirm that "Although the beautiful and heroic aspects of our history should be taught, so must the ugly and exclusionary."[4] The issue is one of balance in our classrooms as we teach both the "beautiful and the ugly" in order to present history in an authentic and realistic manner.

The National Council for the Social Studies has outlined performance expectations for students in the arena of culture and cultural diversity. These include:

- Compare similarities and difference in the ways groups, society, and cultures meet human needs and concerns.

- Explain how information and experiences may be interpreted by people from diverse cultural perspectives.

- Explain and give examples of how language, literature, the arts, architecture, traditions, beliefs, values, and behaviors contribute to the development and transmission of culture.

- Explain why individuals and groups respond differently to their physical and social environments.

- Articulate the implications of cultural diversity, as well as cohesion, within and across groups.[5]

Such lists are important to history teachers for three reasons. First, with the topic of cultural diversity, teachers need to understand that there are underlying assumptions for its inclusion in the curriculum. Second, terms found within the performance expectations such as interpret, contribute, transmit, and respond indicate an active learning agenda for students. And third, beliefs, values, and behaviors are given validity in the acknowledgment of cultural diversity.

Marri found in a focused study of three teachers the need for promoting multicultural and democratic principles when teaching about the nation's history of inequality. She found the three teachers all highlighted the struggles of marginalized groups, engaged students to critically examine the role of human agency (action) in confronting inequality, and created a classroom based on trust and respect.[6] When students can observe that marginalized students' lives were often reflective of their own lives, then the theme of social justice becomes real for the students.

The concept of justice and a just society has been traced to the Greeks, who viewed these as underpinnings for an ideal civilization. In a 1963 nationally televised speech to explain the use of National Guard troops to peacefully assist in admitting two Black students to the University of Alabama, President Kennedy said, " . . . law alone cannot make men see right. We are confronted primarily with a moral issue. It is as old as the Scriptures and is as clear as the American Constitution."[7] It can indeed be traced back to the Old Testament prophets. Martin Luther King, Jr. often used the words of Amos in his sermons, most notably on December 5, 1955, in the midst of the Montgomery, Alabama bus boycott[8]: "But let justice roll down like waters and righteousness like an ever-flowing stream"(Amos 5:22). Another Old Testament prophet, Isaiah, spoke of the poor, prisoners, the blind, and the oppressed (Isaiah 60:1). Jesus repeated Isaiah's words in Luke 4:18 of the New Testament and was a consistent and constant advocate for the poor, the sick, the disadvantaged, females, and ethnicities outside the Jewish race.

In the context of this book, social justice will be defined as an overarching term used to examine the inequitable social arrangements found between individuals or groups that include, but are not limited to, social class, race, gender, ethnicity, disability, and sexual oriention.[9] Nieto and Bode include four components when defining social justice: 1) it challenges, confronts, and disrupts misconceptions, untruths, and stereotypes that lead to structural inequality . . . based on race, social class, and other social and human differences, 2) it provides all students with the resources necessary to learn to their full potential, 3) it draws on the strengths and talents that students bring to their education, and 4) it creates a learning environment that promotes crucial thinking and supports agency for social change.[10]

Two major considerations that are connected to social justice are the inequitable social arrangements that exist between people of privilege and those in poverty and also the redistribution of resources to address these conditions and imbalances. History is replete with examples of such injustices as slavery, exploitation of laborers, discrimination against non-majority peoples and women, unequal protection of the laws, and the failure of society to address the needs of the poor, especially children. Pedagogic strategies for adolescents in history include listening and sharing stories from the past, respecting alternative perspectives, and introducing subject areas that will help develop appropriate social activism.[11]

There is a need for teachers to understand the concept of privilege and how it impacts social justice. One explicit activity was created by McIntosh and called the "Privilege Walk." The activity begins with an exercise where teachers stand shoulder-to-shoulder and then take a step forward or backward depending on the answers to 30 questions. A teacher would take a step forward if they had more than 50 books in their homes growing up, had or have people of color working for them as household servants or gardeners, inherited money, were taken to art galleries by their parents, or attended a private school or summer camp. Teachers would take a step backward if they went to a school speaking a language other than English, had to skip a meal or were hungry due to lack of finances, saw members of their race portrayed on television in degrading roles, lived in an area of high crime or drug activity, or had to move because the family could not afford the rent. Processing questions after the exercise include "What happened or didn't happen during the exercise? Is one person any more privileged than another? How can this exercise apply to your school or your own lives outside of school?"[12]

The major reason for inequitable social arrangements is poverty. As poverty is a constant in history, the opportunities to teach about it are abundant. Teacher preparation programs need to provide diverse socioeconomic settings for field experiences as well as diverse ethnic and racial settings. One middle school teacher has written, "Before my first practicum in the middle grades education program . . . I had never experienced or devoted much thought to the effects of poverty on a community. I certainly had never imagined how a child's learning and behaviors could be altered based on his or her socioeconomic status."[13] One event in American history with abundant opportunities to teach about poverty is the Great Depression. Two examples would be exploring homelessness and hunger and how they affected millions of Americans. It is not difficult to relate the poverty of the 1930s to poverty today. Websites and young adult literature can be found that examine the issues surrounding poverty. Service learning has been suggested as a way for students to engage with issues of poverty experientially.[14]

Another lens to look at social justice has been suggested by Elizabeth Spalding and her colleagues using the 1949 Pete Seeger song "If I Had a Hammer." The hammer is tool to deliver a blow to either build and construct or break down and destroy something. "Hammers" at the disposal of educators include studies in critical race theory, anti-oppressive education, culturally responsive teaching, Whiteness studies, culturally relevant pedagogy, and lesbian/gay/bisexual/transgender (LGBT) education. The "bell" is to send a clear and persuasive message that in order to teach well, teachers must know themselves, their students, and their community. And the "song" of "If I Had a Hammer" references caring—what Nel Noddings and others have viewed as showing a concern and connectedness toward their students.[15]

Teaching about diversity in history classes is in itself a controversial act. Napoleon was reported to have said that the winners of wars write the history. Or at least the dominant class in most cases. Gary Howard holds that "Whites have had the power and the privilege . . . to write our own versions of history. We have been able to determine the structure and content of schooling and in this day have institutionalized our ignorance in the name of education."[16] This "dominance paradigm," contends Howard, "has throughout our history functioned as an obstacle to justice and equity on the river of diversity."[17] Point of view is an essential element that students need to explore in the study of history. Whose history is being written and is there an agenda, hidden or explicit?

Teaching about social justice to privileged adolescents can be fraught with risks for students and teacher alike. Seider has addressed three issues that often cause the goal of teaching social justice to fail with students from high socio-economic backgrounds. First, sometimes the knowledge can be overwhelming. Students may not know how to deal with historical episodes of lynching to modern day stories of global poverty on an incredible, hardly comprehensible scale. A second impediment can occur as teachers attempt to teach social justice as fear. Seider found that when students learned about the challenges of poverty as well as the disparities between affluent and poor communities it actually increased the protectiveness of their own privilege. Third, Seider found that often "radical" arguments aimed at persuading students of their moral obligation did just the opposite. The approach often "triggered suspicions, resentment, and a desire to trivialize" what was happening to people in poverty by students of privilege.[18]

Seider suggests counteracting these potential pitfalls in the teaching of social justice by inspiring positive emotions rather than negative ones. He quotes research that indicates positive rather than negative emotions deepen commitment to social action. To counter fear on the part of privileged adolescents, Seider points to showing students examples where injustice was overcome by those whose stories might first be viewed with apprehension by students of privilege. Finally, to balance prejudicial judgments by even the oppressed by pointing to positive change agents from the privileged class. Examples such as Bill Gates and Warren Buffett, the epitome of privilege, can be used to show how the moral obligations felt by these financial giants have been used to enhance the health, education, and opportunities for the poor.[19] The author remembers meeting with a leader of the Sandinistas in Nicaragua in the 1990s who was amazed to hear that industrialists in America, such as W.K. Kellogg, had become philanthropists, creating foundations to use their wealth for the public good.

An additional question when teaching about diversity in history classes becomes "Can White Teachers Effectively Teach Students of Color?" When Kristin Traudt asked older adolescents this question the response was two-fold. First, most students in the survey reported that relational concerns such as respect and just treatment mattered more than ethnicity. "It doesn't matter as long as the teacher treats everybody equally, no matter what race they are," a student said. The second finding made by Traudt was that having a diverse teaching staff was important to students of color. Common cultures and backgrounds were important also.[20] Therefore, in connection with this second conclusion, it is important that every attempt is made by those responsible for hiring faculty to secure a representative teaching cadre that approximates the community population.

History, as we teach it today, must contain diversity that reflects the nation's population. Gender and race are the most obvious classifications that come to mind. Often, though, when the tandem of race and gender is used, gender tends to get forgotten. Wives of presidents are frequently used as examples when studying history. Martha Washington and Mary Todd Lincoln are often mentioned. But they are usually not viewed as significant in their own right. Abigail Adams, also a president's wife, has fared better in the past decade. Kozol suggests women such as Dorothy Day, Emma Goldman, and Susan B. Anthony for inclusion as key representatives of their gender. Kozol thinks a healthier strategy than looking at models of gender is to discuss in today's classrooms how women and young girls perceive their proper role within society and in the public school itself."[21]

In terms of gender Nel Noddings has written that "If women's culture were taken more seriously in educational planning, social studies and history might have a very different emphasis. Instead of moving from war to war, ruler to ruler, one political campaign to the next, we would give far more attention to social issues."[22] Hanger and Garlock have extensively written about programs and curricula that address the unique needs of the adolescent female learner.[23]

The journalist Richard Whitmire has suggested that young males have become, if not victims, at least under-achievers in the academic realm. Whitmire has pointed out in a set of recent data a pattern of increasingly poor performance by males in schools:

- Twice as many girls as boys were members of the National Honor Society in 2007.

- The National Assessment of Educational Progress (NEAP) has reported that girls have closed the math/science gap with males and are increasing the verbal abilities gap.

- Nearly twice as many boys are repeating a grade as girls. Secondary students with disabilities are nearly 70% male.

- A majority of women receive degrees in all categories—associate, bachelors, masters, and doctoral.

- Males ages ten to fourteen are twice as likely to commit suicide as females in that age range.

- Four times as many males as females are likely to suffer from attention-deficit hyperactivity disorder.[24]

Whitmire provides a list of the "usual suspects" in his analysis for the male achievement gap. They include lack of phonics in the teaching of reading, weak teacher education programs, lack of reading instruction in the upper grades, few male role models for young men, boredom, and a deficiency of books for male adolescents. (While acknowledging a racial divide, noticeably missing from Whitmire's list is poverty.) After identifying a few model schools and programs (which have often been difficult to replicate), Whitmire suggests addressing the above particular deficits by: more phonics and mentoring, more single-sex and charter schools, and more middle school reading and writing skill instruction. More books written for male adolescents and employing E.D. Hirsch's core literacy program are also recommended. No antidote is given for boredom.[25] While Whitmire's prescriptions can be criticized as partisan and predisposed to solutions that tend toward the conservative end of the educational spectrum, the data demonstrate a serious diversity issue in the community of male adolescent learners and ones about which history teachers need to be aware.

Cornel West has written on the primacy of race in American history and the need for all people—adolescents as well as adults—to gain a greater understanding of its impact on everyday life. Since W.E.B. Du Bois wrote in *The Souls of Black Folk* that "The problem of the 20th century is the problem of the color line," we have seen that American history cannot be taught or learned without addressing race. West has written that "From 1776 to 1964—188 years of our 218 year history—this racial divide would serve as a basic presupposition for the expansive functioning of American democracy."[26] It can be argued that race has been the defining and perennial issue in American history.

Disabilities and history is another area that educators often grapple with to make meaningful connections between this form of diversity and the past. (It must be made clear, though, that diversity is not a disability, but disabilities can and often are a category found within the concept of diversity.) Burch has written that "disability is everywhere in history, once you begin looking for it." Burch found that America's deaf population has garnered the greatest attention, yet in 2009 there was no history of deaf education. The question of "normal" emerges in disability studies in works that deal with co-joined twins and whether such cases are medically abnormal. Another area is polio, which was a feared and dreaded disease prior to the Salk vaccine, leaving many children (and adults) disabled. Burch raises a number of other cases from the history of disabilities such as the voyeurism of "freaks" (physically disabled persons) in circuses. The history of mental disabilities and the treatment of these women and men run the gamut from institutionalization, lobotomies, and chemical and surgical castrations.[27] This nation has a long and troubling history in the area of disabilities.

Historically the public has had difficulty in recognizing, even acknowledging, disabilities as part of life. When the Franklin D. Roosevelt Memorial was being planned and constructed in the 1990s, there was a deep difference of opinion over how to depict the former president's disability. During his presidency, FDR was never photographed being carried to and from automobiles and trains or in his wheelchair. To do so, it was thought, would diminish his stature as a leader. After much discussion and debate, those responsible for the FDR Memorial in Washington, D.C. placed a statue within the memorial of Roosevelt in his wheelchair. The stigma of disability had remained in the nation's psyche well into the 20th century.[28]

As James Loewen and others have pointed out, Helen Keller's dual disabilities—blindness and deafness—and how she overcame them, were often the exclusive identifiers for the public. The fact that she was a political activist and socialist has been lost or forgotten in the telling of her story. While greater attention is being paid to veterans of recent American conflicts, especially those with devastating and incapacitating injuries, there is a history of how returning soldiers, their relatives, and the public responded to them. The autobiographical *Gone for a Soldier: The Civil War Memoirs of Private Alfred Bellard* (1891, reprinted 1975) opens the door to the subject of how soldiers disabled by the war reentered civilian society. In World War I, artists were employed to make masks that would cover the disfigured faces of soldiers injured in battle. Burns, a frequent occurrence in World War II, opened the field of reconstructive surgery. And paraplegics and quadriplegics from the Vietnam era, made known by Ron Kovic's 1976 autobiography, and later film, *Born on the Fourth of July*, again brought to light disabilities directly related to history.

Kim Nielsen writes about how biographies can be used to teach about disabilities in connection to history. She has written, "Historical questions about daily experiences of people with disabilities—including topics as employment, use of technology, civic engagement, friendship and family, and courtship—help to address large historical forces."[29] All of these issues as related to disabilities and more can be connected to the history being taught to adolescents.

History teachers may not view themselves as special education teachers, but knowledge of disabilities and how to assist students with disabilities in the classroom can be consequential to successful instruction. Assistive technology is a key element in this area. Assistive technology devices are any piece of equipment, or product system that is used to increase, maintain, or improve the capabilities of a student with a disability. Assistive technology service means any service that directly assists a student with a disability in the selection, acquisition, or use of an assistive technology device.[30]

While the diversity of America cannot be ignored, its appropriate role in our schools has been disputed. Two examples of this debate have been Frances FitzGerald in the 1970s and Arthur M. Schlesinger, Jr. in the 1990s. Both pondered the potential divisiveness of focusing on our differences rather than our commonalities. FitzGerald, in her study of American history textbooks, believed in the need to teach for tolerance and respect when looking at our differences. But she also thought that the similarities between Americans that had bound us together as a nation were minimized. She saw a lack of integration of diversity in history textbooks finding what she labeled a "patchwork." By "patchwork" she meant that texts often placed photos or would mention a Hispanic or Native American in an attempt to assure all races, ethnicities, and cultures were "covered." But then the textbooks would not adequately explain or integrate the material within the narrative. Schlesinger's similar thesis was that by emphasizing our differences in America we were in danger of forgetting what holds us together as a nation.[31]

Directly related to the teaching of history to adolescents is the work of the African American educator James Banks and his lifelong professional study of diversity and multicultural education. Always grounded in the assumption that education must be based on democratic values such as justice and equality, Banks calls for a "balance of diversity and unity." Examples are plentiful. Violent divisions based on culture or ethnicity can be seen in nations and regions throughout history, even in the seemingly homogeneous country of Canada with its separatist movement in Quebec.

Banks also sees the need for balance in how Black and White students look at history. Rather than victimization by the minority culture, alternative examples should be provided of Whites fighting for oppressed groups in American history. These would include Whites who were leading abolitionists and civil rights workers. And for those groups that have been victimized and marginalized, Banks calls for a "transformative curriculum." An example that Banks provides is to select for inclusion in the mainstream curriculum ethnic heroes who challenged the existing social and political order such as Geronimo and Nat Turner. Another example is the courage of Mrs. Daisy Bates, local head of the NAACP in Little Rock, Arkansas, who suffered financial and personal turmoil for her stance in support of the Little Rock Nine.

A final example that Banks provides in teaching history from a diverse perspective is the need for viewing the United States from the concept of a "multidirectional" society. Often American history has been seen as an "east to west" phenomenon—the country moved from Western Europe across the Atlantic Ocean then on to the Pacific. The familiar Manifest Destiny concept is a prime example. Banks suggests that insufficient attention has been paid to the northeasterly directional flow of culture from Africa, the northerly flow from Mexico and Latin America, and the easterly flow from Asia.[32]

Using the personal example of John Hope Franklin, the late Black historian, adds to the discussion of diversity. He was influenced to choose a career in history rather than law by a White professor at the historically Black Fisk University.

And Franklin's contribution was two-fold: construct the history of African Americans while reconstructing mainstream American history.[33] Although produced in 1969, *Black History: Lost, Stolen, or Strayed* (available on DVD) examines how Black history was either distorted or forgotten within mainstream treatments of American history. Hosted by a youthful Bill Cosby, the film is also an excellent artifact that documents the lack of status of Black history forty years ago and the resultant Black Power movement of the 1960s.

Textbooks must also be representational in the areas of diversity. Two studies in the 1990s by the American Association of University Women found that publishers were producing social studies textbooks that were slightly more gender balanced than in the past.[34] One reason for this imbalance has been the dominance of political history, an area in which women have been marginalized. An additional topic that is found within history and social studies curricula is sexual identity and orientation. While a diversity issue, it can also be viewed as a controversial and closed issue for many schools. Margaret Smith Morocco has addressed this topic in her work on gender and sexuality in the social studies.[35]

The addition of social and cultural history into the American history curriculum has ameliorated some of this disparity. But balance is also in the eye of the beholder. Canada, which has been exceptionally sensitive to diversity issues in the past few years, can serve as a case study in connection with the issue of balance. Canada's bilingual society and indigenous population have been an impetus for textbook writers to pay close attention to diversity. An outstanding and innovative history textbook from the past decade for older adolescents titled *Canadian History 1900–2000* can be examined in terms of explaining balance in areas such as gender, race, ethnicity, and marginalized peoples. Significant space in the textbook is given to the role of women in Canadian society including female and minority artists, authors, and politicians. (Admittedly, space allotment and selection of topics and individuals can often be controversial criteria. Judging textbook content in the U.S. during the standards debate of the 1990s is an example.) Substantial sections of the Canadian textbook are provided for narratives of Canada's indigenous peoples, the internment of Japanese-Canadians during World War II (yes, it happened in Canada, too), the role of the elderly in Canadian society, and the rise of an alternative university in the 1960s to meet the needs of adult learners. But, in terms of balance, what about William Lyon Mackenzie King, Canada's Depression-era and World War II Prime Minister? While mentioned in a number places in this textbook, he is never given the complete leadership narrative, description, or space that less famous individuals are provided.[36] Could major events, figures, and movements that were critical to the forming of the Canadian nation have been minimized in order to include a more diverse depiction of the country's history? It will become a legitimate question in the United States with an ever-tightening curriculum and the competition in textbooks for limited page space to include the diverse nature of our society. Again, the answer may lie in the increased use of trade books or self-selected reading by the student.

Another powerful approach to the teaching about diversity through history can be found in Ravi's teaching unit on immigration. This strategy takes into account the students themselves. Their experiences and their own histories, who they are as Americans, and their own personal story or their ancestors' experience as voluntary or involuntary immigrants should be considered when teaching the history of immigration.[37] In addition, language and poverty have been seen as barriers by students from the immigrant experience.[38]

Along with gender and race, social class is a component of diversity that is critical in the teaching of history to adolescents. Jonathan Kozol, urban teacher during the 1960s, has long written about the link between school success and social class. His classic work, *Savage Inequalities*, exposed to the nation how social justice was a promise yet to be fulfilled in American Society. In his most recent book, *The Shame of the Nation: The Restoration of Apartheid*, Kozol demonstrates how different academic and career goals are set for middle and upper class schools than for those students who attend lower socio-economic schools. To remedy this he calls for teaching students about social class and proposes a new Civil Rights movement.[39]

We also know that teaching adolescents about diversity in history is best taught through real-life experiences. Most of all is the need for continuous and authentic interaction amongst cultural and ethnic groups. To this must be added community involvement and visits, guest speakers from various groups, and visual materials that make the experience of groups from the past real to the students of the present. Harvard's Henry Louis Gates, Jr. and his Du Bois Institute have begun to use genealogy with adolescent Black students to both teach and personalize history. He has even provided DNA testing to enable the students to trace their ethnicity.[40] It is again the need, when teaching history to adolescents, to present an integrated, balanced, and accurate portrait of a diverse nation.

Empathy is critical in the teaching about diversity through history. Holocaust survivor (and later victim when he committed suicide) Primo Levi stressed the need for empathy when he wrote of our "inability to perceive the experience of others."[41] Empathy is not feeling sorry for or guilty about others who live in poverty, are persecuted, or are discriminated against due to their color or social status. Empathy then, for the purposes of this book, will mean the ability of students to put themselves in the place of others in a variety of historical situations.

Veteran multicultural educator Ronald Takaki has written one of the most inclusive books on ethnicity, if that phrase is not paradoxical. Within his book, *In A Different Mirror: A History of Multicultural America*, Takaki provides a vast spectrum of content-specific examples of diversity from our history. Takaki moves beyond the traditional examination of Blacks, Native Americans, and Hispanics to include the Chinese, Irish, and Jewish experience. Colonialism, immigration, class divisions, and attempts to bridge racial and ethnic gaps are all depicted through episodes, incidents, and stories from the nation's past.[42]

In conclusion, it should be remembered that celebrating and acknowledging the diversity within our population is not a recent movement. A brave woman educator in the 1920s established what may have been the first real attempt to integrate diversity into the lives of students. The decade known as the Roaring Twenties was also marked by racism and nativism, the rebirth of the Ku Klux Klan, lynchings and racial violence, the introduction of border patrols to limit Mexican immigration, and anti-Catholic sentiment. These were all examples of cultural anxieties on the part of America's dominant White and Protestant citizenry. Viewing minority group identity as a source of strength for the country, educator Rachel Davis DuBois initiated a school assembly program in her New Jersey high school. DuBois attempted to discuss ethnoracial (the term used in the 1920s by DuBois) groups by replacing stereotypes with positive images. DuBois, a Quaker, secured the sponsorship of the Women's International League for Peace and Freedom. Clearly directed at White native-born students, the programs were timed to coincide with holidays. While it is recognized today that the "heroes and holidays" approach to teaching about diversity is too limiting, at this time in our nation's history DuBois' endeavor was innovative and courageous. Known as the Woodbury Plan, it became the foundation for the intercultural education effort that was a part of Progressive education at the time.[43]

Examples of DuBois' programs were contributions by Italians to American life during October, "Negro" history in the month of February, and Hebrew (Jewish) themed programs in March. The programs included contributions by these ethnoracial groups in areas such as art, science, literature, noted women, inventors, and leaders. Activities included presentations, talks, and demonstrations. For example there were posters, dances, music, food tasting, and guest speakers. Even educators were included. During Italian month an assembly program notes acknowledging educators Maria Montessori and Angelo Patri.[44] Patri was an early twentieth-century New York City principal who was a close follower of Dewey's ideas, implementing many of them into his school.[45]

Our schools will only become more diverse in the future. This most obvious of statements, though, also contains an opportunity not always provided to previous generations. Unfortunately, not all educators view that future in a positive way. A colleague of the author related a posting placed on an online class discussion board. When presented with data predicting an even more diverse student population in twenty years, the comment by a teacher was: "Glad I'll be retired by then." The richness of diversity must be viewed as an asset to our classrooms, not a deficit, especially in our history classrooms. The prospect of an increasingly diverse student body providing their contributions to the American experience through their language, customs, and worldviews can only add to how this nation looks at the issues of social justice, empathy, and the past itself.

The World of Practice
Diversity and Room 106
by John Beineke

A number of years ago I stepped into room 106 as a first-year, seventh-grade teacher. Although George Will and others have bemoaned the excesses of the 1960s—and excesses there were—the decade also produced its share of idealism and action. In the arena of public education a group of urban educators, called the "Compassionate Critics" by the late curriculum guru William Van Til, gave voice to the needs of children and adolescents caught in impoverished environments. Jonathan Kozol, Herbert Kohl, and John Holt wrote eloquently of their experiences as inner-city teachers. (Kozol and Kohl are still writing.) Their stories inspired many of us to commit ourselves to teaching and making a difference.

My first school was not in New York, Chicago, or Los Angeles—but it was urban, it was diverse, and it was challenging. The rich racial diversity arose from a school population that included 40 percent African Americans, several Hispanic students, and a few Native Americans. The school was located in a neighborhood that would now be labeled "in transition." As I walked the four blocks to school each day from my apartment, I observed firsthand the troubled settings in which our students spent their lives outside school. As teachers, we saw the aftermath of what occurred in those homes—bruised minds, bruised souls, and too often, bruised faces and bodies. But teachers were there to make a difference, including that lanky new fellow in room 106.

While the concept was certainly evident in both theory and practice, the term diversity was not in use at that time. Neither was pluralism, although multiculturalism was beginning to be discussed in a few of my graduate courses. Yet we knew that our school was diverse. Ideas around race, poverty, and class were raised in the teacher workrooms and in our faculty meetings. It also was the early days of special education. And yet our student population of over 900 students had only one teacher who worked with no more than 15 of our most severely disabled students. Those students not served in this special classroom were placed in our classes. But this, of course, was before mainstreaming or inclusion became an accepted practice in educating the special needs student. The teacher in room 106 was learning that diversity took many forms.

The difficulties and frustrations in the lives of many of our students surfaced in a number of ways. While weapons and drugs were a rarity in our building, assaults and verbal abuse between students and toward teachers were not. The new teacher in room 106 was the recipient of both—and on one occasion received six stitches over his right eye. We knew that one deeply troubled young man was a powder keg waiting to explode. Parent conferences, meetings with school counselors, and the use of new classroom management techniques such as behavior modification were tried. Even simple one-on-one sessions all came to naught. One day, after school, "Eddie" erupted in the room next door and I attempted to intervene to assist my colleague. I asked "Eddie" to step into my room to talk. His anger was then turned toward me and he physically struck out at me. The assistant principal, who was passing by in the hallway, witnessed the episode. Expelled permanently, "Eddie" was eventually sent to some sort of group home in a neighboring state. I wonder whatever happened to him.

But there were victories amidst the challenges. In the curriculum, our goal was to make school more relevant to the learner. In social studies we asked our students to creatively match their own solutions to the myriad of real-life problems they experienced every day. We set aside listing in order the presidents from George Washington to the current occupant of the White House and memorizing the seven major imports and exports of Chile. Instead we examined the issues of urban America and vicariously explored life in big-city settings beyond our borders, including Mexico City, Calcutta, Beijing, and Nairobi.

There was, admittedly, much greater freedom at that time in a teacher's selection of the subject matter to be learned. We studied the history and legacy of race relations in our country, even though my predecessor had received a letter from the KKK warning her to "lay off" the topic. One 16 millimeter film we used in room 106 was Bill Cosby's 1969 documentary *Black History: Lost, Stolen, or Strayed?* (Yes, I know that using 16 millimeter films dates me, but age is diversity too.) It was a groundbreaking piece of work. Child actress Shirley Temple did not seem as cute when Cosby pointed out that she was made appealing at the expense of the dignity of the Black actors that worked alongside her. And how, asked Cosby, were all those Black inventors, explorers, and writers "lost" in the history books? Good question. The psychological damage of institutional racism was considered in the film, as were controversial storefront schools for Black children who were appearing in New York and California. My memories of that film still instruct and enlighten me, and it has been reissued on DVD.

We were convinced that students had to be reached on a personal level. The practice of team teaching was in its infancy, but it provided my three colleagues and me with the opportunity to apply flexible scheduling to meet the needs of the 125 students assigned to us. One example was the Friday afternoon "Quiz Game." The mathematics teacher had constructed eight wooden boxes with lights and buzzers for the two teams of four students each. The weekly "Quiz Game" was used to review the week's academic work. Mildly competitive, but not compulsory, almost all students chose to participate. They really seemed to enjoy getting on the stage of our ancient auditorium at the end of each week.

More importantly, such activities broke down barriers, allowing teachers the opportunity to step outside their traditional classroom roles. Even that new and somewhat reserved teacher from room 106 was seen in a new light when it was his turn to become the "quizmaster." We also played basketball with the students after school, had in-school clubs once a month (what would be called Advisory Groups today), and took seriously these tools to enhance self-concept. Although nurturing self-esteem is an essential building block in creating community and celebrating diversity, it has increasingly become viewed by some of the Essentialist school of educational philosophy as too soft and too anti-academic.

But we knew then, as we know now, that the emotional needs of children and adolescents must be met before any meaningful intellectual endeavors can be pursued. After all, we were aware of psychologist Kenneth Clark's research on the negative impact that segregation and racism had on learning among Black children. Clark's testimony in Brown vs. Board of Education, through the use of Black dolls and White dolls, proved a decisive factor in that landmark decision. I hope that the students in room 106 not only felt better about themselves, but learned something, too. I think they did.

I drove by the school a few years ago—it was located in my old hometown where I had grown up and where I spent the first five years of my teaching career. From the street I could see the five basement windows of room 106. It had been years since I was in that building, but I had little trouble recreating in my mind the sight, the smell, the feel of that room. I wonder if a new teacher entered room 106 this year to begin a career in teaching. What will be the challenges and successes? And what progress will that teacher be able to chart a quarter-century hence? I envy her—and I wish her well.

Endnotes

1   Barton, Keith C. "Research on Students' Ideas about History. " Ed. Linda S. Levstik and Cynthia A. Tyson. *Handbook of Research in Social Studies Education.* New York: Routledge, 2008. 247.

2   Davis, Barbara Gross. *Tools for Teaching.* 2nd ed. San Francisco: Jossey-Bass, 2009. 59–66.

3   Nieto, Sonia and Patty Bode. *Affirming Diversity: The Sociopolitical Context of Multicultural Education.* 5th ed. Boston: Pearson/Allyn and Bacon, 2008. 8.

4   Ibid. 45.

5   *Expectations of Excellence: Curriculum Standards for Social Studies.* Bulletin 89. Washington, DC: National Council for the Social Studies, Fall 1994. 79.

6   Marri, Anand R. "Building a Framework for Classroom-based Multicultural Democratic Education: Learning from Three Skilled Teachers." *Teachers College Record.* 107 (2005) : 1036–59.

7   *John F. Kennedy Civil Rights Address.* 11 June 1963. Retrieved from <http://inspirationalspeakers.wordpress.com>.

8   Branch, Taylor. *Parting the Waters: America in the King Years, 1954–63.* New York: Simon and Schuster, 1988. 141.
9   Gereluk, Dianne. "Education for Social Justice." Ed. Eugene F. Provenzo, Jr. *Encyclopedia of the Social and Cultural Foundations of Education.* Thousand Oaks: Sage Publications, 2009. 728–29.
10   Nieto and Bode, 12.
11   Gereluk, 729.
12   McIntosh, P. "White Privilege: Unpacking the Invisible Knapsack." Independent School *Journal.* Winter 1990.
13   Thompson, Katherine P., P. Gayle Andrews, Courtney S. Jackson, and Mary Reagin. "Who Are My Students and Why Does It Matter? Using Service-Learning to Teach Children Impacted by Poverty." *Middle School Journal* 41.4 (2010): 52.
14   Ibid. 52–61.
15   Spalding, Elizabeth et al. "Social Justice and Teacher Education: A Hammer, a Bell, and a Song." *Journal of Teacher Education* 61.3 (2010): 191–96. See also Noddings, Nel. "An Ethic of Caring and Its Implications for Instructional Arrangements." *American Journal of Education* 96. 2 (1988): 215–30.
16   Howard, Gary R. *We Can't Teach What We Don't Know: White Teachers, Multiracial Schools.* New York: Teachers College Press, 1999. 59.
17   Ibid. 81.
18   Seider, Scott. "Social Justice in the Suburbs." *Educational Leadership* 66. 8 (2009): 54–7.
19   Ibid.
20   Traudt, Kristin. "Survey Says . . . : Can White Teachers Effectively Teach Students of Color?" Ed. Linda Darling-Hammond, Jennifer French, and Silvia Paloma Garcia-Lopez. *Learning to Teach for Social Justice.* New York: Teachers College Press, 2002. 49.
21   Kozol, Jonathan. *On Being a Teacher.* Oxford, England: Oneworld Books, 1981. 2009. 29–34.
22   Noddings, Nel. "The Gender Issue." *Educational Leadership* 49 (1991–92): 65–70.
23   Hanger, Howard and Vicki Garlock. *A Precious Window: A Manual for Teaching and Nurturing Middle School Girls.* Asheville: Lobster Books, 2008.
24   Whitmire, Richard. *Why Boys Fail: Saving Our Sons from an Educational System That's Leaving Them Behind.* New York: American Management Association, 2010. 211–15.
25   Ibid. 108–133, 190–191. See also Kershner, Ivan. "Being Up Front: Motivating Boys to Learn." *Middle Ground: The Magazine of Middle Level Education* 13. 3 (2010): 21.
26   West, Cornel. *Race Matters.* New York: Vintage Books, 1994. xiv, 157.
27   Burch, Susan. "(Extraordinary) Bodies of Knowledge: Recent Scholarship in American Disability History." *Magazine of History* 23. 3 (2009): 29–34.
28   See Gallagher, Hugh *FDR's Splendid Deception.* New York: Dodd, Mead, 1985.
29   Nielsen, Kim E. "Using Biography to Teach Disability History" *Organization of American Historians Magazine of History* Vol. 23, Issue 3 (July 2009) p. 42.
30   Bugaj, Christopher R., and Sally Norton-Darr. *The Practical and Fun Guide to Assistive Technology in the Public Schools.* Washington, DC: International Society for Technology in Education, 2010. 13.

31   FitzGerald, Frances. *America Revised.* Boston: Little Brown, 1979; and Schlesinger, Arthur M., Jr. *The Disuniting of America: Reflections on a Multicultural Society.* New York: W.W. Norton and Co., 1994.

32   Banks, James A. *Cultural Diversity and Education: Foundations, Curriculum, and Teaching.* 5th ed. Boston: Allyn and Bacon, 2006. 23, 143, 209, 213–14, 332–33.

33   Franklin, John Hope. *From Slavery to Freedom: A History of Negro Americans.* 3rd ed. New York: Knopf, 1967.

34   *American Association of University Women.* "How Schools Shortchange Women." New York: Marlow, 1992; and *American Association of University Women.* "Gender Gaps: Where Schools Still Fail our Children." New York: Marlow, 1998.

35   Crocco, Margaret Smith. "Gender and Sexuality in the Social Studies." Ed. Linda S. Levstik and Cynthia A. Tyson. *Handbook of Research in Social Studies Education.* New York: Routledge, 2008. 172–96.

36   Hundey, Ian M., and Michael L. Magarrey. *Canadian History 1900–2000.* Toronto: Irwin Publishing, 2000.

37   Ravi, Anita K. "Disciplinary Literacy in the History Classroom." Ed. Stephanie M. McConachie and Anthony R. Petrosky. *Content Matters: A Disciplinary Literacy Approach to Improving Student Learning.* San Francisco: Jossey-Bass, 2010. 33–61.

38   Garcia, Roman H. "Navigating a New World: The Development of an Immigrant Student in an American Middle School." Ed. Linda Darling-Hammond, Jennifer French, and Silvia Paloma Garcia-Lopez. *Learning to Teach for Social Justice.* New York: Teachers College Press, 2002. 126–7.

39   Kozol, Jonathan. *The Shame of the Nation: The Restoration of Apartheid.* New York: Three Rivers Press, 2006.

40   See the Du Bois Institute at <http://dubois.fas.harvard.edu> for the "African American Lives, Genealogy, and Genetics Curriculum" and the "African American National Biography Project." Also the PBS series *African American Lives.*

41   Levi, Primo. *The Drowned and the Saved.* New York: Vintage, 1980. 151.

42   Takaki, Ronald A. *In a Different Mirror: A Multicultural History of America.* Boston: Little Brown Co., 1993.

43   Selig, Diana. "Celebrating Cultural Diversity in the 1920's." *Magazine of History* 21. 3 (2007): 41–2.

44   Ibid. 43–6.

45   See Wallace, James. *The Promise of Progressivism: Angelo Patri and Urban Education.* New York, NY: Peter Lang Publishing, 2006.

SEVEN

Movies, Movies, Movies

For all of the scandals that have continued to plague the hapless Warren G. Harding, he does need to be given credit for advocating during his brief presidency (1921–1923) the use of film in the nation's classrooms. Coming from a conservative Republican politician, this can be considered a rather progressive stance to take toward the emerging medium of film. In a letter to Will Hayes, director of the Motion Picture Association, Harding wrote:

> Next to studying geography by seeing the world . . . would be studying it with the aid of the moving picture . . . I do not want to be understood as assuming that education can or ought to be made a mere pleasure, a titillation of the fancy, by making it too easy. I would not by any means turn the school room into a moving picture theater. On the other hand, I would use the picture as a means to enlist the pupils' interest in the real work that must be involved in acquiring any education worthy of the name.[1]

In regard to this pedagogical suggestion Harding was prescient—in the future film would play a central role in the education of youth, particularly in the discipline of history. Thomas Edison at almost the same time said that he viewed the motion picture as "destined to revolutionize our education system . . . supplant[ing] largely, if not entirely, the use of textbooks. The education of the future will be conducted through the medium of the motion picture . . . where it should be possible to obtain one hundred percent efficiency."[2]

Many assertions have been made regarding the efficacy of using film in the history classroom. Claims have included that their use can rouse students to higher levels of inquiry, provide students with details of life that are not able to be communicated in writing, and that film makes history "come alive."[3] The authors of *Teaching History with Film* have outlined a thoughtful rationale for using motion pictures in the secondary school classroom. Film can be used to:

- develop empathy.

- develop analytical and interpretive skills.

- teach about controversial issues.

- visualize the past.

- challenge students to examine history with other narratives.[4]

Media in general and film in particular are major components in the life of adolescents. A recent study found that the typical adolescent spends four hours a day listening to music and watching television. Furthermore over 50% of adolescents, the largest film-watching age group of the American population, views at least one movie per month.[5] The amount of film that is available to teach twentieth-century history is remarkable. From documentaries to Hollywood productions, film provides history teachers with a valuable venue for engaging the adolescent learner.

A more in-depth analysis of this data has been undertaken by Sam Wineburg and his colleagues. Their research on the role of film in students' knowledge of history has shown that movies are what can be called "the cultural curriculum." In their study, the award-winning film *Forrest Gump* (1994) was found to be highly effective in teaching about the 1960s—highlighting historical events ranging from the Vietnam War to the hippie movement to various American presidents. The influence of film narratives that students bring to the classroom can be used by teachers to build deeper historical knowledge. Wineburg quotes the president of the Organization of American Historians as "begrudgingly recognizing films as the predominant influence on students' historical understanding."[6]

Nevertheless, there are other educators that give caution to the use of movies with adolescents. Selwyn and Maher have written in connection with movies:

> Students come to school with enormous amounts of misinformation based on movies they have watched; most moviemakers have little interest or concern about historical accuracy. The consequences for us as social studies teachers is

that we have to undo the miss-education our students have suffered before; we need to help them learn a more accurate and useful approach to the study of history.[7]

Selwyn and Maher state that movies such as *Gone With the Wind* (1939) and *The Alamo* (the 1960 John Wayne version) are "miss-histories." Suggesting student research as the antidote, they recommend students seek out historical resources and information that either support or refute what was shown in the film as factual.

Another concern when using film in the history classroom relates to the overuse of the medium. A possibly apocryphal story is told of the history teacher whose colleagues put a sign over his door, "Coffee Cup Theater," due to the excessive use of film in his class. A film should never be used as "filler," a substitute for processing the material at hand, or employed without careful thought as to how the film is to be integrated into the lesson.

Potter has observed that film is a primary source document.[8] Matz and Pingatore have noted that for the first half of the twentieth century, thousands of hours of newsreels were shot documenting current events for moviegoers in the days before television brought news into homes. In addition to such documentaries, they suggest that Hollywood-produced period pieces are most effective for use in history classes. This pair of researchers has listed five categories that students should look for in such films: 1) technology (telephones, televisions, cars) 2) fashion (hair styles, clothes, hats) 3) language ('ice box,' 'That's swell') 4) culture (smoking, Coke in glass bottles, larger families) and 5) the economy (fewer women in the workplace and only in certain jobs, a dime to make a phone call, prices for food and gasoline).[9]

In addition to the categories listed above, students should also look for the depiction of race in film. Pre-1960 Hollywood rarely if ever had Blacks in any roles other than maids, butlers, railroad porters, or chauffeurs. Most films did not even have Blacks in background scenes or as part of crowds. It was as though only Whites existed in America. Sidney Poitier broke the color-line in the 1960s with leading roles and an Academy Award for *Lilies of the Field*. Current actors such as Denzel Washington and Halle Berry are prominent stars, but it could be argued that Blacks, Latinos, and Native Americans are still underrepresented in modern film.

Film scholars often categorize films, and it is helpful to teachers who use film in their classrooms to be aware of them. One of the most common classifications is style. Movies are often placed on a continuum from documentary (factual, real depiction of actual events) to fiction (representations of real or imagined events and people) to avant-garde (abstract and experimental).[10] The final style is rarely used or advantageous for adolescent students.

Furay and Salevouris suggest that films can be categorized by function.[11] For example, film can be a *record*. An example of this is *The Holocaust and Concentration Camps: Jewish Life and Death in Nazi Camps* (2006), which contains actual film footage of the liberation of the concentration camps. The scenes are graphic, however, and the teacher will need to make a professional decision as to what age is appropriate for viewing. Another film in this category is *Image of an Assassination: A New Look at the Zapruder Film* (2008), a digitally enhanced version of the Kennedy assassination. While again graphic, connecting it with the ever-present conspiracy theories surrounding that 1963 November day in Dallas can make for an absorbing lesson.

Another category of film for Furay and Salevouris would be *representation*. These films range from documentaries like Ken Burns' *The Civil War* or the PBS *American Experience* to theatrical releases such as *All the King's Men, Reds,* and *Platoon*. Popular movies about World War II such as *Schindler's List* and *Saving Private Ryan* combine compelling stories with outstanding filmmaking. One will never know the true terror, brutality, and sacrifice of the Normandy invasion on D-Day; however the ferocious intensity of the first twenty minutes of *Saving Private Ryan* may come as vicariously close as one can to what that day was like. Pairing several minutes from Holocaust archives with the opening scenes from *Saving Private Ryan* explains better than any reading why World War II was called the "necessary war."

Cultural artifact is another classification of film that Furay and Salevouris identify. This branch includes historical films that examine and reflect the thinking and values of the period in which they were made. The best example is D.W. Griffith's *Birth of a Nation* (1915), which depicts Reconstruction from a White, Southern point of view on the issue of race. *The Grapes of Wrath* (1940), drawn from author John Steinbeck's Depression-era novel of Dustbowl migrants, is another example. The film captures what women and men of this time period thought about the economic collapse they were experiencing.

Two final categories are *biographical* and *propaganda*. The life of Alfred Kinsey simultaneously generated a Hollywood version of his life in addition to a PBS treatment. Other examples of film biographies are *PT 109, Malcolm X, Patton,* and *Gandhi*. The best examples of propaganda films are by a German and an American. Leni Riefenstahl's *Triumph of the Will* depicts the supposed glory of Nazi Germany. On the Allied side of World War II, Hollywood director Frank Capra produced the *Why We Fight* series. Of course, a teaching point could be made that the Nazis and the Allies each, no doubt, saw their own productions as documentaries, not propaganda.

History teachers who choose to use film need to ensure that their purpose in the classroom is clear. A first step for teachers who may not be film connoisseurs or up-to-date on filmography is to become aware of what is available. Suggested resource websites for documentaries and classic television shows are The Internet Movie Database www.imdb.com, the Internet Movie Archive www.archive.org/movies/movies.php, and Rotten Tomatoes www.rottentomatoes.com. The journal *Film and History*, published by The Historian Film Committee, is an excellent resource for both film selection and background information on the films.

Here, in addition to the films discussed above, are some suggestions and recommendations of films categorized by historical period. The list is far from exhaustive, but it does represent both popular and critical productions that offer much to the history classroom. The films were selected for a number of reasons. Some are historically accurate or inaccurate and therefore can be used as examples to demonstrate to students how events did or did not happen. Another reason behind the selection of the following films is that they reflect a point of view from the period in which they were made. Some films are suggested because they are representational of actual events, whether they be Hollywood or documentary productions. Finally, these films will easily capture the attention of students through their stories, acting, or visual appeal.

The first recommendation may not at first seem to be a film about colonization. *The End of Poverty* (2010) examines the complex question, "Why is there poverty?" The roots of poverty, according to filmmaker Philippe Diaz, are to be found in colonialism beginning with Christopher Columbus and continuing to this day. Military conquest, slavery, and the seizure and theft of land in the Americas and other continents are viewed as the major causes of poverty both then and now. There may not be a better example of a film that makes the connection between history and the real-life issues confronting humans today.

The world of Native Americans as depicted in film makes for an excellent exercise in comparison and contrast. The more recent the films, the more realistic the representation of the Native Americans. Taken from a bestselling novel, *Drums Along the Mohawk* (1939) views the 18th-century colonists as struggling to settle land in western New York already populated by the Mohawks. The topic of land theft by Whites is never explicitly explored. Instead the film focuses on stereotypical depictions of the Mohawks as devious, violent, and cruel. James Fenimore Cooper's novel, *The Last of the Mohicans,* has been produced more than once with the 1936 treatment and the 1992 production considered the strongest. An additional film with Native American themes is *Dances with Wolves* (1990) where a White Army officer, after extensive interaction with the Sioux, comes to the realization that their culture may be morally superior to his own.[12] Native Americans are portrayed in a historically accurate and authentic manner in this film and in *The New World* (2005), which explores the lives of Pocahontas and John Smith.

The West has always been a major theme in history and the movies. The 2004 version of *The Alamo* is considered a historically realistic rendering of the events in 1830s Mexico. Even at this historical distance, General George Armstrong Custer continues to evoke strong emotions in native people. Errol Flynn's rendition of Custer in *They Died With Their Boots On* (1941) left an indelible mark on a generation of Americans as they viewed the events surrounding the Battle of the Big Horn through the eyes of a heroic Custer. An opposite, anti-heroic, and at times irreverent representation of both Native Americans and Custer's Last Stand can be found in *Little Big Man* (1970). In that film, Dustin Hoffman plays the 120-year-old Jack Crabb. Crabb is supposedly the only White survivor of the Little Big Horn. Having been adopted by the Native Americans, the film is told as an oral history of Crabb's remembrances. The film may be more representative of the period, in which it was made than the period it purports to represent, combining comedy, tragedy, and cynicism.

This issue of racism is often viewed in history as a strictly Black/White phenomenon. However, one of the most popular westerns of all time, *The Searchers* (1956), starring John Wayne, has some of the most glaring examples of racism toward Native Americans in modern film. The PBS production *In the White Man's Image* (1992) is a non-Hollywood documentary treatment of Native American/White relationships and racism in late 19th- and early 20th-century America. It is the best film on the subject of Native American/White relations and connects with adolescents and adults on both a strong emotional and intellectual level.

Slavery, the Civil War, and Reconstruction have been portrayed in film since the days of silent films. *Birth of a Nation* (1915) was referenced earlier in this chapter and deals with Reconstruction. Ken Burns' *The Civil War* (1990) is the most comprehensive treatment of the monumental conflict. *Amistad* (1997), an episode of slave-trading in the early 19th century, and *Amazing Grace* (2007), which tells the story of William Wilberforce and the British abolitionists' labors against the institution of slavery in England, both capture the politics and human dimension of slavery.

Other than *Birth of a Nation*, no Hollywood film has provided a better interpretation of the White Southern point of view of slavery and Reconstruction than *Gone With the Wind* (1939), taken from Atlanta resident Margaret Mitchell's bestselling novel. Happy slaves (most of the time), corrupt carpetbaggers, and the White man's right to the Southern "way of life" based on slavery are all found in this film. *Glory* (1989) serves as an antidote to the conventional rendering of Blacks during the Civil War. It is the true story of the Massachusetts 54th regiment of Black soldiers who served with great courage and distinction. *Glory* has been highly recommended for classroom use.[13] One other suggested film for use when teaching about the Civil War is *Ride with the Devil* (1999), which explores the often forgotten Missouri-Kansas border wars of the 1850s and 1860s.[14]

Abraham Lincoln has been a frequent subject on film, leading all other presidential appearances with 123 as of 2007. Most notable would be legendary director D.W. Griffith's 1930 version of Lincoln's life, *Abraham Lincoln* starring Walter

Huston. (Lincoln on film is even the subject of an entire book, Mark S. Reinhart's *Abraham Lincoln on Screen*.[15]) One of the first talkies, it covers the entire span of Lincoln's life from his birth in Kentucky in 1809 to his assassination in 1865. Due to its datedness, using the entire film with adolescents is not advisable; however, using segments, especially in comparison to other Lincoln motion pictures, is most effective. Two back-to-back films concerning Lincoln's pre-presidential years are *Young Mr. Lincoln* (1939) and *Abe Lincoln of Illinois* (1940), which competed with each other upon their releases. The former stars Henry Fonda and of the two films is the most appropriate and useful for young adolescents. It covers the greatly exaggerated (and little documented) romance between Lincoln and Ann Rutledge in New Salem, Illinois, his prowess as a rail-splitter and wrestler, his move to Springfield to begin his law practice, and the meeting of his future wife Mary Todd. The film also focuses on a fictionalized trial where Fonda's Lincoln demonstrates many of the well-known Lincoln characteristics such as his laconic persona, his sense of humor, and his intelligence. The film ends with Lincoln walking up a hill into an oncoming thunderstorm, representative of the yet-to-occur Civil War, as the *Battle Hymn of the Republic* is heard playing in the background.

Abe Lincoln of Illinois, which appeared one year after *Young Mr. Lincoln* with Raymond Massey in the lead, is recommended for older adolescents as it addresses the political issues of the day. Massey, who received an Oscar nomination for his role, also covers the New Salem years and again the Ann Rutledge story. The screenplay was taken from Robert Sherwood's Pulitzer Prize–winning play of the same name. Sherwood later sued 20th Century Fox for plagiarism of his work in their Fonda film. (Sherwood lost in court.) Also of note in *Abe Lincoln of Illinois* is the negative portrayal of Mary Todd Lincoln. A realistic look at the Lincolns' marriage can be found in PBS's *Abraham and Mary Lincoln: A House Divided* (2001).

More recent treatments of Lincoln are the 1988 television mini-series *Gore Vidal's Lincoln* and the PBS documentary by Harvard's Henry Louis Gates, Jr., *Looking for Lincoln* (2009). An array of films on the Lincoln assassination has been produced. The documentary dramatization of *Stealing Lincoln's Body* (2009), based on the 2007 book of the same name by Thomas J. Craughwell, tells the bizarre tale of the forty years it took for Lincoln to finally be laid to rest.[16]

Other than some very primitive filming attempts during the Spanish-American War, World War I was the first war to be documented on film. Tracing the aerial war is the silent, Academy Award-winning film *Wings* (1927). *All Quiet on the Western Front* (1930), from the Erich Maria Remarque novel, caused much debate in United States during the 1930s due to its anti-war theme. *Sergeant York* (1941), starring Gary Cooper, follows the true story of Tennessee native Alvin York's journey from conscientious objector to war hero in the trenches of France. Director Stanley Kubrick's *Paths of Glory* (1957) again pointed to the futility of trench warfare and the politics of war in general. Not political in the sense of the two above films, the 1966 *The Blue Max* looks at the introduction of the airplane into combat as seen from the German side of the Great War. A recent French film, *A Very Long Engagement* (2004), also captures epic scenes of that war in addition to providing a glimpse of the European home front.

America's World War I president, Woodrow Wilson, is portrayed in the 1944 *Wilson*. (*Wilson* is also an example of the fact that some films are difficult to secure. Although put on video a number of years ago, it is not commercially available at this time, but is shown occasionally on Turner Classic Movies.) *Wilson* won five Academy Awards and while explicitly reverential at times (as we shall see below), it does "cover" Wilson's rise and presidency as well as end with a warning as to the dangers of not achieving a lasting peace. Wilson's unsuccessful struggle with the Senate over the ratification of the Versailles Treaty is seen as a heroic and visionary effort to bring about world peace. Released in 1944, just after the November presidential election and during World War II, it was considered too politically partisan. Franklin Roosevelt, like Wilson a generation earlier, was a wartime Democrat looking ahead to the post-war world.

In her biography, *Edith and Woodrow*, Phyllis Lee Levin reveals that Wilson's second wife, Edith Bolling Galt Wilson, still alive when *Wilson* was produced, had a direct hand in how her husband was depicted. The rather swift marriage—seven months after the death of Wilson's wife—and the passionate courting of Edith by the outwardly intellectual and dispassionate president is well hidden in the film. As much of the film was based on the second Mrs. Wilson's memoir, she also curtailed how her relationship with the president was depicted on the screen. She also made sure she was played by an attractive actress. Also concealed is the major role Edith played after Wilson's stroke. Some historians have speculated that she was in fact making presidential decisions in order to protect her husband during his incapacity.[17] There was indeed "talk" about Edith at the time, especially the courtship. The *American Experience* presidential series relates a story about Woodrow and Edith. A news item in the *Washington Post* inadvertently made a typographical error in a story about Edith and the president, stating that "the president was *entering* (author's emphasis) Mrs. Galt" rather than the "president was entertaining Mrs. Galt."

Films about the Great Depression years, produced since the 1930s, document that era well. Documentaries include those on Franklin and Eleanor Roosevelt, demagogues such as Huey Long, and other larger-than-life figures from that decade. The iconic film *Grapes of Wrath* (1940), mentioned earlier, has been considered the greatest film dealing with the Dust Bowl, the Depression, and the lives of those caught up in its tragedies. This is one of the few films that is justifiably worth the two or more days of class time spent to show it in its entirety. Director Peter Bogdanovich's black-and-white *Paper Moon* (1973) provides the viewer, as few films have, with the texture and atmosphere of rural Kansas during this period.

The activities of gangsters and crooks have often been a favorite of adolescents. (See the story of William Van Til and his students in Columbus, Ohio, during the Depression in the chapter "Does the Subject Matter?") Over 200 gangster movies were made between 1930 and 1932.[18] Three of the most popular were Edward G. Robinson's *Little Caesar* (1930), James Cagney's *The Public Enemy* (1931), and Paul Muni in *Scarface* (1932). F.B.I. agent Elliot Ness was re-discovered in the 1960s television series, *The Untouchables*, taken from his autobiography. Ness was given star treatment with Kevin Costner as Ness in the 1987 film version by the same title. Highly stylized and popular, Warren Beatty and Faye Dunaway re-invented the infamous Texas bank robbers and killers in the 1967 *Bonnie and Clyde*. In 2009 *Public Enemies*, drawing on Bryan Burroughs's book about Indiana-born bank robber John Dillinger, starred Johnny Depp. *Road to Perdition* (2002), based on a graphic novel, stars Tom Hanks and captures well the life of Midwest gangsters in the 1930s.

World War II has been the most frequently used and popular setting for historical films. This would include not just films *about* World War II, but films *made* during World War II. The times, and the films that they reflected, pitted dictatorship and enslavement against democracy and freedom. It was indeed a "people's war" as the minister in *Mrs. Miniver* tells his congregation at the film's conclusion. Producers, directors, writers, actors and actresses in the entire film industry contributed to the war effort.[19]

The examples of outstanding World War II films that follow, while not comprehensive, are fairly representative of both movies from the war era and recent renditions of the conflict. Films were often used to build morale on the home front. *Mrs. Miniver* (1941), *Casablanca* (1942), and *This Above All* (1942) all fall into this category. Through the magic of film Sherlock Holmes leaves his original late 19th-century setting to confront Nazis in the early 1940s. Actor Basil Rathbone, as Holmes, ended several of these films with quotes from Winston Churchill that served both literary and patriotic functions.

The 1942 film *In Which We Serve* starring Noel Coward, who co-directed with David Lean, demonstrates naval danger, courage, and patriotism. Two Tyrone Power vehicles—*Crash Dive* (1943), also a navy film, and *A Yank in the RAF* (1941), which covered the celebrated British air arm ("Never has so much been done by so few for so many")—were both representative of wartime Hollywood feature films. Power himself served in the Marines as a pilot seeing action in the Pacific. Other actors who also joined the services included Clark Gable, Henry Fonda, and James Stewart. And Hollywood was active on the home front. Gable's wife, Carole Lombard, lost her life in a plane crash returning to California from a war bonds sale in her home state of Indiana. Another victim of the war was the beloved journalist, Ernie Pyle. A favorite correspondent of the GIs, due to his close relationship to the service men, Pyle has his war years re-told in the 1945 movie, *The Story of G.I. Joe.*

The propaganda element of these World War II films sometimes provided unintended consequences for the filmmakers. *Mission to Moscow* (1943), based on the experiences of U.S. ambassador to the Soviet Union Joseph E. Davies, gave a much too idealistic view of America's ally and its leader Joseph Stalin. Later, especially after the war, it was seen as a much too sympathetic, even apologetic, portrayal of the communist country. Most agree that the attempt to sympathetically connect the United States to its ally the Soviet Union were never as successful as the film industry's linking this country to England.[20]

One of the best Hollywood films to capture the flavor and look of the home front during World War II was *The Human Comedy* (1943). Nominated for multiple Academy Awards including best picture, actor, and director, small-town California is seen through the eyes of Mickey Rooney as a teenager. The middle son of a widowed mother, Rooney experiences the war from mundane occurrences in his own backyard to his high school to his part-time job as a Western Union telegram boy. This meant he often delivered the fateful news of a battlefield death to the soldier's family. Few films examined the contributions of women in the war effort, though *So Proudly We Hail* (1943) and *Cry Havoc* (1944) did pay tribute to the role of nurses in the conflict.

Since You Went Away (1944) was another prestigious home-front movie that provided both subtle and explicit support for war aims and democracy. Its ending also suggests the transition from a war-time footing to the future peace and the coming post-war years. The immediate aftermath of the war as it impacted the returning soldiers is explored in *The Best Years of Our Lives* (1945). Considered a classic, this film is also a home-front narrative, that examines the lives of servicemen returning from the war. A veteran rather than an actor, and also a double amputee, Harold Russell won the Academy Award for his performance in a supporting role in this picture.

As alluded to above and also the chapter on public history, no one has captured the experience of World War II much better than the team of director and producer Steven Spielberg and actor, director, and producer Tom Hanks. In addition to *Saving Private Ryan,* they have collaborated on two HBO series, *Band of Brothers* (2001) and *The Pacific* (2010). Actor and director Clint Eastwood made two companion films about the 36-day battle for the island of Iwo Jima in the Pacific. *Flags of Our Fathers* is told from the American point of view while *Letters from Iwo Jima* (both 2006) examines the same event as experienced by the Japanese. Two other recent films on World War II are *Enemy at the Gates* (2001), about the Battle of Stalingrad, and *The Thin Red Line* (1998), which deals with the Battle of Guadalcanal. Documentarian Ken Burns' *The War* is his homage to four cities during World War II and representative women and men who fought the "necessary war." There is no shortage of film on this monumental 20th-century event.

The morality of war becomes the issue as Wetta and Novelli analyze how World War II films have depicted the air war, particularly the bombing of civilians. Paradoxically, they point out, "the strategic bombing offensive in World War II represents both the most morally questionable allied action of the war and the most popular topic for wartime combat films." *Bombardier* (1943) and *Twelve O'Clock High* (1949) were examples of movies where the tactic of what was termed "precision-bombing" was explored. The same rationale used for the dropping of the atomic bombs on Japan was used in defense of strategic bombing in World War II. The historian Michael Bess is quoted as calling the bombings in Europe "the single greatest moral failure of the Anglo-American war effort." Yet, as Wetta and Novelli point out, the application of this technology was used as a justification in later wars from Vietnam to Iraq.[21] The morality of the bombing of Dresden, Germany, was challenged by novelist Kurt Vonnegut (who was an American P.O.W. in the city during the raid) in both his book and later film *Slaughterhouse-Five* (1972).

The films that deal with the Holocaust are a category unto themselves. An excellent film for teachers that provides an overview and foundational information of Hollywood's treatment of the Holocaust is *Imaginary Witness: Hollywood and Holocaust* (2004). Hollywood was greatly concerned over alienating the German market for American films by being too critical of Hitler's dictatorship. A few brave producers, Warner Brothers being the best example, did make films such as the 1939 *Confessions of a Nazi Spy* that attempted to portray the destructive aspects of Hitler's regime. While the United States was still a neutral nation, Charlie Chaplin starred and produced in *The Great Dictator* (1940). The film, which ridicules a Hitler-like leader (played by Chaplin), has elements that contain both mockery and sober warnings in those years before the U.S. entry into the war.

When the Nazi death camps were discovered and liberated, what was found was so unbelievable that it had to be documented on film. The raw footage of the camps was shown in theaters for about a year after the war, then not widely seen until the late 1960s. The films of the camps were shown within the 1962 movie *Judgment at Nuremburg. The Pawnbroker* (1965), the story of a camp survivor, examined the psychological effects of the experience on one man in New York. Two 1980s television mini-series, *Holocaust* and *War and Remembrance,* graphically reproduced the results of Hitler's Final Solution. The 1970s and 1980s were also a time when survivors of the camps emerged to tell their stories for a number of documentary films.

The documentary *Imaginary Witness* acknowledges the need for film to talk about the Holocaust. It also gives voice to critics, including survivor Elie Wiesel, who powerfully maintain that film is unable to address the reality of this atrocity.

Stephen Spielberg's 1993 *Schindler's List* is seen by the producers of *Imaginary Witness* as probably the most accurate treatment of the topic possible considering the enormity, brutality, and venality of the event. It received an Academy Award for best picture. Other films have used the Holocaust for their subject matter, but it is doubtful any writer, director, or producer will ever fully capture the inhumanity of these horrific events.

The post-World War II intricacies and complexities of McCarthyism—the man and the era—are difficult to encapsulate and then relay to adolescent audiences, even on film. An excellent source, though, are the programs of television journalist Edward R. Murrow, available on DVD. His *See It Now* episode on McCarthy is considered classic 1950s television. It is recreated in the 2004 film *Good Night, and Good Luck* with George Clooney directing and co-starring with David Strathairn as the legendary CBS journalist. Juxtaposing segments of original film with Hollywood treatments can be an effective use of the medium. Two classic political films that both deal with corruption—one fictional and one actual—are director Frank Capra's memorable 1939 *Mr. Smith Goes to Washington* and the factual dramatization of Bob Woodward's and Carl Bernstein's book on the Watergate scandal *All the President's Men* (1976).

Race relations and the Civil Rights movement have provided critical subject matter for what many historians consider the paramount issue in American history. One of the best pieces of journalistic television ever produced is journalist Bill Moyers' *Walk Through the Twentieth Century: The Second American Revolution, Pt. II* (1984). The episode begins with the *Plessey v. Ferguson* case in 1896 and ends with Dr. King's "I Have a Dream" speech in 1963. Moyers traces race relations with *Brown v. Board of Education* at its center and King, Malcolm X, and Thurgood Marshall, pivotal figures in the movement's history. In looking at the life of Malcolm X, Denzel Washington captured the essence and the substance of the man in his portrayal of this American Black leader in the 1992 dramatized biography *Malcolm X*.

A television production from 1969 by Bill Cosby titled *Black History: Lost, Stolen, or Strayed* has been re-issued on DVD. Looking at the historical depiction of Blacks in history books and film, in addition to the impact that "history" has had on children, this production retains the power to inform and emotionally move adolescents and adults. The script was penned by CBS television network writer and commentator Andy Rooney.

How race played out in the lives of Americans during the Civil Rights era has been represented in three theatrical releases—two from the 1960s and one two decades later. *Guess Who's Coming to Dinner* (1967) examined how a liberal White couple (Katharine Hepburn and Spencer Tracy) grapple with the issue of their White daughter marrying a Black physician played by Sidney Poitier. The beliefs, values, and prejudices of all the characters, Black and White, come to the fore. Poitier again is the leading actor in the 1967 *In the Heat of the Night*, playing against Rod Steiger, as a stereotypical White southern sheriff of that time. A final exploration of Black/White relations is the period piece made in 1989, but covering the decade of the 1960s, *Driving Miss Daisy*. A White Atlanta matron and her Black chauffer interact in the changing milieu of the day. Pieces of all of these films, while dramatized, provide glimpses into race relations from that time period.

Almost since the fall of Saigon in 1975, film has been used as a medium to understand and explain the American involvement in Vietnam. *Coming Home* (1978) and *Born on the Fourth of July* (1989), the former fictional and the latter semi-biographical, depict the personal results of war where veterans, in both of these films, are paraplegics. *Apocalypse Now* (1986), *Platoon* (1986), *Full Metal Jacket* (1987), and *Forrest Gump* (1994) are a series of films that examine the Vietnam experience, usually from an anti-war point of view. These films, other than *Forrest Gump*, would be recommended for teachers to use for their own background knowledge.

Films on the wars in the Middle East of the past two decades—from Operation Desert Storm in 1991 to the recent wars in Iraq and Afghanistan—are, due to their violence and often controversial views of the wars, difficult to use in middle level or high school classrooms. These films, though, as suggested above, may provide needed background and supplemental material for teachers. Operation Desert Storm in 1991 seemed too short in length to generate a collection of films about that conflict. The sole example of that conflict is *Three Kings* (1999), which is as much about the politics of war as about war itself. *Black Hawk Down* (2001), which looked at President Bill Clinton's involvement in Somalia, has been praised for both content and style. While still few in number, films about the Iraq War that began in 2003 are mostly anti-war in outlook. The best known may be *Fahrenheit 9/11* (2007) by producer and director Michael Moore. It has been viewed as overly critical of President George W. Bush's policies even by neutral film critics.[22] Moore's films, although labeled as documentaries, are seen by some as lacking objectivity—a requirement necessary for consideration in that genre by some film critics.[23]

Fictional films on the American involvement in the Middle East have gained critical acclaim while questioning the United States' role in these wars. Examples include *In the Valley of Elah* (2008), a story about the sacrifices of war, and *Rendition* (2007), which deals with torture by the United States in the pursuit of terrorists. The Academy Award-winning *The Hurt Locker* (2009), while not patently anti-war, strongly suggests the toll of war on those who fight and their families.

A highly recommended documentary set of DVDs is the *American Experience* series *The Presidents* (2008). The collection of biographies and presidencies includes Theodore Roosevelt, Woodrow Wilson, Franklin D. Roosevelt, John F.

Kennedy (including the lives of his brothers Robert F. Kennedy and Edward "Ted" Kennedy), Lyndon B. Johnson, Richard Nixon, Jimmy Carter, Ronald Reagan, and George H. W. Bush.

Hollywood treatments of presidents are almost their own genre. Sarah Miles Bolam and Thomas J. Bolam have chronicled this genus in their *The Presidents on Film: A Comprehensive Filmography of Portrayals from George Washington to George W. Bush.*[24] Bolam and Bolam, whose work tracks films from 1903 until 2005, document 407 films in their study. They found that presidential appearances in films closely follow polls by historians and the public on presidential greatness and popularity. Lincoln leads with 123 appearances, followed by Washington with 52. Next is Grant with 45, an anomaly as he is considered one of the nation's worst presidents, and then Theodore Roosevelt (33), Jefferson (25), Franklin Roosevelt (22), John Kennedy (21), and Andrew Jackson (15). Richard Nixon has been portrayed 24 times in film, but that, according to Bolam and Bolam, is due as much to notoriety as popularity. Three presidents, all at the bottom of presidential greatness ratings—John Tyler, James Buchanan, and Warren G. Harding—have never been depicted on film.[25]

Presidential films are not always biographical treatments. Early movies, like the three Lincoln films from 1930 to 1940 discussed above, tended to be strictly biographical. While biographical films of the presidents have been made in recent years (for example, *W,* Oliver Stone's 2008 take on George W. Bush's rise to the presidency and his first term in the White House), the chief executives usually play parts related to major historical events.

Two documentaries—one of a candidate who did not win the White House and one who did—are *One Bright Shining Moment: The Forgotten Summer of George McGovern* (2005) and *Jimmy Carter: Man from Plains* (2008). Both of these documentaries provide non-traditional approaches to the lives of these public figures by allowing the two men to speak for themselves. Two Hollywood treatments of recent presidents are director Oliver Stone's *Nixon* (1995) and the 1998 *Primary Colors*, taken from journalist Joe Klein's novel. *Primary Colors* is the fictional telling of a Bill Clinton-like southern governor's rise to the presidency through both luck and at times sham. Both are rated R and are more useful for teacher background (and entertainment, especially the latter) than actual viewing in class, although segments could be used with older adolescents.

Often only a portion of a president's life is rendered. *Sunrise at Campobello* (1960), starring Ralph Bellamy, traces Franklin Roosevelt's pre-presidential battle with infantile paralysis and his victorious return to politics. One of the most effective scenes is Roosevelt's attempt to use crutches rather than staying in his wheelchair; knowing that the public would probably never consider electing a candidate unable to walk. Again, used as a companion piece to documentary footage of Roosevelt standing (using steel braces) or swimming at Warm Springs, Georgia, students can visualize the issue of diversity as seen in FDR's attempt to mask his disability. Roosevelt was never photographed being carried to and from his car or train. There are only one or two rare photographs of Roosevelt in a wheelchair. And a mere three seconds of film show him "walking"—braces hidden under his trousers and appearing to stroll by shifting his weight from one leg to another using a cane with one hand, and holding on to the arm of his son with the other.

Another example of an episode in the life of a future president would be *PT 109* (1963), the story of John F. Kennedy's action in the Pacific during World War II. It focuses on the destruction of the young Kennedy's torpedo boat by a Japanese destroyer and the role he played in rescuing his crew stranded on a small Pacific island. It was made during Kennedy's presidency.

Since the 1960s there have been more presidential films on television than the wide screen. Again, Kennedy has become the subject of several television movies, often focusing on the private life of the young president and his wife Jacqueline. Other made-for-television movies, though, have been historically accurate. An excellent example would be the companion mini-series made in the 1980s, *Winds of War* and *War and Remembrance*. Tracing World War II in thirty hours, Ralph Bellamy would reprise his role as FDR first undertaken in *Sunrise at Campobello*. Bellamy captured exceedingly well the nuances of voice, gestures, and speech of the American wartime leader.

While Hollywood versions of the presidents are not always strictly factual, they can be useful in the adolescent classroom. Historically fictionalized, these films take dramatic license with their material. Examples of these deviations from historical reality would be composite characterizations, changes in chronology, and condensations of events and speeches. But as Bolam and Bolam maintain, if one is not too punctilious, these films can effectively dramatize events and provide for easier understanding of history.[26] This would be especially true when teachers use film with adolescents as introductory material to the past.

An example of a presidential portrayal that simultaneously captures both the historical actions and the stereotypical personality quirks of a president is *Arsenic and Old Lace* (1944). While blatantly politically incorrect in its depiction of mental illness, this Cary Grant vehicle is about Mortimer Brewster's (the Grant character) two aunts. They poison homeless, elderly gentlemen they deem in need of "assistance to achieve their final resting place."[27] Mortimer's brother in the film thinks he is Teddy Roosevelt. (Thinking of oneself as a famous historical figure, like Napoleon, was viewed at this time as a common symptom of mental illness.) Teddy digs locks (graves) in the basement to bury his aunts' victims, thinking they are yellow fever fatalities from Panama. "Teddy" charges up the stairs to his room with sword drawn and bugle blowing in replication of San Juan Hill in the Spanish American War. Local policemen who stop by the Brewster home are seen by "Teddy" as soldiers who must call him Colonel. Teddy also uses the familiar

Rooseveltian expressions "bully" and "delighted" throughout the film. (Historically, Theodore Roosevelt's quirks and exuberance for life and the presidency gave critics to the opportunity to call him "clearly mad" and think that he acted as if he were "about eight.") When Teddy is taken off to Happydale Rest Home under the guise of a hunting trip to Africa, the director of the rest home asks Cary Grant's character if insanity runs in his family. "It gallops," he responds.

Arsenic and Old Lace, when used in connection with the PBS *American Experience* episodes on Theodore Roosevelt, provides an excellent compare-and-contrast opportunity. A section of the *American Experience* documentary offers a number of examples of Roosevelt's real-life personality and eccentricities that match the 1940s film. These include his "point-to-point" marches, toothy smiles, militaristic approach to life, sometimes threatening behavior to others, and overall heartiness and gusto for life that represented his presidency.

As the films approach recent events in our history, the greater the controversy they often engender. This is due to the fact that controversy is based on conflicting points of view. The more recent the issue, the more likely it is to precipitate disagreement. (Race is the exception. It has always been controversial.) An excellent example is director Spike Lee's documentary of the aftermath of Hurricane Katrina, *When the Levees Broke: A Requiem in Four Acts* (2006). The response to the disaster, viewed by some as mishandled by President George W. Bush, began a slide in the polls from which he never recovered.

In terms of recent films, it is not only the works of Michael Moore that produce strong differences of opinion. Former Vice-President Al Gore's film *An Inconvenient Truth* has been divisive not only in public arenas, but in academic ones. Yet the film won Gore an Oscar and the Nobel Peace Prize. Diana Hess, who writes on controversy in the classroom, has related an episode where the consensus view of global warming as a scientific fact was challenged in a pedagogical journal. In relating her exchange with another educator over the veracity of Gore's evidence, Hess concludes that teachers have a responsibility not to accept undocumented opinion as a point of view. Also, a disagreement, even in film, does not make it a controversy. In fact, deciding what is controversial, apparently, can itself be controversial.[28]

The appropriate use of film in the classroom might best be captured by Furay and Salevouris with the following quote:

> The danger [in film] is not that we find it enjoyable to watch the magical images, but that we do so casually and uncritically. When the lights go down it is too easy to turn off the brain and wait to be entertained. But what we see on the screen must be analyzed, discussed and challenged if we are to avoid becoming passive receptacles of whatever messages are broadcast in our direction.[29]

An additional concern is that film is not an academically serious medium. This is especially true in the adolescent history classroom. Some have viewed film as "filler" or time-killer, rather than an approach to engage in serious academic work. The mere showing of a video with vacuous visualizations and no context or analysis could indeed be seen as educationally suspect. If any time spent on film is a potential waste of class time, then showing an entire movie, which usually takes two full class periods, can be especially suspect. This is being addressed by the increasing focus on film studies in academia. The rise of film as a legitimate academic discipline has done much to alleviate some of these concerns. Viewed as a reputable field of study with growing literature to support it, film has especially found a home in English departments in universities. But as a part of popular culture, also a growing field of study, historians are examining how to use film in their research and teaching. It is apparent, as has been seen in this chapter, that the quantity and quality of film available to the history teacher is expanding.

Some of the professional literature is related to teaching about the medium. *Abe Lincoln in Illinois* (referenced above) is a good example. Stone has connected the film to the national history standards, provided learning objectives, and fully developed lesson plans around the film. The sophistication of such research can be seen in Stone's use of the film's year of production (1940) in his analysis. He juxtaposes Lincoln's rebuttal to Stephen Douglas over the ownership of Blacks with the isolationist/interventionist debate of the time equating slavery (1850s America) with dictatorship (1930s Europe.)[30]

Film scholars have asked "How clearly and usefully will [the film] connect . . . with other kinds of materials used or topics covered in the lesson."[31] One response to this concern is the use of study guides, question sheets, and film guides that both provide structure and hold students accountable for what they are viewing. A simple guide for students, generic enough for use with most films, can be divided into three sections on a single sheet of paper. The first question asks students to list "facts" as they observe in the movie. A second section is for students to place material that was new to them. And a third section is for aspects of the film that might have bothered them or with which they disagreed.

Film also allows for differentiation in the history classroom. As noted in other chapters, differentiated instruction is viewed as a highly effective tool for both motivation and increased learning for adolescents. One strategy is to provide a list of approved DVDs that are connected to the historical period being studied and allow for student choice. Rentals are fairly inexpensive, and the number of films becoming available on the Web that are both free and legal is increasing. Teachers need to be sensitive to those students who do not have the resources to rent or technology to download movies. One option is that some schools do lend laptops that have video viewing capability to students. The school can also provide the videos. The idea of personalization through student selection is one that film facilitates by its variety and availability.[32]

The medium of television has itself, on occasion, played an important role in history. Below is a list, by no means complete, of a number of events that were turning points in history due to the fact that they were televised:

- Richard Nixon's 1952 "Checkers" speech

- The Army-McCarthy hearings and Edward R. Murrow's "See It Now" program helped end "McCarthyism"

- The Civil Rights movement with pictures of Blacks being beaten by police and bitten by dogs

- The Vietnam War that brought the fighting via television into American living rooms

- The Watergate hearings and the Nixon press conferences of 1973–74

- The Iranian hostage crisis

- The terrorist attacks of 9/11

- President George W. Bush's Air Force One "flyover" of the Hurricane Katrina disaster

- Barack Obama's 2004 Democratic Convention keynote speech

- The interview of Governor Sarah Palin by CBS News when the question "what do you read?" was asked and her response to it

Films of these events are excellent primary sources for students when teaching about the issues that surrounded these events. They all had an immediate, and in some cases lasting, impact on the nation. Social justice was increased, presidents and candidates were made or destroyed, and wars became unpopular.

A free and copyright-legal source for video online is provided by C-SPAN. As of 2010, the cable network had 160,000 hours of material covering multiple aspects of the past 25 years of political history, featuring 115,000 individuals. Their presidential website is especially useful and there are also lesson plans available.[33] Another valuable source for recent video that is truly "history in the making" is PBS's weekly series *Frontline*.[34]

While most film critics would cringe at the thought, not all films should or need to be shown in their entirety. There are several reasons for this. First, there is frankly some material in some films that is probably not age-appropriate for all adolescent learners. Without raising the censorship issue, most schools have policies on the types of films that can be shown either by using the Motion Picture Association of America rating system or prior approval by the building or district administrator. School policies frequently require permission forms to be signed by parents before screening some films in class. A fairly good rule-of-thumb is that most motion pictures produced prior to the 1960s are "safe" for classroom use. A number of the film recommendations in this chapter are from that era. One film historian has noted that what is shown in classrooms in no way correlates to what adolescents view in theaters, as "teenagers flock to see R-rated raunchy and vulgar comedies and mindless violent action films."[35]

Another reason not to show a film in its entirety is that there are portions of some films that do not lead to any authentic learning in history. Romantic, comedic, or tragic interludes essential to most popular movies, even ones with historical themes, may not be vital when used for educational purposes. And time is always a factor in the classroom setting. A two-hour film in a school day where the history teacher may have students for only 50 minutes calculates into devoting a half-week to one movie. The availability of "chapters" on almost all DVDs allows for the easy selection of portions of a film.

Finally, is it critical that copyright laws be adhered to when using film in the classroom. With the rise of online education, the use of film in classes not only taught on-site, but at a distance, has become an area of ongoing legal uncertainties. To err on the side of prudence is advised. Yet with all the concerns, reservations, and potential difficulties, both pedagogically and with the subject matter, the use of film can be, when used correctly, an essential learning tool for teaching history. In the end, the incorporation of film into the classroom most certainly outweighs the potential problems raised by the use of this unique and increasingly innovative medium.

Endnotes

1   Anthony, Carl Sferrazza. "The Most Scandalous President." *American Heritage Magazine* 49.4 (1998): 58.
2   Cuban, Larry. *Teachers and Machines: The Classroom Use of Technology Since 1920.* New York: Teachers College Press, 1986. 9.
3   Marcus, Alan S., Scott Alan Metzger, Richard Paxton, and Jeremy D. Stoddard. *Teaching History with Film: Strategies for Secondary Social Studies.* New York: Routledge, 2010. 5.
4   Ibid. 10–13.

5   Palmer, Edward. "Schools, Advertising, and Marketing." *Encyclopedia of Children, Adolescents, and the Media.* Ed. Jeffery J. Arnett. Thousand Oaks: Sage 2006; and Brown, Jane D. Jeanne R. Steele, and Kim Walsh-Childers. Introduction and Overview. *Sexual Teens, Sexual Media: Investigating Media's Influence on Adolescent Sexuality.* Mahwah: Erlbaum, 2002. 1–24.

6   Wineburg, Sam, Susan Mosbog, Dan Porat, and Ariel Duncan. "Common Belief and the Cultural Curriculum: An Intergenerational Study of Historical Consciousness." *American Educational Research Journal* 44. 1 (2007): 40, 67–8.

7   Selwyn, Douglas and Jan Maher. *History in the Present Tense: Engaging Students Through Inquiry and Action.* Portsmouth: Heinemann, 2003. 104.

8   Potter, Lee Ann. "Connecting with the Past: Uncovering Clues in Primary Source Documents." *Social Education* 67. 7 (2003): 372–80.

9   Matz, Karl A. and Lori L. Pingatore. "Reel to Real: Teaching the Twentieth Century with Classic Hollywood Films." *Social Education* 69. 4 (2005): 189–93.

10   Giannetti, Louis. *Understanding Movies.* 12th ed. Boston: Allyn and Bacon, 2011. 4–8.

11   Furay, Conal and Michael J. Salevouris. *The Methods and Skills of History: A Practical Guide.* Wheeling: Harlan Davidson, Inc., 2000. 131–34.

12   Giannetti, 416.

13   Marcus et al., *Teaching History with Film*, 159–73.

14   Ibid. 176–89.

15   Reinhart, Mark S. *Abraham Lincoln on Screen: Fictional and Documentary Portrayals on Film and Television.* 2nd ed. Jefferson: McFarland and Company, Inc. Publishers, 2008.

16   Craughwell, Thomas J. *Stealing Lincoln's Body.* Cambridge: The Belknap Press of Harvard University Press, 2007.

17   Levin, Phyllis L. *Edith and Woodrow: The Wilson White House.* New York: Scribner, 2001. 509–11.

18   Giannetti, Louis and Scott Eyman. *Flashback: A Brief History of Film.* Boston: Allyn and Bacon, 2010. 80.

19   For examples of films made during World War II with attendant filmography see both McLaughlin, Robert L. and Sally E. Parry. *We'll Always Have the Movies: American Cinema During World War II.* Lexington: The University Press of Kentucky, 2006; and Milberg, Doris. *World War II on the Big Screen: 450+ Films, 1938–2008.* Jefferson: McFarland & Company, 2010.

20   Milbert, 74 and McLaughlin and Parry, 158–61.

21   Wetta, Frank J. and Martin A. Novelli. "Good Bombing, Bad Bombing: Hollywood, Air Warfare, and Morality in World War I and World War II." *Magazine of History* 22. 4 (2008): 25–29. See also Peter C Rollins and John E. O'Connor. *Why We Fought: America's Wars in Film and History.* Lexington: University of Kentucky Press, 2008.

22   Giannetti, 405.

23   Prince, Stephen. *Movies and Meaning: An Introduction to Film.* Boston: Allyn and Bacon, 2010. 300–01.

24   Bolam, Sarah Miles and Thomas J. Bolam. *The Presidents on Film: A Comprehensive Filmography of Portrayals from George Washington to George W. Bush.* Jefferson: McFarland and Company, Inc. Publishers, 2007.

25   Ibid. 7.

26 Ibid.
27 Ibid. 227–28.
28 Hess, Diana E. *Controversy in the Classroom: The Democratic Power of Discussion.* New York: Routledge, 2009. 118–22.
29 Furay and Salevouris, 138.
30 Stone, Christopher. "Living Words: Using *Abe Lincoln in Illinois* to Teach Film Analysis and Historical Thinking." *Organization of American Historians Magazine of History* 23. 1 (2009): 59–61.
31 Marcus, et al. *Teaching History with Film,* 24.
32 Ko, Susan and Steve Rossen. *Teaching Online: A Practical Guide.* 3rd ed. New York: Routledge, 2010. 108–09.
33 See <http://www.c-span.org/videolibrary>. For lesson plan suggestions contact C-SPAN at educate@c-span.org
34 See <http://www.pbs.org/wgbh/pages/frontline/>.
35 Giglio, Ernest. *Here's Looking at You: Hollywood, Film, and Politics.* 2nd ed. New York: Peter Lang, 2005. xiii.

EIGHT

Differentiated Instruction and Student Research in History

Differentiated instruction for students is highly applicable and most appropriate to teaching history. That is simply because the numbers of topics available, while not infinite, are vast. As will be discussed in the chapter on subject matter, the selection of content in American history can be a daunting task. Within major themes there are innumerable issues that can be pursued in a variety of ways including student research.

Carol Ann Tomlinson and Rick Wormeli are probably the best-known educational gurus in the arena of differentiated instruction. Definitions are clearly helpful when working with a concept such as differentiated instruction, and Tomlinson has provided what she terms its "hallmarks":

> Teachers must be ready to engage students in instruction through different learning modalities, by appealing to differing interests, and by using varied rates of instruction along with varied degrees of complexity. In differentiated classrooms, teachers ensure that a student competes against himself as he grows and develops more than he competes against other students.[1]

Tomlinson adds that differentiated classrooms assume strong standards by the school, hard work by students, and high expectations by the teachers. Another critical element to successful differentiation is the need for prior assessment by teachers to determine where students are academically.[2]

Grouping students has been considered an essential component of differentiated instruction, especially in the teaching of history. Yet grouping has been found wanting by many teachers. Staying on task in a group, interpersonal relationships among the group members, and varying abilities within a group have often led to unsuccessful attempts to employ this strategy. Gregory and Kuzmich have addressed such concerns by outlining guidelines for three types of groups. They write:

> Heterogeneous grouping works far better to close gaps and gets results, especially when students are learning from each other. Flexible grouping to teach a discrete skill when students need enrichment or re-teaching is appropriate since this organization of students is a temporary response of students to data collection for learning proficiency. Homogeneous grouping works only for this purpose when the teacher is leading the flexible or temporary group.[3]

Gregory and Kuzmich also suggest seven attributes for successful group or team work and advocate tracking them on a rubric. The seven are helping or assisting others, listening to others, participating and contributing to the success of the group, persuading and exchanging ideas, questioning other members of the team, respect toward members of the team or group, and the sharing of ideas and findings.[4]

A multitude of questions have been raised about differentiated instruction. A major one is the pressure on teachers to meet standards set by the district, state, and professional organizations. Tomlinson advises that teachers should not attempt to address standards in isolation. Standards can be categorized as facts, concepts, principles, attitudes, and skills. Examples from history would be:

> Facts—The Boston Tea Party helped to provoke the American Revolution. The first 10 Amendments to the Constitution are called the Bill of Rights.

> Concepts—Revolution, Power, Authority, Governance.

> Principles—Revolutions are first evolution. Liberty is constrained in all societies.

> Attitudes—It is important to study history so we write the next chapters more wisely. Sometimes I am willing to give up some freedoms to protect the welfare of others.

> Skills—Construction and supporting a position on an issue. Drawing conclusions based on analyses of sound resources.[5]

What differentiated instruction is not may be as important as what differentiated instruction is. Tomlinson writes that differentiated instruction is not individualized instruction. Individualized instruction called for teachers to do something different for 30 or more students. Differentiation does not assume that each student is functioning on a separate level. (Yet, individualized instruction for the purposes of this chapter will not take on a totally pejorative meaning.) Differentiated instruction should not be considered chaotic. Effective differentiated classrooms are purposeful, not disorderly or undisciplined. Finally, differentiated instruction is not just another way to arrive at homogeneous grouping. A term that is often used in the differentiated classroom is "flexible." Students may be strong in one subject, but weaker in another. The teacher must use different working groups and arrangements so students are not identified permanently with one group in any subject. The two words "not permanent" are key to differentiated instruction.[6]

Displaying what students have learned in history classes often falls into the "favorite four" (or maybe "fatal four") activities of posters, dioramas, papers, and timelines. There are other options. These include reenactments by students, storytelling, displaying and explaining photographs or pictures to reflect insights about history, the use of drama and music to present ideas, using a symposium format by bringing adults into the classroom, and the design or use of websites to share ideas.[7] Again, in the study of history, the possibilities are numerous.

Wormeli has delineated what is meant by flexible grouping—a major tool in the arena of differentiated learning:

> If it's time for some flexible grouping in our lessons, we can group according to many different factors and structures, including whole class or half class, teams, small groups, partners, triads, quads, one-on-one mentoring with an adult or peer, learning centers, online wiki groups, readiness, interest, and learners' profile.[8]

Wormeli expands on readiness, interest, and learner profile. *Readiness* is simply whether a learner is ready for more complexity in their lessons by matching appropriateness to complexity and difficulty. *Interest*, for Wormeli, refers to how students are helped to learn material in meaningful ways. And *Learner Profile* would mean consideration for any factor that affects a student's learning. Examples would be language spoken, reading proficiency, or technology access and ability.[9]

The specific applications to history are evident. While there exist alternative approaches to the teaching of history, the fact cannot be denied that a considerable portion of learning history is still reading. History is replete with topics, issues, episodes, vignettes, personalities, movements, events, and interpretations to allow for flexible grouping that can meet the needs of most learners. Again, though, the history teacher must not only have the pedagogical knowledge to make flexible grouping within differentiated learning work, they must have a rich background in content knowledge and a deep understanding of their discipline.

Thornton has made two valid points in response to the critics of teachers who allow their students to individualize history by following their interests. Some contend that with class loads usually numbering 125 or more in middle level and high school classes, it is virtually impossibile for a teacher to address this many individual topics. Thornton has responded that the idea of "limited choices" can be employed. An example would be the study of Nazi Germany. Some subject matter will be broadly addressed by the teacher that includes the rise of Hitler, the ideas behind Nazism, military aims and ventures, and the Holocaust. But a limited number of other topics could be provided to students to pursue. These could include life on the home front for common Germans, religion under Nazism, Nazi propaganda taught in the schools, or cartoons and comics in the Third Reich. Writes Thornton, "Young people are mostly interested in subject matter for which they have aptitude and vice versa."[10]

Second objection, according to Thornton, is that standards preclude the practice of differentiated instruction. While this is accurate in some cases, standards should not prohibit any kind of differentiated instruction or student choice. Due to the immensity of content in history (which is true for language arts as well), any standards set out must at best be a sample, not a comprehensive corpus of the discipline. Again, Thornton accurately depicts the current standards/testing milieu as limiting rather than broadening the intellectual landscape for students. "Young people learn most effectively and enthusiastically," he writes, "material that is connected to their personal experience and aspirations."[11] Individual strengths and interests should be capitalized on rather than purposefully disregarded by teachers due to policies that ignore how students learn and engage in material. This dichotomy of standards and student interests is very real in the schools of today and will be an ongoing challenge for all teachers in all subjects.

On occasion, a student research project can be a motivator for the adolescent. While the historical researching process is probably not applicable or appropriate for an entire class, using research as a motivator can be effective. For example, students could research the following historical questions: If the Declaration of Independence was signed on July 2, 1776 (and some say over a two-week period), why do we celebrate the founding of our country on July 4? Who actually took the first machine-powered flight? Was Charles Lindbergh the first person to cross the Atlantic by air? Or, if the Constitution states that only Congress can declare war, why has this not happened in the five wars the U.S. has fought in since World War II? Discovering mistakes and errors in long-held or common historical beliefs can draw out the skeptical element within many adolescents.

One of the most common assignments in history classes is to send students to the computer lab, library/media center, or home to do a report on a president of the United States. It is also probably the most ill-used variation in history classes of what might mistakenly be thought of today as differentiation. This most conventional practice within such assignments is the directive for students to select a famous or popular president—Washington, Lincoln, and the two Roosevelts, along with John Kennedy and Ronald Reagan, come quickly to mind and are often the ones chosen. An alternative approach to employing differentiated assignments in connection to "great" presidents is to investigate those occupants of the White House that have been considered failures and why. Differentiated groups could select individual presidents who have been placed in this category, investigate, then come back to the group and pull together their findings. Groups of students would individually study the same president.

How might using the "failed presidencies" idea work? There have been a number of assessments and attendant lists of presidential greatness conducted by both historians and the public. At least five presidents have consistently been considered failures by amateurs and professional students of history alike. (The historical ratings, begun in the 1940s with Arthur Schlesinger, Jr., have continued on within C-SPAN's *America's Presidents* series.) There could probably be as many as five or more men who could or should be placed in the "failure" category just as by consensus there are a total of about ten chief executives who are considered to be great or near-great in terms of performance in the White House. The five sent immediately to the bottom of most lists are Franklin Pierce, Ulysses S. Grant, Herbert Hoover, James Buchanan, and, of course, almost everyone's "dead last" choice, Warren G. Harding. Andrew Johnson, Calvin Coolidge, Richard Nixon, and George W. Bush have also, albeit controversially, received low ratings from historians and the public in recent years. While not always receiving low ratings, the reputations of slave-owning presidents from Washington to Jackson and a few beyond have not fared well in recent polls.

Now, how does this relate to differentiated instruction? In several ways. First, while we wish only success in the lives of our students, reality demonstrates that all too frequently tragedies and disappointments strike at the lives of adolescents. To become aware that even presidents (as well as movie stars, entertainers, and the rich and famous) also have problems lets students see that being a celebrity or even the leader of the free world does not make one invulnerable from the storms of life.

Second, a differentiated assignment that examines a president considered a failure allows students to analyze why and how such a judgment was made. If, as we are told, history helps us learn from the past so as not to make similar mistakes in the future, studying failed presidents can provide worthwhile case studies. A final reason in the form of a question would be: Were these men really that bad and can a case can be made as to why they were not? Parents, teachers, and the general public have observed that a goodly number of adolescents can be argumentative. Therefore, why not put that characteristic to good use? The reverse could also be tested. Were the great presidents always that great? Abraham Lincoln as one example has been skewered over the issue of race, his abridgment of civil liberties, and even his selection of military leaders before Grant.

Back to the historically "dead last" president Warren Gamaliel Harding who, for the purposes of demonstrating differentiated instruction, will be used as a primary example. Although considered a failure, Harding has had much attention paid to him. There is no shortage of material on him by which students can make a judgment. Philip G. Payne, in one of the most recent studies of the 29th president, titled his book aptly enough *Dead Last: The Public Memory of Warren G. Harding's Scandalous Legacy*. In spite of the book's title, Payne, formerly associated with the Ohio Historical Society and connected to the Warren G. Harding Home, is actually a credible apologist for the much-maligned president's legacy. He is not the only one to make such a case. Harding was not a failure at all he attempted. He was the first president to give a speech critical of racial policies in the South; he pardoned the jailed socialist presidential candidate Eugene V. Debs, and was successful in arms-reduction negotiations.[12]

But differentiated student assignments in history, on a president like Harding, could explore a number of particular topics (a major constructive element of individualizing instruction). These could include the role of small-town America in the 1920s from which Harding emerged; his rumored Black ancestry and the role of race in early 20th-century politics; the conflicting views of his legacy in biographies; the public and private scandals that have been examined for the past ninety years, and the mysterious nature of his death.

Harding becomes an excellent example for students in testing the reliability of online sources to be discussed in the chapter on technology and media. Payne has analyzed whether or not Wikipedia is a dependable source for information on the 29th president. He found that there were more than double the words (630) on Harding's extramarital affairs than on the administration's scandals (270) and close to that on his total years as president (350.)[13] Another example of examining the accuracy and currency of sources is to compare narratives from dated encyclopedias and current ones. As many old encyclopedias still exist in classrooms and homes, such a contrast is easily accomplished. A 1962 set of *The World Book Encyclopedia* has exactly the same entry as the online 2010 version. While numerous works and a wide variance of judgments have been published in the last five decades, *The World Book Encyclopedia* has maintained the same account of events on Harding and his presidency. (Inexplicably, the 1962 edition and 2010 edition list different authors.) The assessment over fifty years has remained: "Historians almost unanimously rank Harding as one of the weakest presidents. But these historians have recognized that the very quality that made him weak also made him appealing in 1920. He failed because he was weak-willed and a poor judge of character."[14] Such an identical appraisal should at least instigate a letter to the publishers of *The World Book* by an inquiring student if not the teacher.

Harding also serves as a point of departure in comparing and contrasting his standing among supposed failed presidents with current occupants of the office. Liberal Columbia University historian Eric Foner, halfway into George W. Bush's second term, wrote of his failed presidency in the *Washington Post* using Harding, Buchanan, Pierce, and Nixon as markers for the estimate.[15] Newspapers such as the *Cincinnati Post* and the *Boston Globe,* as well as journals of opinion *The Nation* and *Rolling Stone,* drew similar conclusions in their pages.[16] One of the major claims as to history's importance is its use in making comparisons to the events and individuals of today with whom more students should be familiar. However, due to the age of adolescents and two recent two-term presidents—Bill Clinton and George W. Bush—their memories will probably not go back further than one president or two at most.

Playing off the "failure" premise as a prompt for differentiating instruction, there is also the potential in history for using the "boring" president theme. Although arguable, the case could be made that the eight presidents between Abraham Lincoln and Theodore Roosevelt were, well, boring. No doubt historians could contest that the Gilded Age, one name for the era after the Civil War until the turn of the nineteenth century, was significant. Reconstruction, the rise of labor, and the imperialistic subjugation of the Philippines by the United States are three examples that are without question essential to any study of American history. But one can easily imagine the eyes of students glazing over by the other issues of that era such as the raising and lowering of tariffs, civil service reform, and the silver question.

Not only were the issues of this period unexciting if not mind-numbing; so were the nation's leaders. While Ulysses S. Grant is usually recognizable, most of his successors seem to blur together, defying detection. Even when shown photographs of post-Civil War presidents such as Rutherford B. Hayes, James Garfield, and Benjamin Harrison (all in full beards), students will confuse which one is which, let alone identify where they stood on the issues of the day. (The side-burned Chester A. Arthur, the walrus-mustachioed Grover Cleveland, and the clean-shaven William McKinley provide some variety and distinction at least photographically.) The individualization emerges when students are called on to discover if this set of "boring" presidents actually accomplished anything of historical note or remembrance. Just as the question "Was this president really a failure—why or why not?" was asked, so too can the question "Was this president really that boring—why or why not?"

There are valid defenses students could make for some of these men and the issues and events of their day. There was the impeachment of Andrew Johnson, and Grant did have his share of scandals. The Hayes-Tilden election of 1876 mirrored closely the Bush-Gore election of 2000 right down to the contested electoral votes in the state of Florida. There were two assassinations within twenty years and the severe economic Panic of 1893. The paternity of a bachelor presidential candidate became an election issue, and that same president—Grover Cleveland —surreptitiously had a portion of his cancerous jaw removed, concealing his health problem from the public. While not decisive events or on the scale of world wars, social movements, or a major depression (that is why the period can be considered "boring"), a few of the events and personalities of this period do have the possibility of capturing the attention of students.

Admittedly, what will or will not engage the interest of adolescent students is often difficult to discern. And again, realistically, the issue of standards and the content selected by the teacher must be taken into consideration. While subject matter selection is discussed in a later chapter, teachers should attempt to choose content that has the potential to at least mildly intrigue or interest a student in some way. Here are ten for consideration:

- Sitting Bull and Custer's Last Stand

- The "Public Enemies" of the Depression Era

- The Assassination of President Kennedy

- The Terrorist Attacks of September 11, 2001

- The Watergate Scandal and resignation of a president

- The year 1968 and its political turmoil and tragedies

- The impact on youth of decades such as the Roaring Twenties and the 1960s

- The history of birth control and sex education

- The effect of technology such as iPhones, computers, and media on youth

- The abuse, mishandling, and exploitation of the environment and energy resources

All of these are more than isolated events in the nation's story. They look at race, social justice, citizen responsibility, social trends, and pivotal episodes in American history. They suggest that history is not, as one wag put it, just one "damn fact after another." Differentiated instruction should be compatible even within the strictures of the standards movement.

Some structure does need to be in place when students undertake research projects. In one model, Hedrick and Flannagan have devised a taxonomy that describes a path that history students travel from the novice level to the stage of expertise (apprentice and practitioner are the two levels in between). The stages contain behaviors, skills, attitudes, and habits of mind that support teachers and assist learners to advance along the continuum. Hedrick and Flannagan write:

> The novice student in history does not see the context for historical events, people, and places, nor does the novice understand their relationship to the patterns, trends, concepts, and principles that shape the discipline. The novice studies history primarily through rote memorization, often committing the information to short-term memory and therefore fails to deepen understanding in any significant ways.[17]

Although the third and fourth stages—practitioner and expert—are aimed at the advanced learner, there are applications in the apprentice level that adolescent learners can achieve. One example is developing a clearly defined sense of chronology. Other skills novice adolescent learners could grasp and master would be posing historical research questions such as whether the Civil War was avoidable, or compare and contrast the popularity of President John Kennedy and President Ronald Reagan. A final example within the apprentice category would be to seek connections in order to make sense of historical patterns and trends (e.g. the relationship between World War I and World War II or the correlation between the 1920s and the Great Depression).[18]

A variation of differentiated instruction is individualized instruction. And student research is central to individualization. One of the best structures in place to support student research is the National History Day project. Underwritten by educational and historical organizations, each year it affords students the opportunity to research a selected aspect of history. Students then showcase and share their findings through a variety of venues that include performances, presentations, creating websites, and filmmaking, in addition to traditional research formats. Each year a theme is provided—2009's was the "Individual in History."[19]

When working in the area of student research, writing is inevitably a component. One historian has held that when working with historical accounts "the task of learning to think draws very close to the task of learning to write."[20] Drake and Nelson have suggested a number of guidelines when giving students writing assignments. The ideas are actually options for students when assigned a writing project. One is to have students write to different audiences. These audiences could be a younger student, an individual from outside the United States, a peer, or the public at large. The aim is to have students take the information they have researched and think about who will be reading it. A second idea is to write to specific assertions. Advanced Placement teachers use this approach as they coach their students to prepare for document-based and free-response questions. Writing to assertions can be a difficult task even for advanced students.[21] An example of an assertion question might be:

> The New Deal did not bring the Great Depression to an end. React to this assertion. In your reaction, provide examples that support or refute this assertion.

Finally, although used since the 1960s as part of the New Social Studies, oral history projects can still contribute much to a student's understanding of how history is "done." Often oral history is thought of as merely putting a microphone in front of grandma or grandpa and letting the tape recorder run. For oral history projects to be undertaken effectively, the elements must include proper preparation, the selection of a topic or historical period that coincides with either the content under consideration or appropriate standards, and a formal product at its conclusion. If such a structure is followed, then this now-standard approach to individualization can still provide much for students as they learn history. Oral history also allows students to learn about how historians do their research. Lastly, the final products need to become part of the school library, local library, or local historical society. This will impress even more on students that history is important—important enough to keep.[22]

The World of Practice
Lizard Lick
by Ruth E. Baize

"Hey! Look what I've got!"

"Wow! I've found a button!"

"What is this, Mrs. Baize?"

The words came fast and excitedly as students discovered their first artifacts in what we called the Dig of Lizard Lick. No, Lizard Lick is not a real place in our state but is, rather, a town of the 1930s that I made up. I told the students that the mythical town used to be located near the back of the school property, and that we were going to dig in the area and see what we could find. The unusual name and the pretending aspect caused some of the children to giggle; they were ready for an adventure.

The week before the dig, I sent a sealed letter home to the parents explaining the up-coming project and asked them to secretly bring in objects to the school office that may have been used during the 1930s. This could have included crockery (broken or whole), tools, jewelry, buttons, nails, and small toys. I warned them that the items would be buried in the soil and probably not returned. My expectations were exceeded when one parent sent in a deer skull, and another sent chicken bones from the evening meal. I made a trip to the local discount store and bought odds and ends to add to the growing pile of "artifacts." While there I discovered in the Lawn and Garden section small trowels for children. Adding these to one-inch inexpensive paint brushes and a few colanders for sifting, I had enough realistic tools for the dig.

Before the dig I needed to discuss with the class the role of archaeologists and their tools and methods used in uncovering our past. I had several options open to me: I could have an archaeologist come to my class; I could use technology and *Skype* (an Internet telephone service that offers free calling between computers with/without video) someone from a museum or university to talk with my kids; or I could let the students research the topic. Fortunately, Angel Mounds State Historic Site is nearby, and I was able to bring the director to my students. He brought in the tools and discussed how they were used by archaeologists. He showed several artifacts. The speaker also shared that it was illegal to perform a real dig without a permit. His presentation got the juices going for my students. After his talk, I told the students that they were going to dig the next day at a mythical site named Lizard Lick. I added that they should bring a sack lunch/drink, extra water, and an old towel on which to sit. They were so excited.

After school that day, four parents and I met toward the back of the school property with a cooler of cold drinks, a tiller, a ball of string, and some shortened dowel rods. I measured out two sections of dirt two feet by ten feet with at least three yards of ground between them for ease of movement. (The length was dependent upon if one or two or, even, three classes would be digging on the same day. Each child would have his/her own one-foot square in which to dig. When I had forty students after school participating, I measured for each strip to be two feet wide by ten feet. When I had twenty-four students, I measured a strip of two feet by twelve feet.) After one parent tilled the two strips of ground, all of us started burying the so-called relics, putting some deeper in the ground than others. We were careful to liberally "salt" the dig with many "artifacts." After covering the two strips with soil, we then stood the dowel rods down the center of each strip and on the outer edges at every foot connecting them all by string, thereby outlining each square. As we refreshed ourselves with water and soft drinks by a pickup truck, I was surprised to hear the parents say how they would love to be in the class the next day for all the fun! Of course, I invited all who wanted to come, for extra hands are always appreciated.

The day of the dig was beautiful. Carrying our lunches, towels, and tools, the young archaeologists, two parents, and I made our way to the site. I explained to the children that they would use the trowels to carefully dig; the colanders to sift some soil for smaller artifacts; and the brushes to initially clean the items they found. I also asked them to bring any artifacts they uncovered and cleaned to a central area where they would record in what section they found them. I then directed each student to a square-foot section, and let them begin.

The students had a ball! Some tried to dig too quickly and in large scoops and had to be shown again how the archaeologists carefully dig. All caught on quickly and used their tools to unearth the treasures. The finding of even the smallest nail brought squeals from their mouths and young bodies running to see the latest find! But the greatest excitement was when the skull began to show. It was large enough to be buried in two students' plots. The children wanted to simply pull it out of the ground, but I again cautioned them to do it right. Of course, everyone crowded around to watch the process of unearthing this. Because they could see only a small portion, the children speculated on what it was. Was it a human skull? With that suggestion their imaginations soared! To redirect their thinking, I wondered aloud if it was from an animal. Oh, then the children had to wonder what kind. Finally, the two archaeologists were able to bring the deer skull out into the light where all could admire the find. Again, the students returned to their own plots to find what they could find. Every find, large and small, was important to the finder. We adults just grinned at each other. The kids were so excited.

Before breaking for our picnic lunches, we filled in the holes and scattered some grass seed over the dirt. We then gathered our finds and tools and took them near an outside water faucet. Here the students filled a few buckets and carefully washed their finds and laid them out for drying in the sun.

When this was done, we gathered together to discuss the dig. Each was given the opportunity to show what they found. Then, together, we talked about what the artifacts told us about Lizard Lick. Had toys been found? Did this imply that children had been a part of the community? Were tools uncovered? What would the tools have been used for? One found a horseshoe. What was the importance of this? The questions went on and the children soon were able to grasp what the community would have been like.

The day ended but not the lesson. The next day the students wrote about the dig, their finds, and their conclusions. I later encouraged them to use their imaginations and become one of the people who lived in that area. I asked them to write this in a form of a letter from a person in 1937 Lizard Lick to a cousin "back East." They were to tell their cousin about Lizard Lick, their family, or themselves by mentioning some of the artifacts. Of course, I had to remind the students that the artifacts weren't yet artifacts in 1937!

When all the writing was done, a large display was made. I marked off bulletin board paper in one-foot squares by gluing string down the lines; laid the paper down on a long table; and put all the artifacts and a few tools on it for others to see. I covered the whole table with plastic wrap, so other students could look but not touch. Then we hung the letters to their "cousins" behind the display with some of the photos of the dig.

The students knew that Lizard Lick was not real, but the experience they had was. I have repeated this lesson with different age groups with great success. With older students I have had them document where and what they found in their portions of the grid and write their findings as if writing for a professional journal. The youngest students dug in a child's plastic swimming pool filled with sand and used drawings to show their findings. Lizard Lick is easily adapted to any grade. The ages of the archaeologists may be different, but the excitement, wonder, and imagination are the same.

Ruth E. Baize has been an Indiana History Teacher of the Year, a Walt Disney American Teacher Award Nominee, a Wal-Mart Teacher of the Year, and the Indiana Outstanding Geography Teacher of the Year. She is active in multiple professional education organizations and teaches in the Evansville-Vanderburgh (IN) School Corporation.

Endnotes

1   Tomlinson, Carol Ann. *The Differentiated Classroom: Responding to the Needs of All Learners.* Alexandria: Association for Supervision and Curriculum Development, 1999. 2.
2   Ibid.
3   Gregory, Gayle H. and Lin Kuzmich. *Student Teams That Get Results: Teaching Tools for the Differentiated Classroom.* Thousand Oaks: Corwin, 2010. 161.
4   Ibid. 166.
5   Ibid. 40–41. For an extended example of a differentiated history classroom, see pp. 56–60.
6   Tomlinson, Carol Ann. *How to Differentiate Instruction in Mixed-Ability Classrooms.* 2nd ed. Alexandria: Association for Supervision and Curriculum Development, 2001. 2–3.
7   Ibid. 55.
8   Wormeli, Rick. "Flexible Grouping in the Classroom." *Middle Ground* 13. 4 (2010): 31.
9   Ibid. 31–32.
10 Thornton, Stephen J. *Teaching Social Studies That Matters: Curriculum for Active Learning.* New York: Teachers College Press, 2005. 50–51.
11 Ibid. 50–52.
12 Payne, Phillip G. *Dead Last: The Public Memory of Warren G. Harding's Scandalous Legacy.* Athens: Ohio University Press, 2009. Additional scholars and writers that

have found some positive things to say on behalf of Harding include Farrell, Robert. *The Strange Deaths of Warren G. Harding.* Columbia: University of Missouri Press, 1996; Anthony, Carl Sferrazza. "The Most Scandalous President." *American Heritage Magazine* 49. 4 (1998); and Dean, John W. *Warren G. Harding.* New York: Times Books, Henry Holt and Company, 2004.

13 Payne, 213.
14 Mayer, George H. "Warren Gamaliel Harding." *The World Book Encyclopedia.* Chicago: Field Enterprises Educational Corporation, 1962; and Walch, Timothy. "Warren Gamaliel Harding." *The World Book Online Reference Center.* Web. <http://www.worldbookonline.com>.
15 Foner, Eric. "He's the Worst Ever." *Washington Post* 3 Dec. 2006: B1.
16 Payne, 220–21, 256.
17 Hedrick, Kelly and Jenny Sue Flannagan. "Ascending Intellectual Demand in the Parallel Curriculum Model." Tomlinson, Kaplan, Renzulli, et al. *The Parallel Curriculum: A Design to Develop Learner Potential and Challenge Advanced Learners.* Thousand Oaks: Corwin Press, 2009: 272.
18 Hedrick and Flannagan, 273.
19 "The Individual in History: National History Day 2009." Web. <http://www.nhd.org>.
20 Pocock, J.G.A. "Working on Ideas in Time." Ed. Perry L. Curtis. *The Historian's Workshop.* New York: Knopf, 1970: 161.
21 Drake, Frederick D. and Lynn R. Nelson. *Engagement in Teaching History: Theory and Practice for Middle and Secondary Teachers.* 2nd ed. Upper Saddle River: Merrill/Pearson, 2009. 188–89.
22 Excellent resources for the process of oral history and the final product of such products can be found in Whitman, Glenn. *Dialogue with the Past: Engaging Students and Meeting Standards through Oral History.* Walnut Creek: AltaMira Press, 2004; and Sommer, Barbara W. and Mary K. Quinlan. *The Oral History Manual.* Walnut Creek: AltaMira Press, 2002.

NINE

Public History: Bringing History to Life

On a frigid winter night in Minneapolis, Minnesota, during the Great Depression, the historian Carl Becker gave his presidential address to the American Historical Association. Its title was "Everyman His Own Historian." Becker maintained that history must be "an imaginative reconstruction of vanished events, its form and substance are inseparable." Just as an unseen painting by Van Gogh hanging on a museum wall or the unheard music of Beethoven in an empty symphony hall have no meaning, so too with history. For Becker, "The history that lies inert in unread books does no work in the world. The history that does work in the world, the history that influences the course of history, is living history."[1]

Every student, to update Becker's "Everyman" talk, can benefit from having dormant imaginations revitalized with immediate experiences. There is a genuine need to connect adolescents with real-life applications in the study of history. The theme of relevance again. One approach to make this happen would be what is termed public or living history. The practice of public history could be defined as simply broadening the public's appreciation and understanding of the past. The National Council on Public History has provided a number of more complete definitions of public history. Their website defines public history as "where historians and their various publics collaborate in trying to make the past useful to the public." These experiences generally take place in settings beyond the traditional classroom. Public history practitioners include museum professionals, government and business historians, historical societies, historical consultants, archivists, cultural resource managers, curators, film and media producers, policy advocates, and oral historians.[2]

Stanton, writing in *Issues of Public History*, the quarterly newsletter of the National Council for Public History, has chronicled the dialogue and changing view of public history since its inception in the 1970s. A few terms and phrases used currently and in the past to describe public history include making history accessible and useful to the public, social activism, collaborative history, and just plain "doing history." Examples of "doing history" would include genealogy, community celebrations, and reenactments. Other terms used to describe aspects of public history over the years have included methodology, enterprise, and even ideology.[3] The search for a definition might be generalized and encapsulated in a few words—broadening the public's appreciation, understanding, and engagement in history.

Patricia Mooney-Melvin has further addressed a definition of public history through the professionals that work in the field. For her it was historians who were employed in non-academic settings with the goal of communicating to a broader public. The field of public history has matured through a number of advances. These include the creation of professional associations such as the National Council on Public History and the Society for History in the Federal Government. In addition there has been the establishment of professional journals such as *The Public Historian*. The American Association for State and Local History, with its emphases on local historical resources and preservation, has welcomed public history from the 1950s onward. Also, well recognized organizations such as the American Historical Association have legitimized public history by including features about the field in the pages of its journal and acknowledging the diversity of the work by individuals from outside history's traditional role in academics.[4]

Public history, while not always called that, has its own history. One recent nomenclature shift has been to refer to it as "living history." Adapted in the United States at the turn of the 20th century from what were originally preservation activities and open-air museums, living history's first outdoor museums emerged in the 1930s. Usually a collection of restored and re-created historical buildings, often pioneer villages, the conception moved to include houses, farms, plantations, trading posts, forts, naval ships, and battlefields. Outdoor living history sites have become highly popular. Old Town San Diego Historic Park annually hosts seven million visitors, Valley Forge National Historic Park over four million, and Greenfield Village and the Henry Ford Museum and Colonial Williamsburg near one million each.[5]

The goal of students visiting public history sites should be to learn about the past in an interactive, alternative setting to the classroom. Having increased their knowledge about history should be the outcome during a historic site visit. The term now being used for the variety of activities that take place in these settings is *interpretive*. The terminology for those who work in public history has also changed. Rather than guides or docents, the term is now "interpreter." These individuals—professionals, amateurs, and volunteers—are responsible for making history real. In writing about interpreters Mark Howell has said:

> History museums that survive into the twenty-first century will be institutions *about* the past, not shrines to it. History as an accumulation of facts is no history, but history that draws a distinction between past and present creates a valid reason for a family to stop by and see what antiques and famous (and not so famous) dead people can tell us not only about them but about us.[6]

The words students or classrooms can easily be used in place of Howell's "family" when talking about public history. Howell also maintains that it is the emphasis on interpretation that makes history relevant. When public history is analyzed by an interpreter "the slant given to the analysis is often prompted by current society." Interpreters in various public history settings can do this by explaining the relationship between information and objects.[7] Lige Benton Miller has written that interpreters "must give meaning to a physical part of the past. While not being able to bring the past to life, the historian (interpreter) can give life to the past by making its ideas and experiences useful to the contemporary visitor (student)."[8]

One of the most popular and effective roles that interpreters have taken on is first-person interpretation or re-enactors. This technique has also been called "living history" and often encompasses the use of period costumes, dramatic presentation, and the re-creation of historical settings. "Character interpretation" is the interaction of the re-enactor with the audience. Re-enactors can be a powerful learning tool for adolescents (and adults) when well done. When poorly done, though, it can trivialize or over-simplify history.[9] Often professional actors take on the role of re-enactors. One of the most well known is James Whitmore. In his one-man shows he has "become" Teddy Roosevelt, Will Rogers, and Harry Truman.

Interpretative public history first appeared in the National Parks Service (NPS). The perception has been that the NPS was about *parks* not *history*. But the concept of "parks" has long extended beyond the common belief that Yellowstone and Yosemite are parks, not history. Parks include the Chesapeake and Ohio Canal, Valley Forge, and Little Rock High School in Arkansas. Huyck and Pitcaithley have written that "Interpreters serve as the public face of the NPS as they provide walks, talks, and tours that the public has come to expect at parks."[10] Interpretation can include everything from house tours and living history demonstrations (how Mount Rushmore was carved for example) to services such as films, park newspapers, and visitor center exhibits. Whatever the venue, the interpreter must make the past come alive. Huyck and Pitcaithley have also noted that "Because the public learns so much of its history here, interpretation must be of the highest quality, well-grounded in scholarship, and professionally communicated."[11]

But can public history engage (that word again) the adolescent learner? To do so, student encounters, as a result of public history, must move beyond visits to "big houses" like Mount Vernon and relate to "big houses" in their own community. There is absolutely nothing educationally inappropriate with students visiting well-known historical sites like Mount Vernon if the school is within reasonable distance. (Mount Vernon, in fact, has recently updated their interpretive center to be more youth-friendly and accessible.) Using homes as one example, many states and localities have historic homes that serve as superb sites "to do" public history. The Thomas Edison home and laboratory in Ft. Myers, Florida, the Frank Phillips (founder of Phillips 66 Petroleum Company) home and ranch in Bartlesville, Oklahoma, and the W.K. Kellogg home in Battle Creek, Michigan, all present life as it was lived during the early part of the 20th century.

Historical sites are everywhere and becoming increasingly diverse. On Mount Rushmore in South Dakota, Gutzon Borglum carved the faces of four presidents in the 1930s and it is now a National Monument. Located in the Black Hills, considered hallowed ground by Native Americans, another mountain sculpture, this one of Crazy Horse, is being created. Another example of the more recent sensitivities to diversity has been the addition of a Native American burial site next to the cemetery where General George Armstrong Custer and his men fell and are buried near the Little Big Horn River in Montana.

Living history sites (and we will see later public history in general) have not escaped criticism. Danilow cites concerns over their being too celebratory and overly patriotic. In addition they have been known to distort or excessively romanticize portions of the nation's past. The charge has also been made that public history has overlooked the contributions of all Americans, especially people of color and ethnicities. Other criticisms, according to Danilow, have included "poor training and implementation of interpreters and re-enactors, inadequate restoration and care of historical structures and overlooking . . . less favorable aspects of colonial, pioneer, and military life."[12] Again, these real and potential problems have been countered by an increasingly strong interest in the past by the public, the enhancement of living history interpretation, and fewer static displays and exhibits.[13] A familiar criticism has been aimed at outdoor museums, the first of their kind to appear in terms of living history. The problem has been the domination of pioneer villages which are often repetitive and, in some cases, of questionable quality.

Professionalization of the field of public history, sometimes known in university settings as heritage studies, has grown to over one hundred graduate programs and numerous undergraduate majors, minors, certificates, and concentrations. While the number of academic career opportunities in the field of teaching history has shrunk over the past several decades, occupations in public history have grown. Examples include a broad range of docents, from public school and college-age students to senior citizens, working and volunteering at state and national parks, museums, and historical sites.

A significant connection can be made between public history and adolescents in their study and understanding of history by capturing a vision of future vocational possibilities in the field. Public history can be viewed as a field to use the skills of research, interpretation, and writing in a broad variety of public settings. It can also be seen as solving problems, bringing enjoyment of the present, and preserving the past. Working with artifacts, buildings, oral histories, and more recently electronic records are all a part of the work of public historians.[14] By witnessing the work of public historians, adolescents can "see and feel" what history is all about in a very practical way. The actual vocations that are a part of public history are numerous. There are, of course, traditional practitioners such as archivists and museum directors. In addition the field needs editors and publishers who work for historical presses that provide journals, magazines, and books for the public through outlets for state and local historical agencies. Librarians and curators for special collections of books and artifacts are needed. Demonstrating to adolescents the career or volunteer opportunities in the field of public history makes history relevant to adolescents.

A program in California called "Link Learning" connects students to vocations and is keeping students in school, providing them the motivation to move into post-secondary education. The program is funded by both the James Irvine Foundation and the California Department of Education. At one school, for example, a student has seven career-themed programs from which to choose. Some of the areas include the performing arts, architecture, technology, health professions, and education. These sites, which are much like internships, are matched with strong college preparation classes and teachers who are trained for this program. The program is also known as Multiple Pathways to Student Success. The point is that public history sites have the potential to provide similar student opportunities for vocational careers in public history-related fields.[15]

The position of curator may not necessarily be the stereotypical role of those who work with art collections or in public museums. For example, in addition to being the historian of the Indianapolis Motor Speedway (IMS), a part of the position that David Donaldson holds is curator of the IMS collection of antique automobiles and race cars. Beginning his career as an unpaid "Mr. Memory" of Indianapolis 500 Mile Race facts, figures, and trivia, Donaldson soon took on the mantle of historian and is on the staff of the IMS. The IMS has a world-class museum which is visited by thousands of students each year. Donaldson often hosts guests of the IMS for tours of the public and private auto collection and has also written authoritatively on the history of the IMS.[16] Letting students know that this is history as much as what they may read in a textbook opens new avenues of exploration and study.

History is often taught from a federal perspective through national events and issues—the elections and lives of the presidents, the passage of laws by Congress, pivotal Supreme Court decisions, and wars. To bring the relevancy of the national scene to adolescents, history should also be viewed through the lens of a state or community. Excellent models for applied history have emerged through public history projects. One of the best is the Marion, Indiana, Community History Project that was created by a dedicated and creative teacher and high school students in that city. A major part of the project has been to display student historical projects about the community on a website.[17]

Connecting students to the community can be done online or face-to-face. The level of activity of local community or county historical societies varies. Students can gain much from an active local historical society, especially if there is participation by the adults in the community. Even historians who may wish to write on what they consider the grand national themes of our nation have discovered that topics connected to local and state history are most worthwhile and often of greater value to the field.[18] Historians have found if they write only for their fellow academics, and not for the public at large, they may end up only talking to themselves. Public history is an antidote to that challenge.

Film and media producers are central to public history. As with much about the teaching of history to adolescents this is a category that overlaps with another chapter in this book on movies. One of the best examples of the blend of public history and public entertainment has been the collaboration of director Steven Spielberg and actor Tom Hanks, referred to in that chapter. It is a case study of how public history goes public. Looking for what he calls "entertainable history" Hanks, on his own, first explored the potential for a film on the Vietnam era. But by the 1990s that war had been deeply culled through a number of movies. He still purchased the rights to *Forrest Gump* (1994), though, and won an academy award for his performance as the "Zelig-like" hero of the film that seems to be present at all the major events in U.S. history from the 1950s to the 1990s. In his search for subject matter, Hanks came to the conclusion that academic histories were "too dull to grab regular people by the lapel."[19]

Ken Burns' *Civil War* series in 1990 on PBS—with great period music, captivating talking heads, and the pan and scan use of photographs—convinced Hanks that television (HBO in his case) had the capacity to bring history alive for the American public. Using what has been termed the "non-fiction novel," from Truman Capote's *In Cold Blood*, Hanks' productions are "historical events and figures . . . drawn together along fictionalized story arcs where characters have the psychological interiority of characters in novels."[20]

Hanks and Spielberg, having produced numerous films as well as their own solo work, have brought history, especially World War II, to the public domain as no other players on the Hollywood scene. Hitting on their mutual fascination in World War II, the perfect storm of public interest was created with their joint collaboration on the production of *Saving Private Ryan*. That film and NBC television journalist Tom Brokaw's book *The Greatest Generation* both appeared in 1998. Brokaw's highly personal account of the generation that weathered both the Great Depression and World War II struck a chord in the American people. From that point, *Band of Brothers* and *The Pacific*—produced 8 years apart in the first decade of the 21st century—have focused the public's attention on this truly unique and transformational World War II generation.

A *Time* magazine cover story in 2010, written by historian Douglas Brinkley, was aptly titled "History Maker: How Tom Hanks is Redefining America's Past."[21] According to historian Douglas Brinkley, Hanks has made ". . . our back pages come alive, to keep overhauling the history we know and, in the process, get us to understand not just the past but the choices we make today." The purpose and motivation for undertaking such history for the actor was clear. "Public education," writes Brinkley, "was an integral component of Hanks' vision."[22] Hanks' film work has connected to public history projects that include the National World War II Memorial in Washington D.C. and the National World War II Museum in New Orleans. The National World War II Museum was a pet project of the late historian Stephen Ambrose, and Hanks has done much to support that ongoing work.

Hanks has stepped outside the World War II era to produce the critically acclaimed and highly watched HBO series *John Adams* (2008). Drawn from the biography on Adams by David McCullough, both the book and television series are the work of a skilled storyteller and popularizer in the vein of Ambrose and Brokaw. In addition to these projects, Hanks was both the leading actor in and producer of *Charlie Wilson's War* (2007), which is a rendition of a congressman's work to fund Afghan rebels against the Soviet Union in the 1970s and 1980s.

Non-Hollywood, private sector entities such as foundations and historical societies have also produced films for both the public sector and classrooms. The Winthrop Rockefeller Foundation produced *The Elaine Riot: Tragedy and Triumph* (2001) that documents the race riots in that Arkansas community in 1918. Tied to state history standards and frameworks for grades 5–12 and narrated by actor Ozzie Davis, the film is a model for what foundations can do for classrooms. Another example is the Indiana Historical Society's *Ernie Pyle's War: A Documentary on Ernie Pyle, World War II Correspondent* (2005). Both of these films are less than 30 minutes long, an appropriate length for middle school and high school students.

Public history implies, maybe even suggests, that studying history will advance adolescents toward greater civic involvement. A *Washington Post* article reported that high school dropouts are less likely to vote, trust government, do volunteer work, or go to church than better-educated Americans.[23] (At a time when education is usually tethered to economics in terms of productivity and earning power, it is refreshing to see a study, although one that brings troubling news, that reports on meaningful societal values.) Three areas that have been identified as indicators of civic involvement—civic activities (volunteering, community work), electoral activities (voting, working in campaigns), and having a political voice. The last one, having a political voice, is most closely connected to public history.[24] Indicators of civic involvement under the rubric of "having a political voice" include contacting political officials, as well as print or broadcast media, protesting, boycotting, taking part in petition drives, and canvassing.

Cox-Petersen has stated that while civic involvement studies have usually been aimed at young Americans ages 15–25, programs for adolescents in grades six and up are now being advocated.[25] Many of the activities listed as having a "political voice" can be found in our history—from the call for redress of grievances during the American Revolution, anti-Vietnam War protests, and the year 2008 when the youth vote made the difference in the election of a president. All of these activities are examples for adolescents of civic involvement in the public arena and when youth took part in the movements.

Most public history venues provide a plethora of school-related features. These include outreach programs, tours directly related to student interests, and in some cases connections to academic standards. Both pre-trip and post-trip activities are encouraged to maximize the educational experience. While at the museum or cultural institution, Cox-Petersen has made the following recommendations:

- Provide learning tools such as notebooks, clipboards, or prompt sheets.

- Provide graphic organizers, outlines, maps, and photographs that assist students as learning clues.

- Prevent too much docent or teacher talk by mixing the direct instruction with the experiential.

- Provide time for free (but monitored) exploration.

- Plan ahead for connections to school curriculum, standards, or experiences of students from their classroom.

- Always look for opportunities to stress diversity in visiting public history venues—or the lack of diversity for future discussion.[26]

British museums and historical sites are models for student visits. It might be the fact that history is literally "around every corner" on those isles, but from the youngest child through adolescents, the way the British "use" their history is quite effective. The visits to public sites are structured. Students are often seen carrying notebooks, responding to questions, and sharing ideas with others. Some have expressed the concern that Britain has basically become just a large "theme park." But that notion is probably inaccurate considering the wealth of authentic historic sites, museums, and parks in Britain and how its citizens use them for educational purposes.

One concern that is often expressed by educators is the lack of proximity to public history sites. It is a legitimate point. Yet new (really "old" since they are historical) sources for public history are regularly appearing. Presidential sites are an excellent example. William Clotworthy has done an admirable job of creating a directory of places associated with United States presidents.[27] Containing over 1,000 sites, the entries move beyond the usual presidential birthplaces and cemeteries. The list includes homes, churches, colleges, libraries, museums, monuments, and memorials. Clotworthy's research is impressive—he has listed all seven apartments in Washington, D.C. that Harry Truman lived in before becoming president. (He did leave out President Eisenhower's summer visit to the Custer State Park in South Dakota while listing Calvin Coolidge's, but who's counting?) The gamut of entries runs from FDR's home at Hyde Park on the Hudson River in New York to Calvin Coolidge's pre-presidential law office on the second floor of the Masonic Building in Northampton, Massachusetts. Some of the sites are as grand and famous as Jefferson's home, Monticello, in Virginia to an isolated, maybe even unnoticed statue of James A. Garfield in Long Branch, New Jersey, the town where he died after being assassinated in 1881.

Covering presidents from George Washington through Bill Clinton, Clotworthy lists sites with brief annotations for each. Forty-eight states are listed with only Hawaii and Idaho not cited. With the election of Barack Obama and his connections to Hawaii, that now leaves only Idaho without representation. For the record, Minnesota, Nevada, and Utah have only one presidential site and Wyoming and Washington each have two. Virginia and Ohio lead with the most entries due to the large number of presidents each state has sent to the White House.

Taking the presidential sites example a bit further, the least popular presidents have the fewest entries. James Buchanan, Franklin Pierce, Andrew Johnson, and Warren G. Harding all garner fewer than 10 citations each. Admittedly, some of the places are dubious in terms of educational worth. (See Truman's apartments and Coolidge's law office above.) Would a group of adolescents really want to visit the house in Petersburg, Virginia, where President Lincoln and General Grant met to discuss the war in the spring of 1865? Probably not. The point is, though, that the directory proves one need not live in Washington, D.C. to have access to historical sites, however humble they may be.

While on the topic of access, there are students who live in rural communities distant from metropolitan areas where public history sites are likely to be located. But due to demographic shifts in population, more families are moving from remote rural areas to urban/suburban centers. Even if students live in rural areas, many are located within proximity of larger cities. Non-urban areas near Kansas City, Missouri, are within reach of two new museums in the heart of the Midwest—the World War I Museum and the National Negro Baseball Museum. Being new venues, both facilities have focused on the various applications of public history that will connect to students.

Although rare, some historical sites are in amazing proximity to each other. An example is one location in the United States that is both rich and tragic in the history it encompasses. Court Square, located in Montgomery, Alabama, is the terminus of six streets that come together at a statue of Hebe, goddess of youth, in the midst of a public fountain. At one time Court Square served as a site for slave auctions. From Court Square the Alabama state capitol is visible—where Jefferson Davis was sworn in as president of the Confederacy and from where he sent instructions for his troops to commence shelling Fort Sumter, South Carolina. The location was also the main transfer point for the buses that would be boycotted by the city's Blacks in 1955. And finally, from Court Square, Dexter Avenue Baptist Church can be seen. It is the church that in 1954 called a young theology student, Martin Luther King, Jr., to be its pastor.

Another example of public history, this one with a great deal of creativity on the part of historians and a state highway department, can be found along the New Jersey Turnpike. Twelve rest areas along the turnpike are named for famous New Jersey natives with brief pieces of information provided about them for travelers. They include Clara Barton, Walt Whitman, James Fenimore Cooper, Woodrow Wilson (although not a native of the state, he was president of Princeton), Molly Pitcher, Thomas Edison, and Vince Lombardi. Who knows, maybe Frank Sinatra could be next.

Paradoxically, while the aim of public history is to shift away from the dominant print-oriented approach to studying the past, a new form of living history has appeared—books. Two of these volumes or "museums in a book" (a trademarked phrase—titles cannot be copyrighted) are *The Declaration of Independence: The Story Behind America's Founding Document and the Men Who Created It* and *America's Presidents: Facts, Photos, and Memorabilia from the Nation's Chief Executives.*[28] The latter contains facsimiles of a campaign poster from 1888, Albert Einstein's

1939 letter to Franklin Roosevelt about the potential for a uranium bomb that would be "extremely powerful," John Kennedy's "doodles" drawn during the Cuban Missile Crisis, and the April 5, 1917, joint resolution of Congress declaring war on Germany and signed by Woodrow Wilson. These artifacts provide a flavor of the individuals and the times.

Almost every state produces publications as part of their historical societies or organizations. Examples would be the Florida Historical Society's *Florida Historical Society Quarterly*, which partners with the University of Central Florida, and the *California History* magazine produced by the California Historical Society. The Indiana Historical Society, in addition to operating its own book press, produces two publications: *Traces of Indiana and Midwestern History* contains popular history that spans the cultural, political, and biographical history of the state and *The Hoosier Genealogist*. The latter addresses family and local history in addition to primary sources such as diaries, ledgers, and public records. Its name was recently changed to *THG: Connections* to reflect its additional online presence.

Most state historical publications contain articles, book reviews, and photographs. Place is often central to the content of any public history publication. For example, *South Dakota History*, from the South Dakota State Historical Society, is a mix of western and agricultural themes in addition to biographies and how state history has dovetailed with events on the national scene. Staying with South Dakota, *South Dakota Magazine*, while not scholarly in mission, does provide amateur historians the opportunity to publish pieces on a variety of topics from the historical to the recent, from travel to wildlife. Entrepreneurs in larger cities are increasingly publishing magazines that capture modern day life in particular locations. That too is public history.

In spite of much evidence to the contrary, there are critics of public history. While much of the material in this chapter supports and endorses the idea of public history as a key tool in the teaching of history to youth, other viewpoints can always inform any practice. Historian David Lowenthal has drawn a distinction between the terms history and heritage. (Heritage, as has been seen, is at times used interchangeably with public or living history.) Lowenthal does not see heritage as history, but rather a field that borrows from and enlivens historical study. Heritage is not "an inquiry into the past but a celebration of it, not an effort to know what actually happened but a profession of faith in a past tailored to present-day purposes."[29]

The goal of heritage, according to another critic, Bruce VanSledright, is to "spark faith, enhance identity, and create a sense of pleasure and joy in being who we are."[30] William Pannapacker has been concerned about the reality of what might be called the "Barnum Effect" on museums. (P.T. Barnum and his American Museum in the 1800s featured all kinds of fakes, which he claimed was acceptable because people like to be "fooled.") Confronted with the artificial and technological reproductions of dinosaurs found in natural history museums, Pannapacker also worried about other museums. He maintains that "one of the fundamental attractions of . . . museums is the aura of authenticity and the power they have to inspire the imagination, particularly for children in an era that is increasingly virtual and simulated." Attempting to emulate the entertainment industry, Pannapacker warns, only "generates spectacles that do not cultivate quiet reflection and cannot sustain repeated encounters."[31]

William Hogeland has suggested that there has been a failing by those who work in the area of public history such as museums, state and national parks, and even popular historical works of fiction, non-fiction, and biography. Hogeland advocates for greater connection to the "non-specialist" (student) in our society through public history thereby inspiring the untapped imagination of the youth and citizenry.[32] It is the use of venues such as historic and preservation sites, archival work, museums, or learning first-hand what historians do that students relate best to in the field of history.[33]

There is also the issue of revisionism within public history. Revisionism has been a cottage industry for historians for centuries. What would historiography be without spirited debates on the changing views of history? Two recent examples of this phenomenon appearing in the public history arena and attaching themselves to two of the United States' most iconic public sites are the Alamo in San Antonio, Texas, and Ellis Island in New York Harbor.

The dominant portrayal of the Alamo battle has been challenged over the past two decades as scholars are rewriting and revisiting the scene of what many consider well-worn historical ground. Baby-Boomers saw Fess Parker (on television) and John Wayne (in the film) playing Davy Crockett and dying heroically in defense of the Mexican? (Texan?) mission. The Daughters of the Republic of Texas (DRT) are the official custodians of the Alamo having been given it by the state of Texas in 1905 when it was in a state of disrepair. Writing about conflicting views of history, Richard Flores points out factual errors in the DRT film shown to Alamo visitors. An alternative conclusion is that the Tejano (Spanish-speaking citizens living in the state of Coahuila-Tejas, Mexico which later became Texas) fought and died with the Anglos at the Alamo. Flores also reports that Mexico attempted to control immigration into this area due to the large influx of U.S. citizens into their country. Mexico even passed an emancipation proclamation of their own outlawing slavery in this area. Mexico did not practice slavery; the law was to discourage these new arrivals. Flores concludes that "Invoking the past, as a fact of history or a mythical reality, is to judge according to the needs of the present."[34]

The variance of opinion over the public history of Ellis Island has been in dispute by some due to reasons related to diversity. The issue is that the public history being portrayed at Ellis Island focuses only on the peak years of immigration—1886–1924—and not on the history before or after. Writer Daniel Walkowitz, editor of the volume from which this example and that of the Alamo are drawn, has concluded that the thrust of the exhibit "is implicitly one of adjustment, assimilation, and ultimately the 'whitening' of the immigrants." The response to this concern, according to Walkowitz, is more history. An expansion of the story of the immigrant experience is needed, he believes, and "an enriched interpretive analysis of the Ellis experience."[35]

While not a critic of public history per se, James Loewen, whose work in debunking textbooks is reviewed in an earlier chapter, has undertaken a similar mission in connection to historic sites in America. This volume is titled *Lies Across America: What Our Historic Sites Got Wrong*. He has exhaustively investigated hundreds if not thousands of memorials, monuments, homes, cemeteries and other historic sites including historical roadside markers. Loewen's thesis in this book might be encapsulated in the phrase there is a "critical distinction between what happened in the past versus what we say about it."[36] Drawing examples from all fifty states, he includes an appendix that lists ten questions to ask at a historic site. (He warns not to ask about Franklin Roosevelt's mistresses at FDR's home in Hyde Park, New York, or Woodrow Wilson's racial policies at his home on S Street in Washington, D.C.)

Loewen's legitimate concern is the lack of seriousness and substance that are at times a part of public history. He contends that guides will prattle on about the silverware used, the food that was served, and relate boring anecdotes that took place in historic homes—all superfluous, inconsequential, and a waste of the visitor's time. Loewen maintains that avoiding negative or controversial aspects of the sites does a disservice to history. Inventing and perpetuating "blemish free" heroes and events manufacture a falsity that students or adults "don't really buy." In another appendix Loewen suggests twenty historic sites that need in his word "toppling" or to be removed. Most are in the South and are connected to the Confederacy.[37]

In the author's hometown an episode not so different from Loewen's own experiences occurred. A small stone memorial to those from the county who died in the Great War (World War I) was located on the grounds of the court house. About two dozen men were listed. Behind the names of three of the men in parentheses were the three letters "col." An observant local high school history teacher investigated the meaning of the "col" and found out it did not stand for "colonel." He found photographs of the three soldiers on the stone and discovered that they were all Black. The "col" had stood for "colored." Segregated while living, the three soldiers who made the ultimate sacrifice for their country remained segregated on a memorial even in death. The teacher informed a local veterans organization which, to their credit and with great embarrassment, replaced the memorial stone with a new one absent the inappropriate appellations.

The old debates about public history will surely continue and new ones will no doubt emerge. The lesson to be drawn is that when teachers do use public history to engage students they make the best judgments they can. Are the activities they are providing real learning experiences or merely "history lite"? While there are truly many aspects of American history that are most worthy of being celebrated, and should be, the issue is again one of balance. Successes in our nation's history have always been matched with failures and costs compared to achievements. In the quest for relevancy the teaching of history through public history holds great promise. As can be seen from these assorted examples, bringing history to life becomes easier when students can be "taken to it" rather than "it being brought to them." Again, the emphases on experiences and active learning make history real to adolescents.

The World of Practice
Colonial Williamsburg in the Twenty-first Century Classroom
by William E. White

There is a remarkable moment in American history in the mid-eighteenth century when all across the eastern seaboard of North America individuals throw off their role as subjects of the King of Great Britain and take up the mantle of citizen. It was a remarkable transformation. Americans overturned the doctrine of divine right of kings—the idea that all rights and privileges are vested in rulers who then select the rights and privileges of their subjects. Philosophers had theorized that rights were vested in individuals who in turn granted rights and privileges to government, but no one had dared to put that into practical application until Americans did in 1776.

I am privileged to have worked my entire career at an institution dedicated to the implications of that transformational moment. The Colonial Williamsburg Foundation tells the story of the revolutionary generation as they took up the responsibilities of citizen. It is an educational mission that we today refer to as "education for citizenship." This is the story of how "We the People"—every generation of American citizens—engage the challenges of our time to build the republic for ourselves and for a new generation. These are the instructive stories that show every American their role as a citizen of their community, state, and nation today.

For nearly 100 years, Colonial Williamsburg has supported its "education for citizenship" mission with public interpretive programming. The general public tours the sites, exhibitions, and programs in the 301–acre historic area, and school students have always been an important part of our audience. While on-site visits are still a central part of our mission, Colonial Williamsburg is increasingly engaging twenty-first century technologies to transform our role in the community.

Colonial Williamsburg is no longer a static place or institution. It is a national and international forum for teaching the history of our republic—the history of our citizens.

Teacher Professional Development

For thirty years Colonial Williamsburg has sponsored on-site elementary, middle school, and high school teacher workshops. The week-long Teacher Institute provides an opportunity to use the historic area as a laboratory where teachers learn to create an interactive and engaging American history environment in their classroom. Colonial Williamsburg staff also conducts professional development seminars on the road, visiting dozens of school districts every year with content, methods, and costumed interpreters. In the 2010–2011 school year, Colonial Williamsburg will also begin hosting online distance learning opportunities for teachers.

Teacher development is a central component of the Colonial Williamsburg education outreach initiative. History education begins with our nation's elementary teachers, but too often the teachers instructing our fourth and fifth grade students characterize history as the memorization of names, dates, and places. We want teachers to engage students with the excitement of primary sources and active learning. Through our teacher development, we work to transform history education into the most exciting and relevant subject in the classroom.

Colonial Williamsburg Online

Colonial Williamsburg hosts the Digital History Center with primary source materials from a variety of collections, including Colonial Williamsburg's manuscript collection, more than seventy-five years of research reports by Foundation historians, the *Virginia Gazette* online, and the York County Virginia probate inventories. We also host eMuseum, an online catalog providing access to more than 60,000 fine, decorative, mechanical, and folk art objects owned by Colonial Williamsburg. Each entry includes a photograph, description with label text, and provenance for most objects.

These collections offer easy access to documents, objects, and images of all kinds, and serve as a reminder to students that a primary source is not just a written or printed document. As historians, we also interpret curatorial objects, prints, drawings and paintings, archeological artifacts, and buildings and landscapes to understand the past. By delving into these online collections, students can try their hand at the work of historians and curators, and they learn to gather research and think analytically when approaching a topic of interest.

The Internet also provides opportunities for teachers and students to engage the newest research by the institution's historians, archaeologists, architectural historians, and tradespeople. Online resources range from research reports to "podcasts" (sound files), "vodcasts" (video files), and blogs, as well as online exhibitions and content web applications. These tools provide conversations with researchers and tradespeople working on a host of projects: underwater archeology at Yorktown, excavations at Historic Jamestowne, historic area presentations, the history of performing arts, and current historical research. An online exhibit can take students into an exhibition gallery with curators to closely examine artifacts, such as in our current exhibit, where students use infrared, raking light, and x-ray images to see how conservators work to preserve and restore a 1794 painting.

Electronic Field Trips

Electronic Field Trips are another way Colonial Williamsburg reaches outside physical boundaries to the classroom. Monthly from October to April, the museum broadcasts a special classroom event to schools across the nation. Topics run the gamut of colonial and early American history, covering topics from colonization to daily life to slavery to the Revolution, and going as far forward in history as the Civil War. Each year the schedule also includes a program on how we study history, whether it be an in-depth look at archaeology, historical research, artifact conservation, or some other aspect of the profession.

An Electronic Field Trip is designed to create a special event in the classroom. Every program has teacher materials, lesson plans, interactive web activities for students, suggestions for additional reading, additional web resources, literacy strategies, suggestions for using the program with an interactive whiteboard, and more.

At the core of all these resources is a one-hour live interactive television event for the classroom. Classes view the television broadcast by watching their local public or educational television station or by streaming the live broadcast on the Internet. The program has three dramatic television presentations followed by an opportunity for students to call Colonial Williamsburg with their questions. Live-from-the-studio student questions are answered by characters that students met during the history dramatization and a historian who helps provide context. There are always many more questions than time available, but we make sure that every child who calls Colonial Williamsburg on the day of an Electronic Field Trip receives an answer to his or her question. A group of nearly 40 staff and volunteers answer a bank of telephones and computers and spends the day responding to student telephone calls, emails, and message board postings.

The Idea of America

The Idea of America is designed to examine themes in American history and connect high school students with our revolutionary founding. What is, for example, the role of religion in our republic? There is no easy answer, and engaging in conversation or debate on the issue requires understanding issues from the colonial period, the Second Great Awakening, nineteenth-century religious reformers, and onward. Students might examine the role of the military in the republic, but understanding how that role changed in the post-World War II era also means that students should understand what the founding generation thought about a standing army and how the republic has dealt with the military over the course of its nineteenth- and early-twentieth-century history.

The Idea of America helps students with that kind of critical historical thinking. We ask students to envision the United States as an enduring debate about values that are critical to us as a people. Those values, however, are in tension with each other. For example, we celebrate our individual freedom and we celebrate equality, understanding all the while that these two values are actually in tension with each other. We must temper our freedom in order to gain some equality, and in like manner, we must compromise our equality in order to obtain individual freedoms. The American debate embraces the challenge of finding a balance between our freedom and our equality, between our unity and diversity, between our private wealth and our common wealth, and between our law and our ethics.

Students examine American history in the context of this enduring debate in a digital format that provides access to primary sources (textual, graphical, and artifact-based), historian commentary, and stories about individual citizens engaged in the work of the republic. Colonial Williamsburg also maintains a related website called *The Virtual Republic*, supported by an IMLS grant, which engages students with current events issues in the framework of the Great Debate and with historical context.

Moving Toward the Future

Colonial Williamsburg and our sister museums and institutions around the country are becoming a new and different kind of educational institution. We are no longer bound by the physical location and structure of our institution. Digital media and communications technologies offer an opportunity for us to expand our reach and scope—an opportunity to connect millions with the mission of our institution. Nowhere is that potential more palpable than in K–12 education. We are on the cusp of a new era where museums—like Colonial Williamsburg—will be essential classroom resources.

William E. (Bill) White is the Theresa A. and Lawrence C. Salameno Director, Educational Program Development at the Colonial Williamsburg Foundation. White leads the Colonial Williamsburg Teacher Development initiative, the Emmy-winning Electronic Field Trip series, an extensive K–12 media publishing program, and is the author of Pearson Scott Foresman's History-Social Science for California for grades K–5. He has also authored the American history digital curriculum entitled *The Idea of America* distributed by Pearson Education.

Endnotes

1   Becker, Carl. "Everyman His Own Historian." *The American Historical Review* 37. 2 (1932): 233–34.

2   "What is Public History?" National Council on Public History website. <http://ncph.org/cms>.

3   Stanton, Cathy. "What is Public History? Redux." National Council on Public History website <http://ncph.org/cms/what-is-public-history/>. Retrieved May 13, 2010.

4   Mooney-Melvin, Patricia. "Professional Historians and the Challenge of Redefinition." *Public History: Essays from the Field*. Malabar: Krieger Publishing Company, 1999. 14–15.

5   Danilow, Victor J. *Living History Museums and Historic Sites in the United States*. Jefferson: McFarland and Company, Inc., 2010. 1. In addition to providing a background on the field of living history, Danilow's volume is a comprehensive catalog of outdoor living history sites.

6   Howell, Mark. "Interpreters and Museum Educators: Beyond the Blue Hairs." *Public History: Essays from the Field*. Malabar: Krieger Publishing Company, 1999. 142.

7   Ibid. 143 and 145.

8   Miller, Lige Benton, Jr. "History on the Drawing Board: The Historian as Developer of Interpretive Media." Barbara J. Howe and Emory L. Kemp. *Public History: An Introduction*. Malabar: Robert E. Krieger Publishing Company, 1986. 199.

9   Ibid. 146–48.

10   Huyck, Heather, and Dwight Pitcaithley. "National Park Service: Historian in Interpretation, Management, and Cultural Resources Management." Barbara J. Howe and Emory L. Kemp. *Public History: An Introduction*. Malabar: Robert E. Krieger Publishing Company, 1986: 361.

11   Ibid.

12   Ibid. 19.

13   Ibid.

14   Ibid. 32–33.

15   See Canales, James E. "Linking Courses to Careers Improves Graduation Rates." *San Francisco Chronicle* 25 July 2010: E-5; *Multiple Pathways to Student Success* at California Department of Education website <http://www.cde.ca.gov>; and *Irvine Quarterly*, Summer 2010 at James Irvine Foundation website <http://www.irvine.org>.

16   Davidson, Donald, and Rick Shaffer. *Autocourse Official History of the Indianapolis 500*. Silverstone, UK: Crash Media Group, Ltd, 2006.

17   See <http://wikimarion.org/Marion_High_School>.

18   Giglierano, Geoffrey J., and Deborah A. Overmyer. "Why Are You Studying My Neighborhood?: Reaching a General Audience with Local History Projects and the 'New' Social History." Ed. J.D. Britton and Diane F. Britton. *History Outreach: Programs for Museums, Historical Organizations, and Academic History Departments*. Malabar, FL: Krieger Publishing Company, 1994. 177–90.

19 Brinkley, Douglas. "The World According to Tom." *Time* 175. 10. 15 Mar. 2010: 45.
20 Ibid. 46
21 Ibid. 40–45.
22 Ibid. 45.
23 Goldstein, A. "Civic Involvement Tied to Education." *Washington Post* 19 Sept. 2006: A19.
24 Cox-Petersen, Amy. *Educational Partnerships: Connecting Schools, Families, and the Community.* Thousand Oaks: Sage Publications, 2010. 148.
25 Ibid. 149.
26 Ibid. 170.
27 Clotworthy, William G. *Presidential Sites: A Directory of Places Associated with Presidents of the United States.* Blacksburg: The McDonald and Woodward Publishing Company, 1998.
28 Gragg, Rod. *The Declaration of Independence: The Story Behind America's Founding Document and the Men Who Created It.* Nashville: Rutledge Hill Press, 2005; and Wills, Chuck. *America's Presidents: Facts, Photos, and Memorabilia from the Nation's Chief Executives.* Bellevue: Becker and Mayer Books, 2007.
29 Lowenthal, David. *The Heritage Crusade and the Spoils of History.* Cambridge: Cambridge University Press, 1998: x, xi.
30 VanSledright, Bruce. *In Search of America's Past: Learning to Read History in Elementary School.* New York: Teachers College Press, 2002. 11.
31 Pannapacker, William (aka Thomas H. Benton). "Getting Real at the Natural-History Museums." *The Chronicle of Higher Education* 2 July 2010. A29 and A31.
32 Hogeland, William. *Inventing American History.* Cambridge: MIT Press, 2009: xiii–xiv.
33 Percoco, James A. *A Passion for the Past: Creative Teaching of U.S. History.* Portsmouth: Heinemann, 1998. 12–16.
34 Flores, Richard R. "The Alamo: Myth, Public History, and the Politics of Inclusion." Walkowitz, Daniel J. and Lisa M. Knauer. *Contested Histories in Public Space: Memory, Race, and Nation.* Durham: Duke University Press, 2009. 122–35.
35 Walkowitz, Daniel J. "Ellis Island Redux: The Imperial Turn and the Race of Ethnicity." *Contested Histories in Public Space: Memory, Race, and Nation.* Durham: Duke University Press, 2009. 137–54.
36 Loewen, James W. *Lies Across America: What Our Historic Sites Got Wrong.* New York: A Touchstone Book. 3.
37 Ibid. 429–36.

TEN

Does the Subject Matter?:
Content Selection and Emblematic Episodes in American History

An unavoidable question is: "How do history teachers choose what they teach?" Bruce VanSledright has written that:

> No matter how one teaches history, choices must be made about what to teach. The past and the stories we tell about it are too rich, too varied, and too many; we are always forced to choose among them. Making decisions about historical significance involves navigating a swamp; there is no way through it without entanglements.[1]

Another teacher, Monica Edinger, has also confronted the conundrum of what should be taught. She views the process this way:

> Curriculum content is an ongoing issue for us teachers, a quagmire of endless dilemmas. How I wish that it could all be settled, that someone would give me the magic solution to all this contention and controversy. The arguments have been going on forever. From Plato to Rousseau, from Hirsch to my hairdresser—everyone seems to have an opinion as to what I should teach. I read . . . I listen to, argue, and talk with colleagues. I have three concerns when considering what content to teach: outside demands, students' interests, and my own passions.[2]

Edinger's comments make a good point for departure. She is reading, talking, and listening. And the three concerns she has about the history curriculum are all well grounded. Teachers must realize that there are and will be external forces making requirements as to what is taught. All good teachers must be sensitive to and knowledgeable about students' interests. And finally, teachers became teachers because they had a zeal to share with students what made history exciting for them.

The selection of content within the history curriculum is a critical decision for teachers. What is called subject matter is often defined, some may think narrowly, as synonymous with curriculum. It is commonly understood, though, that curriculum cannot be divorced from instruction. And that curriculum is more than the subject matter being taught. This chapter will examine the importance of course content selection. In addition, a rationale for content selection will be offered along with examples drawn from American history to demonstrate possible avenues for teachers to follow in that process.

First, an additional word about the standards movement in history as it relates to curriculum development. There has been less attention paid to national standards in history since the aborted attempt in the early 1990s to create these standards which were a part of the Goals 2000 agenda of both President George H. W. Bush and his successor President Bill Clinton. The University of California at Los Angeles National Center for History in the Schools was given the task of working on national standards in history. But the task quickly turned political when Lynne Cheney, former head of the National Endowment for the Humanities, and others such as conservative talk radio host Rush Limbaugh, attacked the standards. Three California historians have documented the event surrounding the episode in the book *History on Trial: Culture Wars and the Teaching of the Past.*[3] The debate that ensued was indeed caught up in the "culture wars" of left and right, conservative and liberal, progressive and traditionalist both inside and outside the field of history. The U.S. history standards were finally killed in Congress (in the Senate by a vote of 99–1) when Senator Slade Gorton asked who should be included in the history books—Bart Simpson and Roseanne Arnold or George Washington and how America defeated communism. The culture wars had to do with whether the story of America was one of triumph or tragedy, whether to showcase the challenges America has faced and how it confronted them or highlight the nation's successes and accomplishments.[4]

As alluded to earlier, the standards movement has been viewed as both narrowing the curriculum and restricting the choices students and teachers have in the selection of subject matter. This is accurate up to a point. With policymakers and legislatures focused on mathematics and literacy, subjects such as history, science, and the arts have been under less scrutiny, thus less control. However, most teachers agree that the role of history and social studies has diminished. This status quo, though, may or may not hold. Most citizens and educators will agree as to the importance of history. But unlike mathematics or literacy, where achievement can often be calibrated into skill sets, history (and also literature), due to the vast potential of topics and content, is not so easily encapsulated and then measured in terms of assessment. Any attempt in the future to nationalize the history curriculum, beyond what textbooks and states do in terms of uniformity, may run into the same controversies of the 1990s.

But there are standards. In history the National Center for History in the Schools has set forth curricular and grade level guidelines, topics, skills, and expectations in the history and social studies arena.[5] Although not as recent, the National Council for the Social Studies produced a set of standards that covers all the disciplines within the social studies.[6] U.S. history standards usually take the form of outlines beginning with eras or periods of time such as Colonization, the American Revolution, Civil War and Reconstruction, the Progressive Era, and the Great Depression. From there additional topics, content, and details are added.

Every state has its own history standards for history taught to adolescents. Released test items drawn from the standards for history are usually available from state departments of education on their websites. Additional student assessment information tied to standards can also be found on these sites.[7] The key to the use of standards is to work within the parameters that policymakers have set out, but make sure that teachers do not become discouraged or lose the creativeness that makes the classroom meaningful for students. But the standards debate continues unabated with each side, the pro and the con, having an array of experts who not only provide research, but strongly held positions on the role standards play in the nation's schools.[8]

A simple duality within history content delivery would be either a) a broad survey of content within a history course, or b) a thematic/topical/episodic selection of content. Both approaches are valid and have advocates within the history teaching communities. A survey—a detailed or abbreviated overview of American history—allows for a comprehensive coverage of historical eras. The disadvantage to surveying American history is the likely possibility of superficiality and lack of depth within the topics examined. Historical topics cannot be given adequate attention and thereby the result can be a limited understanding by the student of the material.

Thematic or episodic treatments provide a more limited coverage of content and an opposite set of challenges. Greater depth in fewer topics can allow for greater understanding of sometimes difficult material. Thematic teaching (known at one time as "post-holing") allows for delving deeper at various points along the fence that runs through history. An antithetical rendering of thematic teaching would argue that gaps will be present in a study of American history. What movements, individuals, events, trends, and issues do we choose to incorporate in a course—and which of these do we choose to discard or spend less time on?

While the standards movement has decreased the amount of student and teacher choice in terms of the curriculum and the pedagogy, choice remains a powerful tool in the history classroom. Choice can run the gamut from topics and themes the student selects to choices that the teacher puts forth to the class. Student ideas may have come about from television or movies they have seen to books or magazines they have read. One of the most compelling pieces of evidence endorsing student choice in the classroom is an episode in the young career of the progressive educator William Van Til.

One of the more intriguing vignettes in Van Til's autobiography, *My Way of Looking at It,* relates to his very first years of teaching in the 1930s when his beliefs in the mission of progressivism were tested. Since Van Til had come to his new school with a modest reputation as a "reform school teacher," he was immediately given a behaviorally and academically challenging class of high school boys. By his own description he was at the time "a primitive progressive," attempting to follow Dewey's advice to employ "interest and effort" and Kilpatrick's suggestion of "purposeful activity." He began, innocently enough, by asking the boys what they wanted to study. The boys responded that they wanted to study "crooks." "I was at a crossroads," Van Til later wrote. He could have obfuscated the issue, claiming that crooks were not in the English-social studies curriculum. Instead, he followed the Frostian "road less traveled."[9]

Van Til acquiesced and the students undertook a problem-solving curriculum of real life problems using the city of Columbus, Ohio, as their classroom. They visited a police station, examined demographic data, made maps, photographed troubled inner-city neighborhoods, and read widely—even a dusty, little-used sociology dissertation on crime. Their findings were collected in written form and, with the assistance of the art teacher, placed on display for the other students to view and examine. The experience proved both profitable and productive for the young men in the class and the student body as a whole. The inquiry approach led to history, sociology, creative writing, extensive reading, photography, and research. The young teacher had tested progressive theory and become a lifelong adherent to its tenets.[10] Choice can make a difference.

Yet the standards, usually at the state level, do not entirely set out in advance the complete history curriculum. The state history standards are usually topical, mostly name individuals deemed worthy of inclusion, rarely provide a narrative, and never dictate how a teacher should go about teaching the curriculum. That is where teachers must decide what their approach will be and what will be added to the subject matter required in the standards. Epstein reported multiple studies that suggested the selection of a few well-chosen topics or themes and the study of them in depth through a discipline-centered approach was most effective. Learning to study history as a historian would be such a methodology. Other examples would be examining concepts such as continuity and change, cause and effect, making judgments and interpretations on primary sources, and searching for motivation and human agency (action) in historical figures.[11]

Both the thematic (or topical) and the survey approaches are accepted and practiced in the teaching of history. It should also be noted that most history courses tend to be a "mix" of these two approaches. For the purpose of examining subject matter selection this chapter will explore how teachers of adolescents in history courses make those choices. And four of what will be called "emblematic episodes" will be offered with supporting narrative as examples of subject matter selection.

Lists of what students should know have been popular for many years. Often they are used to indicate what a student does not know. (For example, only sixteen percent of high school seniors could provide the years the Civil War began and ended. Only four percent of high school students could name the Chief Justice of the United States.) Sometimes content is selected by teachers from what they think students should know. Lists of the one hundred most important events in American history or the one hundred most important women and men in American history are abundant. *Time* magazine has named a Person of the Year (formerly Man of the Year) since the 1920s. One could form a list from that list.

An example of an entire book titled *What Every American Should Know About American History: 200 Events That Shaped the Nation* by Axelrod and Phillips demonstrates the problem with such lists.[12] The book is actually a fairly good representation of American history if one is limited to just 200 events. The issue of what is placed in such a list and what is left out usually becomes the fodder for debate among adults, but rarely students. Axelrod and Phillips include the writing of the rules of baseball, but not the invention of basketball by James Naismith. Bank robber Jesse James makes the list, but not John Dillinger. A number of important Supreme Court cases make it and a number of them do not. Painter Albert Bierstadt is included, but not Jackson Pollock, Mark Rothko, or Norman Rockwell. We have McGuffey, but not Dr. Seuss. The issue is not to criticize this effort. If the book is picked up by a middle school student who enjoys history, then what it contains will do them no harm and probably a great deal of good. And actually, teachers will need to make similar decisions about the content they choose to include in their courses.

A popular activity for some historians and teachers, and considered a waste of time to others, is the endeavor known as "speculative history"—what if? What if Oswald had missed when he fired on President Kennedy's motorcade? What if the isolationists had prevailed against Franklin Roosevelt in the 1940 presidential election? The most familiar is what if Truman had decided not to drop the atomic bombs on Japan to end World War II? A comparable historical activity, and one that connects to the topic of the selection of historical material for a course, is to suspend the laws of physics and time travel and ask the question, "If you could have been at any event in history, what would it be?"

Twenty well-known historians were allowed to enter a Wellesian time machine and do just that. *I Wish I'd Been There* is a mix of the obvious and the obscure, the imaginative and the reflective. Well-known choices include the Salem Witch Trials, the assassination of Lincoln, and the March on Washington in 1963 that culminated in the "I Have a Dream" speech. Several of the more imaginative selections were being present when John Brown raided Harper's Ferry, the surrender of Chief Joseph, and the meeting between President Kennedy and his brother Robert when they discussed Vietnam.[13] Two "wish I'd been there" choices not included in the book are whether Edith Boling Galt Wilson was really the president of the United States during her husband Woodrow Wilson's incapacitation and how did U.S. Chief Justice Earl Warren secure a unanimous decision on the *Brown v. Board of Education* case?

More of the "thematic" than "survey" school of historians, Loewen has a more circumscribed list of approximately 35–40 topics that he believes are essential to the understanding of American history. There should be a standard, goal, aim, or purpose for the selection of these topics which could also be labeled as themes or episodes. Loewen believes that developing such a list is a critical exercise for teachers. Unwilling to divulge his own list, he believes that every history teacher needs to make these professional curricular decisions on their own. He has suggested, though, several criteria to gauge historical significance. Four from his list of ten include 1) taking the land, 2) the individual versus the state, 3) technological developments, and 4) historiography.[14] For the episodes selected in this chapter, these additional guidelines and concepts were applied:

- Some realignment or attempt to realign the institutional or structural status quo of the society took place.

- There is a connection to the present.

- Personalities that had an impact on the events are involved.

- The ideas and ideals of democracy and social justice are present.

- The episode could be considered a "change" event in the history of the nation.

- Diversity, broadly defined, was an element of the episode.

- Some element of controversy was involved.

- There was a socio-political component to the episode.

Most, but not all, of these guidelines will be present in the selected emblematic episodes below. This does not mean that every episode selected by history teachers must match these templates. But a number of them should. The four emblematic episodes selected by the author as examples of content selection (one from each century beginning with the 17th and going into the 20th) are: 1) King Philip's War, 2) the creation of the Bill of Rights, 3) Reconstruction, and 4) Franklin Roosevelt's attempt to restructure the Supreme Court in 1937. An overview of the events that comprise the episode will be provided. And a rationale for their inclusion in the content of an American history course—either thematically or within a survey approach—will match the above guidelines and criteria. By happenstance, the episodes progress from the first two being more appropriate for younger adolescents in terms of academic conceptual difficulty to the last two that lend themselves to older adolescents.

Here are four emblematic episodes with a historical description. The events meet most of the criteria set out above as to relevancy and significance to the study of American history. There are also a few pivotal questions at the end of each section around which the subject matter at hand can be connected to adolescents in their examination of our nation's past.

King Philip's War (1676):
Race, Culture, and the Meaning of Nationhood

Loewen's criterion of "taking the land" is essential to any understanding of how America came into being. The treatment of Native Americans, in addition to having ethical and legal implications, has currency in the 21st century. Every continent—even Europe—has grappled with the issue of indigenous peoples. The 17th-century conflict between Europeans and Native Americans, known as King Philip's War, is representative of many episodes and movements in our nation's history. Diversity, colonialism, and militarism all played a part in this event. This selection focuses on eastern Native Americans, often given less space in textbooks and class time in lieu of the western Native Americans, from the Spanish conquistadors to Wounded Knee and beyond. The examination of the eastern Native American nations often neutralizes the stereotypes many adolescents have in their minds from previous learnings.

The son of Wampanoag leader Massasoit, the historically touted "friend to the Pilgrims," Metacom (sometimes referred to as Metacomet) was to lead a series of coordinated assaults on English villages and outposts in 17th-century New England. Schultz and Tougias, in their *King Philip's War: The History and Legacy of America's Forgotten Conflict* and Tebbel and Jennison in their *The American Indian Wars* have suggested that the episode had both a catastrophic and profound impact on both the colonists (Whites) and the indigenous peoples of eastern North

America.[15] Metacom, renamed King Philip by the English, was to lead a coalition of Native Americans in what is present-day New England. Although the war erupted in 1675, the conflict had been brewing for years.

At least six causes can be listed for the outbreak of hostilities. Land rights were a major reason. Both Whites and native peoples wished to occupy the same land. Second, and attached to the first point, was the legal confusion brought about by English settlers, whose idea of land ownership and the Native American belief in hunting, fishing, and other territorial rights were profoundly different. Third, a gradual economic subjection of the native population took place as the English traders made native villages more and more dependent on imported goods from overseas.

While land, legal disputes, and economic issues were the major reasons behind the friction between the two peoples, at least three other secondary causes could be listed. Eastern Native Americans were geographically caught between the Whites to their east and the powerful Iroquois Confederacy to their west. Then there was religion. While not as aggressive as the Catholic Jesuit missionaries of the time, the English did press their faith on the Native Americans undercutting the leadership of both chiefs and medicine men. Finally, there was race. Whites considered the native peoples as inferior.

The conflict did not occur in a flash. In the early 1660s Metacom was courted by the Whites and given, in what they viewed as an honor, the name King Philip. Anglicizing the names of non-majority people in a society is considered today a highly demeaning practice and lent credence to the disdain colonists held for the native culture. (Metacom apparently accepted the name King Philip, though, so it will be used in this narrative.) With all of the issues roiling around at this time, King Philip was extremely patient. Other than patience as a reason for not commencing hostilities, the native leader knew he could not prevail in a struggle against the colonists with only his own Wampanoag nation. A single episode put the events that were to follow into motion. In 1675 John Sassamon, a native man, who had been raised and educated by Whites at Harvard and had become a "white Indian" returned to his own people seemingly rejecting his newly adopted culture. Apparently he was a spy though, who was killed by three Wampanoags and hanged by the English. Although the three alleged killers were his friends, King Philip still held back from any overt hostilities.

Inevitably, another incident occurred. A group of Wampanoags attacked a village, killing and mutilating ten citizens. Although it may have been against Philip's wishes, further attacks took place with villages burned and more deaths occurring. A group of English reinforcements from Boston pursued the Wampanoags and took the first scalps of the conflict. Philip then become fully engaged, leading a series of hit and run raids on the weakly protected western English settlements. At the height of the discord in the summer of 1675 it appeared as though the colonists would be driven from their western land conquests back to the Atlantic seashores.

While the conflict has numerous episodes, the siege of the village of Brookfield took place with a grisly outcome that spiraled into even more violence and atrocities. One settler was beheaded and his head kicked around for sport before being stuck on pole. The Wampanoags then attempted to use fire to destroy the village, which almost succeeded if not for a downpour of rain that doused the blaze. Colonial reinforcements arrived in almost Hollywood movie fashion, saving the small community.

Attacks and counter-attacks continued. Algonquins from the northeast region such as the Nipmucks, Pocumtucks, Narragansetts, and Abenakis joined the war against the English. But Native Americans could not withstand the attacks from the colonial forces who had been joined by their Mohegan and Pequot allies. King Philip's wife and son were captured as the Wampanoag leader cut his hair and escaped. Finally, being cornered with a few of his dwindling supporters, King Philip was shot dead, then drawn, quartered, and beheaded. His head was placed on a gibbet for twenty years as a warning to other potential opposition leaders. King Philip's remains were left to rot in a field.

The result had exacted a heavy toll. Twenty-five English villages, more than half of those in existence when the war commenced, had been destroyed. Several thousand settlers had been killed and a debt amounting to a hundred thousand pounds was placed as the cost for the war. As a percentage of loss, the death rate of the war was nearly twice that of the Civil War two hundred years later and seven times that of World War II. The Native American losses are unknown. The essential loss, though, was their freedom.

King Philip's War slowed the westward progression of the English for several decades. But in the end the Native Americans of New England were disbanded, defeated, and destroyed. Jill Lepore, in her book *The Name of War: King Philip's War and the Origins of American Identity*, maintains that the conflict commenced a never-ending war between Whites and native peoples. She also challenges the use of the word war. Three alternatives she provides are 1) a Puritan Conquest (putting forward the proposition of colonial aggression), 2) Metacom's Rebellion (suggesting an Indian resistance), and 3) an Indian Civil War. In actuality, Lepore concludes, the war included all three.[16] The book, not written with adolescents in mind, contains according to the author "fascinating characters, bizarre happenings, strange tales . . . a murder mystery, an adventure story, and a tale of peril on the high seas."[17]

The lessons and legacy from King Philip's War are several. It became a model for how the colonies and later the United States would deal with native populations—from Tippecanoe to the Trail of Tears to Wounded Knee. The war also teaches that conflicts rarely have a single cause. This war is an excellent example of what historians call multiple causation. That is when more than one reason is needed to explain an event such as war. In addition, there is the paradoxical use of King Philip's name in modern day Bristol, Rhode Island, for streets, schools, motels, and even automotive repair shops.

Lepore concludes her penetrating analysis of this critical event in American history with these thoughts:

> King Philip's War, in all its reincarnations, also traces shifting conceptions of Indian identity—from tribal allegiances to campaigns for political sovereignty to pan-Indianism, and, today, to struggles for cultural survival and political recognition.[18]

Potential questions for students: Was land the only issue that divided the colonists and the Native Americans? Was it possible for the English and the Native Americans to share the land? If so, how? How could King Philip be considered a good leader? Are there possible legacies of this episode in 21st-century America?

The Creation of the Bill of Rights (1789–1791): The Roots of Our Civil Liberties

Some schools still have on the walls of their hallways laminated posters of the major political documents in our nation's history—among them the Declaration of Independence, the Constitution, and the Bill of Rights. Often placed there by civic organizations with their hearts in the right place, they are an attempt to provide youth in the community a way to inculcate good citizenship by reading these documents. There is no data as to how often they are read by students or their effectiveness as a learning tool. But there is also no doubt that the words on those documents have carried monumental meaning in the years since they were first penned.

The first Congress took on the task of drafting a number of amendments to the Constitution that became known as the Bill of Rights.[19] The Bill of Rights has been considered a definition of "inalienable rights" as found in the Declaration of Independence. They were also based upon a fear of English power in the way the crown had abused personal rights in the colonies. Nine of the thirteen states had either bills of rights or common law liberties in their constitutions.

James Madison, so instrumental and influential in the drafting and ratification of the Constitution, at first saw no need for a Bill of Rights, thinking they might limit rather than expand personal rights. He viewed them as redundant, pointless, and mere "parchment barriers" to possible future abuse by authority. (The Red Scare of the 1920s, internment of American citizens during World War II, and then McCarthyism in the 1950s all proved Madison not that prescient.)

Thomas Jefferson, in France at the time and no doubt influenced by his environment, called for some kind of document that would protect the rights of the people. In the end, Madison relented and drafted the Amendments himself, guiding them through Congress. Upon the ratification of the required nine states, they became part of the Constitution by the end of 1791.

The First Amendment protects the freedom of religion, speech, the press, assembly, and to redress of grievances against the government. The First Amendment prohibition against the establishment of religion is compatible with the Constitution which, unlike the Declaration of Independence, is a wholly secular document. In addition to the freedom of religion the amendment also contains the rights of free speech and a free press, to peaceably assemble, and for the people to petition their government for redress of grievances. It has been considered the most important amendment in modern times. The Second Amendment addresses the need for a well-regulated militia and ensures that the right to bear arms shall not be infringed. Due to the framers' inability to draw a distinction between a collective and an individual right to bear arms, this Amendment has been highly controversial in recent times between gun owners and gun control advocates.

The Third Amendment deals with limiting the housing of soldiers in private homes. Prohibitions of unreasonable search and seizure of persons and property are found in the Fourth Amendment. The Fifth Amendment speaks to the rights of those suspected of a crime and prohibits the taking of private property by the government without just compensation. The Sixth Amendment recognizes the rights of criminal defendants and the Seventh Amendment protects the right to a jury trial. The mid-20th century would see a number of court decisions further define these three amendments.

Excessive bails, fines, and cruel and unusual punishments are prohibited in the Eighth Amendment. The Ninth Amendment declares that rights not specifically mentioned in the Constitution were "retained by the people." This suggested an incomplete document that later opened the door for rights not found in the actual text of the Constitution. The right to privacy, upon which the abortion case Roe v. Wade was based, is an example. Finally, the Tenth Amendment reserves to the state or the people all powers not delegated to the federal government or prohibited to the states.

More than one historian has noted that the Bill of Rights generated little attention upon ratification. They literally lay dormant for a hundred years, even ignored. They were, though, to become essential to American freedoms in the 20th century. It appears as though this lack of interest, first occurring in the 18th century, has journeyed to the 21st century. A survey by the John S. and James L. Knight Foundation of 100,000 students, 8,000 teachers, and 500 school administrators was undertaken to determine what teachers and administrators think and what students know about the First Amendment. Only one in twenty-five Americans could list all five freedoms of the First Amendment. The findings showed a lack of knowledge and understanding about the essential elements of the First Amendment which incorporates the five freedoms of religion, speech, press, assembly, and petition. The study also found students less tolerant than teachers and administrators in allowing the expression of unpopular opinions and more than one-third of the students thought the First Amendment goes too far in the rights it guarantees. A sample of the public at large, though, did no better than the students when they were queried. [20]

The First Amendment consists of 45 words:

> Congress shall make no law respecting an establishment of religion, or prohibiting the free exercise thereof; or abridging the freedom of speech, or of the press; or the right of the people to peaceably assemble, and to petition the government for redress of grievances.

Chaltain has advocated several remedies to student disinterest and apparent lack of knowledge of the First Amendment. One way is to have schools honor freedom of expression in their policies and practices rather than rebuking or penalizing students who express their political or religious beliefs. This can be done by encouraging debates in respectful and informed ways making schools a true "free market place of ideas." First Amendment school projects have given students the opportunity to address issues such as dress and speech codes, revisions in the student handbook, and the inclusion of students on the school board. Even allowing students to take part in the textbook adoption process or the hiring of new teachers would demonstrate an openness that conveys the message of inclusion rather than exclusion. Finally, Chaltain suggests the study of media literacy, especially in the area of journalism, and the revival of school newspapers, which have been eliminated at an alarming rate over the past decade.[21]

Actually, the press itself, in addition to educators, has taken on the role of advocate for the First Amendment through education. In addition to the McKnight Foundation, Schurz Communications Inc., the First Amendment Center, and the Newseum (the museum in Washington, DC dedicated to the history of the news media) have collaborated to launch a non-partisan educational initiative called "1 for All"[22] to help Americans better understand the First Amendment. In the upper Midwest the *Aberdeen* (SD) *American News,* a Schurz Communications newspaper, stated in an editorial:

> Those 45 words might be the most important words in the U.S. Constitution. They form the bedrock of our democratic form of government, the diagram for our personal freedoms and the symbol of an open society. They assure us that our government will be responsible to us and will respond to our wishes.[23]

The editorial went on to state that "First Amendment freedoms touch each of our lives in some way nearly every day." Either by voicing our opinions, receiving our news uncensored by the government, or practicing the religion of our choice (or none at all) Americans are relying on the 45 words written over 225 years ago. This South Dakota newspaper concluded by calling on Americans to put into practice the rights in this amendment by standing up for others, talking about freedom of faith in places of worship, and exploring and sharing freedom-themed books with friends, family, and colleagues.[24]

Adolescents can connect to the Bill of Rights by providing stories of children and youth who were denied their First Amendment Rights. Gay Ivey has identified two cases where Bill of Rights cases directly involved teenagers and the First Amendment. One was the right to carry a purse with a Confederate battle flag on it and the other dealt with the right of students to post signs with religious messages on a high school football field.[25] An additional example is the Eighth Amendment's proscription against cruel and unusual punishment as applied to sentencing juveniles to life imprisonment with no possibility of parole. In 2009 there were approximately 2,500 lifers in U.S. prisons charged while under the age of eighteen. Of 109 children whose offenses were not murder, 74 were fourteen years old or younger when the crime was committed and 77 of the 109 were in Florida with 84% of them being Black.[26] With high-profile school shootings in public settings such as Jonesboro, Arkansas, and Columbine, Colorado, such cases are highly relevant to adolescents. Even a classroom discussion of the definitions of the words "cruel" and "unusual" could lead to new learning and demonstrate that the meaning of some Constitutional amendments continues to be open to debate.

With the framers of the Constitution well aware of the potential conflict with a state church via their experience with England, the establishment of religion clause in the First Amendment has been central in this nation's history. The spectrum was wide in terms of religious practice in relation to the government in 18th century America. The religious gamut ran from established churches in several states to dissenters who wished to practice their own religion to those with no religious beliefs at all. Thomas Jefferson, probably the most outspoken Founder on religion, saw established churches as infringements on liberty. He is reported to have said, "If a man believes in one god or fifty gods he neither picks my pocket nor breaks my leg."

The debate on religion continues to this day with those who believe the United States was founded as a Christian nation to those who view the establishment of religion clause as meaning a strict separation between church and state. Both sides find support with Presidents George Washington and John Adams proclaiming national thanksgiving or prayer days and President James Madison's refusal to uphold such proclamations. Issues of religious freedom remain germane today to both adolescents and adults. They include the display of religious object or images such as the Ten Commandments or a nativity scene and the use of tax-funded vouchers to pay for religious schools. Another potential freedom of religion issue to be debated is whether a police officer can be compelled to provide security to casinos or abortion clinics if the practices taking place in these edifices go against their religious beliefs.[27]

A strategy to make the Bill of Rights relevant to students is to use agree/disagree statements that are connected to certain amendments. Examples include: If a person is suspected of a serious crime, the police should be allowed to hold that person in jail until enough evidence can be found to officially charge them. (Sixth Amendment) The right to bear arms is different today than it was in colonial times. (Second Amendment) The death penalty by chemical injection or electrocution is a cruel and unusual punishment. (Fifth Amendment) The media, such as newspapers, television, and the Internet, should be allowed to report on any story even if the government believes it is harmful to our nation. (First Amendment) It is acceptable for police to use new technology that can capture a conversation in a room after the individuals have left. (Fifth or Sixth Amendments or none?)

The use of such opinion questions relates to various opinion polls in the past that have found that Americans believe in the Bill of Rights as an idea or concept, but when given specific examples a majority really do not support certain civil liberties. This approach can be used to initiate inquiry into civil liberties and its historical context, helping students better understand what these freedoms mean in current American society.

Finally, there are materials that facilitate such discussions. The Opposing Viewpoints Series from Greenhaven Press has a volume titled *Civil Liberties: Opposing Viewpoints*. In a pro and con format between scholars and civil liberties organizations a number of issues related to the Bill of Rights are debated. These include freedom of expression issues such as restricting free speech or hate speech, flag burning, and legislation regarding pornography. Also debated are drug tests of student athletes, criminal investigation practices, school prayer, and finally a plethora of issues arising from the world of the Internet.[28] The Bill of Rights and the civil liberties that are drawn from the first ten Amendments are a rich field for student exploration with highly relevant topics and a seemingly endless source of new ones each year.

Questions that could be used with students in exploring the meaning and interpretations of the Bill of Rights could include: What is the purpose of a constitutional amendment? How does a document more than 200 years old still remain relevant today? Which three of the first ten Amendments are the most important and why? Which one of the ten is least controversial today and why? In the first 130 years of our nation's history we had nineteen amendments—in the next 60 years we have had only eight and none since 1992. What might be the reason for fewer amendments in recent years?

Reconstruction (1865–1877):
The Ongoing Legacy of the Civil War

Arguably, the Civil War was the major event in our nation's history. But as with many military episodes, the aftermath became an equally important part of American history. Historian Alan Brinkley has written that "Few periods in the history of the United States have produced as much bitterness or created such enduring controversy as the era of Reconstruction."[29] Attempts are made to neatly enclose Reconstruction within the years 1865 to 1877—often by textbooks. In fact, if the case can be made that race is the most important issue in our history, then it could be maintained that the process of Reconstruction continues today. The roots of current racial conflict and debate can be found in the legacy of Reconstruction by Jim Crow laws, the "separate but equal" Supreme Court ruling of 1896, the Civil Rights movement, affirmative action, and charges of "reverse discrimination." Even the way the nation is responding to its first Black president is all part and parcel of the period we label Reconstruction. In addition, from this period can be traced stereotypes about Blacks and the legacy of the 13th, 14th, and 15th Amendments to the Constitution. And, there was a presidential impeachment during Reconstruction.

Reconstruction commenced almost as soon as the military conflict ceased. The central question of Reconstruction was first thought to be "How would the Confederate states be returned to full and equal standing with other states in the Union?" Before his assassination, Lincoln had argued that the states had never left the Union. But it soon became apparent that bringing formerly enslaved African Americans into full and equal citizenship would emerge as the major goal of Reconstruction. Vice President Andrew Johnson entered the White House on Lincoln's death but he was both intellectually limited and temperamentally unsuited for the office. A series of steps were undertaken to bring the states that had not really left the Union—Johnson's view as well as Lincoln's—back into the Union. These included calling state conventions, invalidating secessionist ordinances, mandating the ratification of the 13th Amendment that ended slavery, and the creation of the Freedman's Bureau to assist Blacks in entering into full political citizenship. Operating at cross-purposes were Southern legislatures that passed Black Codes which were a mix of limited rights and severe restrictions on the former slaves in the South.

In Washington, Congress was controlled by the Radical Republicans. With single-minded purpose they focused on obtaining and maintaining the rights of the newly emancipated and enfranchised Black citizens. The "radical" moniker was earned by their strong beliefs in how the South should be dealt with during the post-war period. The Radical Republicans came out of the anti-slavery movement. House Leader Thaddeus Stevens and Massachusetts Senator Charles Sumner became the faces of Radical Republicanism. Battles between Congress and President Johnson consumed the year 1866 with a series of vetoes and veto overrides. The 14th Amendment to the Constitution was ratified in 1868, promising citizenship in addition to "due process of law" for any attempt to deny persons of life, liberty, and property. Another phrase from that amendment, "equal protection under the law," would be applied to numerous court rulings in the future. Congressional, not presidential, Reconstruction proceeded with ten of the eleven Confederate states being placed into five military districts. Further restrictions were placed on presidential authority and when Johnson attempted to remove Secretary of War Stanton from the office he was impeached, surviving conviction in the Senate by a single vote. When it appeared to the Radical Republicans that the Supreme Court was going to limit their plans, especially in the military arena, they pressured the highest court in the land by threatening to pass a bill that would require a two-thirds vote of the justices to overrule a law of Congress. The Court backed down.

All states had regained admission to the Union by 1870. Ratification of the 15th Amendment, which forbade denial of citizenship on the grounds of race, color, or previous servitude, was a sticking point for Georgia, but it finally followed the other secessionist states and rejoined the Union. What could be called White Terror ensued in the South with the creation of the Ku Klux Klan and other paramilitary groups. Blacks did play a central role in state legislatures and two Blacks were elected to the United States Senate and 14 served in the House of Representatives. Radical state constitutions did much for the former slaves in terms of rights and education. But the ongoing tension between Blacks and Whites in the South increased as state by state Republican control faded away, disappearing almost entirely after the election of 1876.

The presidency of Ulysses S. Grant, from 1869 to 1877, was a failure. A lack of leadership, several scandals, and an economic downturn in 1873 made the issue of Black rights in the South diminish further and further from the nation's mind. The presidential election of 1876 brought to office Rutherford B. Hayes. Under what has been called the "Compromise of 1877" federal troops were withdrawn from the South in return for pledges from the former Confederacy of fair treatment for Blacks. The troops left, but just actions toward Blacks would not occur. One by one, Southern Republican governments fell as Northerners lost interest in the fate of Blacks in the South.

The legacy of Reconstruction was mixed, which has led to the highly contentious historical controversy. African Americans did benefit some with a redistribution of income and land. And Southern Whites did rebound to some extent economically within ten years. For a conquered people, they fared well—some very well. And yet Reconstruction was also tragic. While the Confederate states had rejoined the Union, the first attempt at dealing with the race issue had failed and it would be a century before another attempt to address the question was made in earnest.

Reconstruction is one of the best examples in American history of historiography—the history of what historians have said about individuals, events, or periods in our past. In selecting Reconstruction as an emblematic episode students are able to observe how the past has been created, framed, and changed. Reconstruction demonstrates how the historian's craft is carried out and how a major experience in our history has been both represented and misrepresented. Therefore, the historiography of the Reconstruction can be as instructive to students learning history as the event itself. Historians David Kennedy and Lizabeth Cohen concur. They have written that historically "Few topics have triggered as much intellectual warfare as the 'dark and bloody ground' of Reconstruction."[30]

In the early 1900s historian William A. Dunning provided a sympathetic reading of the period by siding with White Southerners. In his view they were punished by vindictive Northern Radical Republicans who were both corrupt and oppressive in the pursuit of their plan. Howard Beale in the 1920s added to the "Dunning Thesis" by providing a motive for Radical Republican exploitation of the South—by advocating Black voting rights they could politically make inroads into the solid Democratic South. According to Beale, the unfortunate president at the time, Andrew Johnson, was punished with impeachment by standing up against the Radical Republicans.

National Association for the Advancement of Colored People (NAACP) co-founder W.E.B. Du Bois provided an antidote to these interpretations in 1935 by viewing Reconstruction as a valiant, though failed attempt, to extend rights to the long disenfranchised Blacks in the South. Kennedy and Cohen write that after World War II Kenneth Stampp and Black historian John Hope Franklin endorsed and added to the Du Bois thesis that the Reconstruction was both "radical and noble." However, while being genuine in motive, its accomplishments were flawed and tragic, although leading to eventual victories in the 20th century through the Civil Rights movement. And Steven Hahn in his book *A Nation Under Our Feet: Black Political Struggles in the Rural South from Slavery to the Great Migration* credits the courage and assertiveness of African Americans in creating their own new opportunities through family, religion, and education.[31]

While Southerners became the target of historians of the revisionist view of Reconstruction, the North was not left entirely free from blame. William Gillette in his book *Retreat from Reconstruction, 1869–1879*, reminds us that Northern racism was fully evident during this period. In addition there was opposition toward Black suffrage. Black rights would be supported by Northerners if Blacks stayed in the South. The Radical Republicans, although in control of Congress, were in the end unable to protect and sustain Black rights in the South. The federal troops, when they left the South, moved West to subdue and subjugate the Native Americans (Sitting Bull and Custer fought the Battle of the Little Big Horn in 1876), and then returned to the North to quell and even suppress the labor movement. For Gillette, Reconstruction ended because Black freedom could not have been sustained without more violence on a Southern society unwilling to live alongside Blacks as equals. But violence did continue for another century in the South, and sometimes the North, at the expense of Blacks.[32]

The work of historian Eric Foner has extended the previously cited work of Du Bois and Hahn by viewing Reconstruction as both a social and political process, not just political. In his 1988 *Reconstruction: America's Unfinished Revolution, 1863–1877*, Foner wrote that Reconstruction can only be judged a failure as an effort to secure Black rights as citizens and free laborers. It opened the economic door and remains an unfinished process. In his 2006 *Forever Free: The Story of Emancipation and Reconstruction* Foner focuses on the enormity of slavery both economically and politically. Only then can the radicalism of emancipation and Reconstruction be appreciated. While giving Lincoln and the Radical Republicans credit for advancing what he calls a "revolution," he sees African Americans as the spark for that revolutionary drive. It is revolutionary because the 13th Amendment abolished slavery without gradualism as it had in the North or by compensation to the slave owners. As Hahn, in a review of Foner's *Forever Free*, writes, "His (Foner's) picture depicts Black men, and Black women, transforming political skills they had developed under slavery and, in the process, creating the possibilities for the first genuine democracy that the South ever had.[33]

Foner has even weighed in on the misconstruing of Reconstruction by filmmaker Ken Burns' PBS *Civil War* series. While the content of the series was the war, Foner has written that "for all his cinematic talents, Burns had chosen to reinforce a vision of the war as essentially a family quarrel among White Americans, and to celebrate the road to reunion without considering the price paid for national reconciliation."[34] For Foner and others, as with most wars, the nation may have gotten the war "right," but it got the peace wrong.

There has been debate over whether Reconstruction ended when the federal troops were withdrawn from the South in 1877 or when Blacks were disenfranchised a decade later. That debate is not as important to Foner as Reconstruction being viewed as the beginning of political democracy, citizenship, and social justice for Blacks. The movement that began in the nineteenth century would come to fruition in the twentieth century with the civil rights revolution. And as with Reconstruction first, the advancement of civil rights would be led by African Americans and remake the nation.[35]

The historiographic debate then becomes a tool for students to explore how history, which now seems to many adolescents (and adults for that matter) immutable, is actually malleable. Not that every opinion carries the same weight or the same import. Those judgments are also part of the study of history and the work of historians. But Reconstruction provides a useful example of how the process of history is carried out and conclusions are reached.

Questions that will lead to the creation of lessons on Reconstruction include: Can a case be made that Reconstruction was as important as the Civil War? Were there options other than military occupation to resolve the issue of Reconstruction? Why have the interpretations of historians about the legacy of Reconstruction changed so frequently over the years? How did both the North and the South need to be reconstructed? Is Reconstruction still going on today?

Franklin D. Roosevelt and the Supreme Court (1937): Constitutional or Political Crisis?

The dispute, controversy, or clash—these three terms and many more have been used to describe what occurred in 1937 between the president of the United States and the Supreme Court—is one of the more dramatic episodes in American history. It is best known by the phrase "Franklin Roosevelt's attempt to 'pack the court'" which in itself could be considered a biased expression for the episode. It explores the workings of the least known branch of government, the Supreme Court.

But it is also about more than just the Supreme Court. The actual inter-relationship of the three branches of government is seen in this episode at probably its most stressful and high-stakes points in history. The three branches of government (executive, legislative, and judicial), their particular and enunciated powers, and the separation of those powers are basic to our understanding of how our government functions. Examples in history can be given of how any two of these entities interrelate in the Founders' system of "checks and balances." Some of these include judicial review (the judicial and the legislative), the law-making process (executive and legislative), and the power of appointment (executive and judicial). But it is rare when all three branches of the government encounter and interact with each other in a single episode. This occurred in the 1937 series of events between President Franklin D. Roosevelt, Congress, and the Supreme Court which began over the constitutionality of New Deal legislation.

During the Great Depression, the most severe economic downturn in American history, the actual survival of the nation's democratic system of government was thought by many to be at stake. With 25% of the nation's workforce unemployed, with farming and industry at historic lows in terms of profitability, the economic policies—or lack of them—on the part of Herbert Hoover seemed lifeless and obsolete. Hoover the man and the leader seemed both insensitive and unresponsive.

The election of the buoyant and energetic Franklin D. Roosevelt in 1932 brought hope to the nation. In a series of activist and experimental legislative moves by Roosevelt and Congress, known collectively as the New Deal, the nation slowly began to respond. Based on a series of programs known by their acronyms and referred to as "alphabet soup agencies," government assumed a new and forceful role in American life. With Democratic majorities in each house of Congress, Roosevelt appeared to have a free hand in moving the country in a new direction. Then the Supreme Court made its presence felt. Two pivotal, yet controversial programs—the National Recovery Act and the Agricultural Adjustment Act—were declared unconstitutional in 1936. A number of other acts, including state minimum wage laws, were also discarded by the highest court in the land.[36]

But this battle, and a battle it was, had to do with power. The rationale from the Court through its decisions seemed to be that the New Deal experiment had gone too far, too fast. This had occurred by the executive branch delegating too much authority to the legislative branch—and quite a bit to itself as well. The response from FDR and other progressives was that the Court was out of step with the times. New times and new problems called for new thinking and new responses. Roosevelt even used the term "horse and buggy" to capture his thoughts about the lack of understanding by the Supreme Court as to the monumental economic issues facing the nation. This in part was extrapolated from the fact that the Court, with an average age of 71 in 1935, was the oldest in the nation's history. There were also no retirements in sight. The term "Nine Old Men" soon found its way into the nation's lexicon.

To many there seemed to be an imbalance within the three branches of government, and the Supreme Court appeared to yield the power and the final word. With New Deal legislation being declared unconstitutional, and new legislation being proposed by FDR in jeopardy of a similar fate, a number of ideas emerged to limit the Supreme court's power, vis-à-vis the legislative and executive branches. Even the practice of judicial review that John Marshall asserted in *Marbury v. Madison* was questioned. "Where in the Constitution does it say the Supreme Court has the power to do that?" critics asked.

There were a number of remedies proposed to counter this real and perceived imbalance. Legislators could impeach judges, withhold funding, "pack" or add members to the Court, or restrict the Court's jurisdiction. Constitutional amendments were suggested, several in fact, but the ratification process was viewed as too slow. Senator Robert LaFollette, sympathetic to court reform, thought changing the Constitution every time progressive legislation was needed was unworkable. The idea of packing the Court had been raised in several newspapers two years before FDR put his plan forward. The number ranged from two additional members to as many as six.

The actual number of nine justices on the Supreme Court is not stipulated in the Constitution. The power to set the number of justices on the nation's highest court rests with Congress. In 1789 Congress placed the number at six. In 1801 the number fell to five. Then, in 1837, at the end of Andrew Jackson's two terms, the number was increased to nine. Lincoln, needing the Court's support for his war policies, was able to persuade Congress to increase the number to ten only to have it fall to seven at one point during Reconstruction. President Grant, unhappy over the Court's ruling that paper money was unconstitutional, got Congress to increase the numbers to overturn this ruling, which the Court did. Set at nine in 1869, this is where the number had rested as the battle lines were drawn in the 1930s. The number of justices sitting on the high bench, it appeared, could change.

On February 5, 1937, coming off a historic landslide election in 1936 and at the height of his popularity with the American public, FDR decided to make his move against the Court. He put forth the idea of asking Congress for legislation that would allow the President to name a new justice for each justice over the age of 70 who would not retire. The first (and fallacious) reason given by Roosevelt was that the Court was behind on its cases and needed more justices to accomplish its work. Chief Justice Charles Evans Hughes next produced evidence that the Court was not behind in its work. The issue of age was next used by Roosevelt to express the need for justices who were more in touch with the needs (economic and social) of the time. That argument was countered by the fact that Justice Louis Brandeis, a liberal in his early 80s, was the oldest member of the Court. A final underlying reason was the worry that with so many 5–4 decisions, government could not function on the impulses of one or two judges. With the "Four Horsemen"—the solid conservative block of justices—and three reliable liberals, the close decisions were often in the hands of Chief Justice Charles Evans Hughes or Associate Justice Owen Roberts, both appointed by Republican presidents and who voted with the conservatives most of the time.

The actual reason had been given by Roosevelt when he first announced the plan in February of 1937. "A constant and systematic addition of younger blood," he had said, "will vitalize the courts and better equip them to recognize and apply the essential concepts of justice in the light of the needs of an ever-changing world." The real reason was a difference in judicial philosophy and FDR saw his New Deal was being destroyed by what he viewed as an out-of-touch judicial branch of government. Was the Constitution a "living document" to meet changing needs or was it an immutable text set in stone by the Framers?

The reaction to the court packing plan was sizeable and significant. The conflict was as large, if not larger, than Wilson's League of Nations fight in 1919–

1920 or even, some thought, Reconstruction. At a time when dictatorships were flourishing around the world, the irony was whether FDR's idea, if passed, would place too much power in the hands of one man. Always ready with an apt analogy, Roosevelt responded that when a team of three well-matched horses work together as a team then "the field would be plowed." If one horse lies down or plunges off in another direction, "the field would not be plowed." The uncooperative horse did not need to be identified. An example of the obtuseness of the Court is reflected in the words and actions of the reactionary and racist Justice James McReynolds (he hated Blacks and Jews and called Roosevelt "that cripple in the White House"). He described the Depression as a "temporary inconvenience" and said citizens needed to pay more attention "to their obligations than their so-called rights." One journalist called McReynolds' performances despicable, unsympathetic, and just plain mean.

But the attack on the plan was strong and led by disaffected Democrats, not Republicans. Progressive Democratic Montana Senator Burton Wheeler, followed by a number of Democrats, led the charge against the plan. FDR's own Vice-President, John Nance Garner of Texas, did not support him, and as usual the country's newspapers, the majority anti-Roosevelt, were against the plan. The task of getting the court bill through the Senate fell to the Majority Leader Joe Robinson of Arkansas. Although a strong FDR-man, he was conservative and probably not as sympathetic to the New Deal as his votes indicated. To complicate the matter, Roosevelt, in a political deal made years earlier, had promised Robinson the next open seat on the Court. Now wishing to place a dependable liberal on the Court, Roosevelt was not sure Robinson was that man.

Then, in a series of events that could have been taken from a novelistic rendering of politics and history, the story took an unexpected turn. First, the Court reversed itself on a case involving a minimum wage law in Washington State. Elsie Parrish had sued for $219 in back wages due to her from her job as a hotel chambermaid. In a 5–4 decision, Owen Roberts changed sides and decided in Parrish's favor. He had just recently voted the opposite way in a similar case. A saying attributed to no one, but claimed by many, was that a "switch in time, saved nine"—a play on the eighteenth-century adage "a stitch in time, saves nine." This was followed by a series of other pro-New Deal decisions by the court. The reason for Roberts' change of heart was never made clear, but many give Chief Justice Hughes credit for persuading his younger brethren to shift his vote. After these decisions some thought Hughes had read the tea leaves and used his influence to save the Court and maybe the country.

By the time the Court adjourned in June 1937, it had not struck down a single one of the dozen New Deal measures it heard. And then, 76 year-old Willis Van Devanter, one of the conservative "Four Horsemen," announced his retirement. Although events had moved in his direction, Roosevelt, never one who liked to lose at anything and unsure of the "conversions" of Roberts and Hughes, still wanted his Court bill. Pushing Majority Leader Joe Robinson, the likelihood of passage became slimmer as June turned to July. Then, Robinson dropped dead with a heart attack. Roosevelt got a minor bill that reorganized the lower federal courts, but there was no change in the makeup of the Supreme Court. On Constitution Day in September FDR still claimed victory. Additional appointments would follow. By 1942, Roosevelt had appointed seven of the nine sitting justices and before the end of his presidency he named one more. Many said he had lost the battle with the Court, but in the end had won the war.

The autopsies of the famous "Court Packing Plan" have been many and ongoing. Jeff Shesol has written that Roosevelt was overconfident, impatient, and politically out of tune with both the public and politicians. When asked after the plan had failed if he regretted it, FDR said no, it was inevitable. But Shesol also saw "The Court at long last, had reconciled itself to the twentieth century." The New Deal had lost its momentum and Roosevelt had squandered his mandate.[37]

Burt Solomon seems to agree with many of the newspapers of the time—it was the worst drubbing a president had taken since Woodrow Wilson's attempt to take the United States into the League of Nations. Yet he balances that tough assessment with the ideas that when the Nazis were sweeping across Europe, FDR had learned his lesson by allowing the public reaction to develop before he took the issue to the people. The "spectacular failure of trying to pack the Supreme Court was balanced by his performance when the stakes were much, much higher."[38] David Kennedy believed that the "high pressure front that had been building for months" did have an impact on Hughes and Roberts. Even before his own appointments began, Roosevelt had brought about a "momentous judicial transformation" and in countering the Court-packing plan Hughes and Roberts gave birth to what has rightly become known as the "Constitutional Revolution of 1937."[39]

Roosevelt biographer James McGregor Burns, in evaluations more than fifty years apart, has found the president's plan not hastily conceived, and mild considering the alternatives being put forth. And that stubbornness was a quality that had served FDR well in the past. "Certainly Roosevelt made mistakes in the court fight, but so did his opponents. While calling what happened a "stunning defeat," Burns blamed the method more than the plan.[40] In a more recent recounting of the episode, Burns found the devious "efficiency" charge by Roosevelt to have hobbled the president, when he should have bluntly attacked the Court on ideological grounds. FDR should have broadened his fight rather than narrowing it, thereby demonstrating a lack of courage in contrast to fights both before and after the Court battle.[41]

Many have considered the court packing episode pivotal in American history. It has continued, 75 years later, with a stream of articles and books. A recent defender of Roosevelt's court packing move has been professor of law and litigator Barry Friedman.[42] What FDR attempted, according to Friedman, was well within reason especially in the context of public opinion and the path the court had taken in response to the New Deal. First, he points out that there should have been no surprise that Roosevelt was going to take some kind of action against the Court. He had made clear, or as clear as Roosevelt made things, that the Constitution, in his view, was a "living" document. By this he meant it was open to modern interpretations to meet the needs of modern times. In addition to words like "living," the president and his supporters employed terms like flexible, adaptable, progressive, and liberal.

Second, if Owen Roberts had not changed his vote, then Roosevelt would have prevailed with his plan, supported by a public that may have finally seen the Court as too out of touch with modern problems. In 1936, a year before the crisis, Friedman quotes a poll that indicated the public supported a mandatory retirement age for justices. The move by Roosevelt was clearly political to bring about change in a court that was churning out 5–4 decisions (albeit eventually in the New Deal's favor) and could "switch" back again if the pressure from the executive branch ceased. Years later Owen Roberts said that it would have been difficult for the court to have resisted the popular urge for change in the court's pronouncements.

Third, why there was a switch is less important, writes Friedman, than the fact that there was a switch. Friedman posits that if the court had not changed direction (and Van Devanter not retired) then the public would have been open to either FDR's plan or some other restraint or disciplining of the court by Congress and the president. And then there were the votes of Hughes to the liberal side against the "Four Horsemen." "For all of history's frequent talk about the independence of the judiciary," writes Friedman, "that independence exists only at public sufferance." The lesson to be taken from the great "court packing" episode was that judicial decisions dare not "wander far from the mainstream of American belief about the meaning of the Constitution."

Michael O'Donnell, writing in the liberal pages of *The Nation*, sees the move by Roosevelt as too political, coming close to harming judicial independence which is a cornerstone of the separation of powers. O'Donnell concedes Friedman's point that justices are influenced by politics through public opinion. But he views Roosevelt's plan "to browbeat the justices like a group of freshmen Congress members until they got in line" as far too political. An independent judiciary does not mean zero political interference, and when the Court tries to stop a president, O'Donnell believes that the Court "should expect some heat." His opinion is that using the smallest amount of interference is the best policy in that the separation of powers was put in place as "an excellent wedge against tyranny."[43]

Questions that can be raised with older adolescents from this episode include: Is it always possible for all three branches of government to work together? Does our system of government ever allow one branch to dictate over the other branches? What other steps might Roosevelt, the Congress, and/or the Court have taken to avoid this encounter? What role does personality play in politics? Is age a factor in terms of competency for judges and politicians? Was Roosevelt a "winner or loser" in this battle? Would it be possible now or in the future for two of the three branches of government to reach an impasse on issues such as health care, immigration, energy, or homeland security? Is the Constitution a "living" document or is it a document "set in time" by the Framers? If you were going to re-create the Supreme Court, what would it look like?

Final Issues in Content Selection

In any discussion of content selection, the thought and work of the late historian and social activist Howard Zinn must be considered. While Zinn wrote textbooks, he was very much anti-textbook. Zinn's view of content selection was not in the mainstream of historians, past and present. And while Zinn's choices included people and issues and events, they were different people, issues, and events than are seen in most course outlines and standards. Eric Foner has written that Friedrich Nietzsche said there were three approaches to writing history: the monumental, the antiquarian, and the critical. Nietzsche's monumental history would be the celebration of great men and great events. Zinn took the alternate path of the critical approach offering profound and differing views. He wrote of "ordinary Americans' struggles for justice, equality, and power," writes Foner.[44]

Foner has also been critical of Zinn, calling his view "oversimplified" with a strong tendency toward the Manichaean dichotomy of good and bad, light and dark. The critical approach does not necessarily have to be a negative perception of American history. Zinn celebrated the social movements and radicals such as Frederick Douglass, Susan B. Anthony, and Eugene V. Debs.[45] The title of his book (he probably did not view it as a textbook) was *A People's History of the United States*. What else would he have called it? He made no attempt to demonstrate objectivity. History was partial because choices are made as to what is included and excluded in addition to what is promoted and what is criticized. Zinn made clear his intentions. In his *A People's History* he wrote:

> I prefer to try to tell the story of the discovery of America from the viewpoint of the Arawaks, of the Constitution from the standpoint of the slave, of Andrew Jackson as seen by the Cherokees, of the Mexican War as seen by the deserting soldiers of Scott's army, of the rise of industrialism as seen by the young women in the Lowell textile mills, of the Spanish-American War as seen by the Cubans,

the conquest of the Philippines as by the black soldiers on Luzon, the First World war as seen by socialists, the Second World War as seen by Blacks in Harlem.[46]

Bigelow has written that in spite of the perceived focus of Zinn on America's detriments, defeats, and dreadful decisions at times, his "history is both more honest than traditional histories but also more hopeful." Bigelow quotes Zinn as saying: "To be hopeful in bad times is not just foolishly romantic. It is also based on the fact that human history is a history not only of cruelty, but also of compassion, sacrifice, courage, kindness."[47] Even the Progressive Movement was not Zinn's kind of movement. It protected capitalism at the expense of the more people-oriented socialist initiatives. More to his liking was the New Deal, based on people wanting a new direction from the leadership of the 1920s with programs like Social Security. Another example is the legislation of the 1960s that attempted to assure equal protection under the law for Blacks and also Medicare and Medicaid to assist the healthcare needs of the elderly and the poor. For Zinn these were victories for the people's movement, not accomplishments of the great leaders of the time.[48]

One additional area to consider in the history curriculum selection process is how to deal with recent events. There has been a conventional point of demarcation in many college level and Advanced Placement courses when American history is taught. Whether in courses on the college level or by semesters in middle school and high school, the division of the American story has usually fallen on or near the period of Reconstruction. This artifice has been in place for at least fifty years. With an additional fifty years of history "in the books," it is more difficult for teachers, scholars, or even textbook publishers to maintain this arbitrary partition.

Not only is this "split" in American history artificial, it is becoming more and more difficult to defend for either pedagogical or subject matter reasons. Consider the past fifty years:

- the presidencies of John Kennedy and Lyndon Johnson

- social and cultural changes of the 1960s

- Vietnam

- Watergate

- the conservative political revolution of Ronald Reagan

- the fall of communism

- the presidencies of Bill Clinton and George W. Bush

- the current era of terrorism and multiple wars in the Middle East

- financial malfeasance, economic uncertainty, and the Great Recession

- the election of the first Black president, Barack Obama

This is a vast amount of history that has become impossible to "shoehorn" into a predetermined timeframe or structure—call it course, semester, or school year.

This is not to suggest that any history before the twentieth century needs to be abridged or deleted. It is to note that a rationale for increased attention to recent history can be made. Teachers and historians are beginning to examine this realignment. Sean Wilentz and Julian E. Zelizer have written about the importance of recent history and why curricula have shied away from repositioning traditional course parameters in American history courses. One reason is the belief that assessing any historical event or person needs "time" to truly determine what is important and what is not. A case in point is Harry Truman. Held in low estimation by both the public and historians when he left office, his reappraisal and revival in the 1970s to "top ten" status among great and near-great presidents has been used to confirm the hazards of judgments made too soon. Wilentz and Zelizer also contend that the best work on some periods of history, like the New Deal, was written soon after the events occurred. They have also, albeit on the college level, taught courses on George W. Bush, out of office less than two years.[49]

An additional line of reasoning to incorporate more recent history into classes for adolescents is what might be termed content currency. An adolescent deep into the second four-year term of a president will probably not remember that president's predecessor. But the adolescent may indeed remember events that have taken place during the last four or five years. Any connection to real experiences on the part of the student assists in the teaching of new material. By making the world just that much more real to the student will make the past more comprehensible. Teaching recent history can accomplish that goal.

Finally, the issue of textbook selection and its impact on the history curriculum. Politics have most definitely entered the process. It is quite reminiscent of the early attempts to write standards for history that were described earlier in this chapter. The most high profile episodes of recent times have been the battle in the Milwaukee, Wisconsin, public schools and in the state of Texas. The debate is almost always drawn over political differences that reflect the red state/blue state political division in which America finds itself in the 21st century. On the political left are those who believe that social movements and injustices need to be taught. These would include the labor, women's, environmental, and peace movements. In addition, racism needs to be fully addressed in all U.S. history courses. Conservatives advocate more traditional history curricula that show the more positive aspects of the American story—presidential successes, the strong role the United States has played in world affairs, the economic power of the capitalist system, and the role of religion in the nation's life.[50] The point of the textbook selection process is wider than what gets in and what gets left out. It is about how we go about making decisions that impact youth and how we do so in a democratic way.

Every teacher needs to make the critical curricular decisions about the selection of history content in their own classrooms. Choosing to teach from a survey or thematic approach to deciding which periods of history to teach is not a mundane exercise to be taken lightly. Neither is the politicalization of the textbook adoption process. All of these elements are essential and inescapable responsibilities for each and every teacher in the history classroom as they go about the work of content selection.

Endnotes

1   VanSledright, Bruce. *In Search of America's Past*. New York: Teachers College Press, 2002. 140.

2   Edinger, Monica, and Stephanie Fins. *Far Away and Long Ago: Young Historians in the Classroom*. York: Stenhouse Publishers, 1998. 7.

3   Nash, Gary, Charlotte Crabtree, and Ross Dunn. *History on Trial: Culture Wars and the Teaching of the Past*. New York: Vintage, 2000.

4   Marshal, J. Dan, James T. Sears, Louise Anderson Allen, Patrick A. Roberts, and William H. Schubert. *Turning Points in Curriculum: A Contemporary American Memoir*. 2nd ed. Upper Saddle River: Pearson/Merrill Prentice Hall, 2006. 226–30.

5   See <http://nchs.ucla.edu/> for the *National Center for History in the Schools* website.

6   National Council for the Social Studies. *Expectations of Excellence: Curriculum Standards for Social Studies*. Washington, DC: NCSS, 1994.

7   For an example see <http://www.arkansased.org/testing/assessment.html> for the *Arkansas Department of Education* website on standards and assessment.

8   Barton, Paul E. "National Standards: To be or Not to Be." *Educational Leadership* 67. 7 (2010): 22–29.

9   Van Til, William. *My Way of Looking at It: An Autobiography*. San Francisco: Caddo Gap Press, 1996. 124–29.

10 Beineke, John A. "William Van Til: The Consistent Progressive." Ed. Kridel, Craig, Robert V. Bullough, Jr. and Paul Shaker. *Teachers and Mentors: Profiles of Distinguished Twentieth-Century Professors of Education*. New York: Garland Publishing, 1996. 225–232.

11 Epstein, Terrie. "Research on Teaching and Learning History: Teacher Professionalization and Student Cognition and Culture." Ed. Diana Turk, Rachel Mattson, Terrie Epstein, and Robert Cohen. *Teaching U.S. History: Dialogues among Social Studies Teachers and Historians*. New York: Routledge, 2010. 197–98.

12 Axelrod, Alan, and Charles Phillips. *What Every American Should Know About American History: 200 Events That Shaped the Nation.* Holbrook: Adams Media Corporation, 1992.

13 Byron, Hollinshead, ed. *I Wish I'd Been There: Twenty Historians Bring to Life Dramatic Events That Changed America.* New York: Doubleday, 2006.

14 Loewen, James W. *Teaching What Really Happened: How to Avoid the Tyranny of Textbooks & Get Students Excited About Doing History.* New York: Teachers College Press, 2010. 19–22.

15 The description of this episode is drawn from Schultz, Eric B. and Michael J. Tougias. *King Philip's War: The History and Legacy of America's Forgotten Conflict.* Woodstock; The Countryman Press, 1999; and Tebbel, John and Keith Jennison. *The American Indian Wars.* London: Phoenix Press, 1988. A more recent treatment of King Philip's War, demonstrating its staying power as a pivotal event in American history is Mandell, Daniel R. *King Philip's War: Colonial Expansion, Native Resistance, and the End of Indian Sovereignty.* Washington, D.C.: The John Hopkins University Press, 2010.

16 Lepore, Jill. *The Name of War: King Philip's War and the Origins of American Identity.* New York: Random House, 1998. xv.

17 Lepore, xxii.

18 Lepore, 240.

19 This narrative is drawn from Foner, Eric. *Give Me Liberty: An American History.* 2nd ed. London: W.W. Norton and Company, 2009; Kennedy, David M., Lizabeth Cohen, and Thomas A. Bailey. *The American Pageant.* 14th ed. Boston: Wadsworth Cenage Learning, 2010; Wood, Gordon S. *Empire of Liberty: A History of the Early Republic, 1789–1815.* New York: Oxford University Press, 2009. Highly recommended is *The Oxford History of the United States*, of which this last volume is a part, a series of a dozen planned volumes of which about half are complete.

20 See <www.firstamendmentfuture.org> for more information on the study and a subsequent study on the efficacy of the 2004 Constitution Day federal law that mandates September 17 as day devoted in all schools that receive federal dollars to teach about the Constitution. For additional ideas about teaching the First Amendment see <www.teachfirstamendment.org>.

21 Chaltain, Sam. "Does the First Amendment Have a Future?" *Social Education* 69. 3 (2005): 126–31.

22 "1 for All" website is <http://1forall.us/about/the-first-amendment/>. Teaching lessons on the First Amendment can be found at <http://1forall.us/about/the-first-amendment>.

23 "First Amendment: Learn All About It." Editorial in *Aberdeen* (SD) *American News.* 1 July 2010. 4A or at <www.aberdeennews.com>.

24 Ibid.

25 Ivey, Gay. "Texts That Matter." *Educational Leadership* 67. 6 (2010): 22.

26 William, Patricia J. "Absolutely No Excuse." *The Nation* 7 Dec. 2009. 9.

27 Hamm, Thomas D. "Disestablishment and Free Exercise: The Religion Clauses of the First Amendment." *Magazine of History* 22. 1 (2008): 28–31.

28 Leone, Bruno, ed. *Civil Liberties: Opposing Viewpoints.* San Diego: Greenhaven Press, Inc., 1999.

29 Brinkley, Alan. *The Unfinished Nation: A Concise History of the American People.* 6th ed. New York: The McGraw-Hill Companies, 2010. 370.

30 Kennedy, Cohen, and Bailey, 534.

31   Kennedy, Cohen, and Bailey, 535.
32   Gillette, William. *Retreat from Reconstruction, 1869–1879*. Baton Rouge: Louisiana State University Press, 1980.
33   Hahn, Steven. "The Other American Revolution." *The New Republic* Aug. 2006. 26.
34   Foner, Eric. *Who Owns History: Rethinking the Past in a Changing World*. New York: Hill and Wang, 2002. 189–90.
35   Foner, Eric. *Forever Free: The Story of Emancipation and Reconstruction*. New York: Alfred A. Knopf, 2006. and Hahn, 28.
36   The relating of the story of Franklin Roosevelt's battle with the Supreme Court in this book is based on material drawn from several works. These include Shesol, Jeff. *Supreme Power: Franklin Roosevelt vs. The Supreme Court*. New York: W.W. Norton & Company, 2010; Solomon, Burt. *FDR vs. The Constitution: The Court-Packing Fight and the Triumph of Democracy*. New York: Walker and Company, 2009; and Kennedy, David M. *Freedom From Fear: The American People in Depression and War, 1929–1945*. New York: Oxford University Press, 1999.
37   Shesol, 508–09, 520.
38   Solomon, 257, 265.
39   Kennedy, 337–38.
40   Burns, James McGregor. *Roosevelt: The Lion and the Fox, 1882–1940*. New York: Harcourt, Brace, and World, 1956. 313–15.
41   Burns, James McGregor. *Packing the Court: The Rise of Judicial Power and the Coming Crisis of the Supreme Court*. New York: The Penguin Press, 2009. 154.
42   The material relating to Barry Friedman's hypothesis is drawn from Friedman, Barry. *The Will of the People: How Public Opinion Has Influenced the Supreme Court and Shaped the Meaning of the Constitution*. New York: Farrar, Straus and Giroux, 2009. 205–36.
43   O'Donnell, Michael. "The Wedge Against Tyranny." *The Nation* 291. 7 & 8. 16/23 Aug 2010. 39–42.
44   Foner, Eric. "Zinn's Critical History." *The Nation* 290. 7 (2010): 6.
45   Ibid.
46   Zinn, Howard. *A People's History of the United States, 1492–Present*. New York: HarperCollins, 1999. 10.
47   Bigelow, Bill. *A People's History for the Classroom*. Milwaukee: Rethinking Schools Ltd., 2008. 7.
48   Zinn, 349–54, 401–03, 450–67.
49   Wilentz, Sean and Julian E. Zelizer. "Teaching 'W' as History: The Challenges of the Recent Past in the Classroom." *The Chronicle of Higher Education Review* 16 July 2010. B4–5.
50   Alter, Gloria. "Challenging the Textbook." *Educational Leadership* 66. 8 (2009): 72–75.

ELEVEN

Media, Technology, and the Internet

Adolescents live in the ubiquitous age of instant communication with its attendant texting, twittering, Googling, and blogging. It is therefore not surprising that the emergence of the Internet has added a new dimension and tool to the teaching of history. One survey found that 90% of American adolescents between the ages of eleven and eighteen have access to the Internet and 80% percent have an Internet connection at home which most use daily.[1] A number of sites are most impressive with many highly useful to teachers as well as students. New sites that incorporate lectures and course outlines, lesson plans, readings, and audiovisual materials include TeacherTube, HippoCampus, and MIT's OpenCourseware.[2]

Jessica K. Parker has looked deeply at the multiple implications of the digital media on the adolescents of today. She captures this "brave new world" of media for youth as she writes:

> Today's student is likely to engage in numerous literate practices, from print to film to multimodal forms such as Web and video games. She lives in a media saturated world and averages nearly six and a half hours a day with media. She is a media multitasker, watching television as she instant messages and completes her homework. She searches for information on the Internet, displays herself on myspace.com and takes pictures on her cell phone, then chooses between a number of media sharing sites in which to upload them. She expects her teachers to guide her through this information era, not dictate "correct" answers to rote questions that Google can provide in seconds through multimodal means.[3]

A word of caution regarding technology and the Internet may be in order before delving further into these topics. Nothing other than the explosion of knowledge—of which technology and the Internet are part and parcel and a main contributor—changes as fast as the high-tech world of information and the vehicles that convey it. There is hesitancy, therefore, to reference any website or platform for fear that within months or even weeks its mere mention will date the entirety of a work. Just a quarter century ago, John Goodlad in his authoritative study of public education, *A Place Called School*, wrote that "purchasing microcomputers is becoming the 'in' thing for school districts to do."[4] Today such an observation almost seems quaint, even from a visionary in the field of education like Goodlad.

A brief review of Neil Postman's work in the 1970s and 1980s serves as foundation for the world of technology and information we live in today. Postman called the major medium of his day—television—the "first curriculum." School, by default, was the second curriculum. Postman saw television and school as both having characteristics. They both had a requirement about how to attend to them—both were compulsory, but school used legal means and television used psychological. Both had subject matter, a way to organize time and defining knowledge. Postman saw the characteristics of television as:

- Non-punitive

- Affect-centered

- Image-centered

- Non-analytical

- Non-hierarchical

- Authoritarian (information moves in one direction)

- Discontinuous in content and highly segmented

- Intrinsically gratifying

- Present-oriented

As for school, the characteristics Postman identified were:

- Hierarchical

- Analytical

- Sustained concentration

- Historical

- Semi-authoritarian

- Abstract and symbolic

As can readily be seen, the characteristics of media, not just television but most media, even the Internet, diametrically work against what is taking place in the schools. Take history as an example. If school is historical in that it builds on what has come before, whether the subject is literacy, mathematics, or even history itself, the student must have a historical background in place. With media, old and new, each new show, game, or hit on the Internet is an experience unto itself. Another example, derived from Postman's analysis, that impacts school and the teaching of history is the segmentation of media. School does call for sustained concentration, analysis of what is being read, and the ability to think abstractly. With few exceptions media does not have such requirements. An hour program, a video game, or viewing a clip on YouTube is a complete experience unto itself. For Postman, then, media works against what schools are trying to accomplish. Postman's antidote was to use the characteristics of school to counter the characteristic of media. This is what he called "media literacy." Students should be taught how the media works, which would lead them to be intelligent consumers of media.[5]

Information literacy, as it has been called today, is similar to what Neil Postman called media literacy in the 1980s. While computers were only beginning to be used at that time, the concept is similar. Locating and evaluating online sources, managing data, and producing results from the research are indispensable skills in the Internet age. And such resources to accomplish this process are increasingly available.[6]

Piscitelli has defined it as knowing what information you need, where to find it, how to evaluate it, and how to use it properly.[7] Take one of these areas as an example—how to evaluate a website. If a student is researching the late 19th-century labor union movement, how would that student know if the information located on websites was reliable and valid? While no process is flawless, Glanz has suggested several approaches drawn from research in the field. Authoritativeness means that the authors represent credible institutions or organizations. Admittedly, the student may have difficulty determining this, but by "drilling down" deeper into the website, legitimacy can usually be established. Does the site look well established and is the information current? In addition, can the author or webmaster be contacted? Other ways to evaluate reliability and validity would be to find out if the site loads easily, are the graphics educational rather than commercial, and are links to other sites are provided? Finally, when was the website established and when was it last updated or revised?[8]

Examples of this increase in knowledge may seem obvious, but it places in perspective what technology has done to subject matter and content that students will be learning. The sheer size of Internet content can also be a drawback. The number of sites increases daily, but a recent number given for just primary sources was in the "hundreds of millions."[9] A 2005 study on using the Internet for research in history provided an excellent example. In 1996 Franklin D. Roosevelt yielded fewer than 100 hits. In 2005, a decade later, the number had increased to 150,000. (The author's own 2009 search yielded 2,100,000. And a year later the figure had exploded yet again to 3,550,000.[10]) It would take a half million new libraries the size of the Library of Congress print collection to hold the amount of information produced in just one year in the first decade of the 21st century. Ninety-two percent of this information is not in print form—and much of the new and old information may not be.[11] Google is attempting to scan and digitize more than 50 million books from the five largest research libraries in the world.

The production of content is truly mind-boggling. A longitudinal study illustrates how the expanse of information has become a major challenge. A comparative study of supply and demand of media content produced and consumed has been tracked over the past 40 years. Neuman has reported that in the 1960s media basically consisted of radio, a few television stations, daily newspapers, mail, film, records, and books. If each person is allowed a 24-hour day, then 98 minutes of content was being produced five decades ago for each one minute of time in a person's day. (We do not, of course, have 24 hours a day due to sleeping, eating, and other non-content media consumption time.) By 2005, in addition to the above outlets, were added hundreds of cable and satellite television channels (in the 1960s there were usually 3 network channels with maybe an independent or public broadcast channel also available), DVDs, VCRs, video games, cell phones, and the Internet. Phones, for example, were not new, but mobile phones allowed for more content to be produced and consumed from any location. The Internet was considered as a single television channel in the study, which we know it is not. The new ratio in 2005 was 20,943 minutes of content for each minute in an adult's 24-hour day.[12] The implication for history teachers in the selection of content to teach—and students to "consume"—becomes overwhelming. The challenge can only be met if teachers, students, and the public at large become much better at discerning what information is important and how to find it.

These examples of the exponential increase of information are demanding that we reconsider how we think about content and curriculum. For several years the technology that allowed this information growth to occur has been likened to other shifts in history such as Gutenberg's printing press or the Industrial Revolution. (Thomas Freidman has written about the change globally in his *The World is Flat: A Brief History of the Twenty-First Century*.[13]) Richardson has written of the "Big Shifts" that are coming in this new world of technology. A few of these include: 1) Open-Source Classrooms—where contributions to the curriculum are not limited to finite sources, 2) Many Teachers and 24/7 Learning—where teachers have access to primary sources such as authors, historians, and researchers any day at any time, 3) the Web as Notebook—where it becomes not just a source for information, but a platform for sharing learning with audio, video, and more, and 4) Mastery as a Product, Not the Test—where students display mastery beyond percentages on tests through the creation of digital content.[14]

By extrapolating from Richardson's conclusions about the Web, the implications for the teaching of history are many. History teachers will need to redefine what it means to teach. History teachers will be *connectors* of people, not just of content. Teachers will need to become *content creators*. The possibly much overused word *collaborator* means that teachers and students will work alongside each other, not in a hierarchy. Teachers will need to think of themselves as *coaches* who model the skills that students need to be successful. (A paradox: The most successful coach in the history of college basketball, UCLA's John Wooden, viewed himself as a teacher.) And finally Web-oriented history teachers will need to be change agents moving away from unproductive traditional paradigms of instruction.[15]

Technology is and must be an integral part of what teachers do. The key is for educators to have a variety of instructional tools at their disposal, some of which may be high-tech and some low-tech. Australian technology gurus and proponents Lee and Winzenried have written "A well-told story can be as effective as a quality interactive multimedia presentation. Pens, paper, and whiteboards have an important and continuing role to play in teaching for some time yet."[16] With that said, Lee and Winzenried make a compelling case for greater use of technology when they unequivocally state:

> The digital can enrich the teaching, make the learning more relevant, engage all manner of students, individualize much of the teaching, enhance the efficiency of the teaching, open new unexplored worlds, reduce teachers' workload and when successfully used across the schools of the nation can assist and enhance national productivity in knowledge-based economies. A predominantly digitally based mode of teaching has only just begun to realize its potential.[17]

There remain, though, reservations regarding the use of technology. Some school systems have limited or even reduced their use of technology based on concerns over its efficacy as related to culture and student achievement. Two authors, Mark Bauerline and Todd Oppenheimer, are 21st-century skeptics about technology. Bauerline laments the decline in reading due, in his opinion, to the substitute of computers that consume too much student time. Individuals have abandoned the stacks while computer stations are full.[18] Oppenheimer provides a number of examples of school districts spending heartily on technology yet are reporting low test scores. Other school districts are dropping technology by eliminating laptop computer programs.[19]

Accessibility also needs to be kept in mind when assigning research in history to adolescents. The familiar "digital divide" that separates the haves and have-nots in terms of technology access is very real. Using Australia as an example, that country has three mobile phones, three televisions, two computers, two DVD players, two portable mp3/mp4 players, a VCR, and two game consuls per household.[20] Average does not mean everyone. Assigning projects that are dependent on technology should always be made with assurances built in that all students will have an entrée into the digital world. This may mean that the home cannot always be relied upon to support the technology needs of students.

Schools too must work hard to maintain a viable technology platform to meet the needs of educators. This includes constant professional development tied directly to the subject matter, appropriate content and software, and infrastructure that includes both technical and trained personnel. There must also be designated specialists within the school district or building who are knowledgeable leaders in and advocates for technology.

One strength with regard to teaching history is the rich and abundant amount of visual material available. With photographs beginning in the mid-19th century and film and video available of most major events of the 20th century, there is no lack of material to support history instruction. It is preferable to show students how Adolf Hitler appeared and sounded than for the student to read about him in a textbook or for the teacher to try to explain his extraordinary hold over the German people. The same holds true for historical figures such as Malcolm X, John Kennedy, Eleanor Roosevelt, Ronald Reagan, or Sandra Day O'Connor. And events such as the Vietnam War (the first televised war), inspiring speeches by Martin Luther King, Jr., and presidential elections bring to life the history of the nation. The amount of video available is truly extraordinary. Vast collections of media are now obtainable from cable, satellite, and online feeds. (For additional suggestions on the selection and use of visuals, see the chapter "Movies, Movies, Movies.")

In their book *Digital History: A Guide to Gathering, Preserving, and Presenting the Past on the Web*, Cohen and Rosenzweig strongly encourage history teachers to "critically and soberly assess where computers, networks, and digital media are and are not useful for historians." They see a number of advantages as well as hazards on the "information superhighway." Positive factors include: 1) capacity—the cost and storage ability that digital media allows; 2) accessibility—websites that allow students to vicariously enter the Library of Congress, archives, and national museums; 3) flexibility—the capability of students exploring history to study, preserve, and present the past in multiple media formats; 4) diversity—the Web as a platform for a broad array of authors who come from disparate backgrounds and multiple viewpoints; 5) manipulability—the ability to use electronic search engines in the study of history that antiquates print sources and processes; 6) interactivity—opportunities for dialogue and feedback on history websites that facilitates collaboration and debate; and 7) hypertextuality or nonlinearity—the ease of moving through narratives or data in undirected, unique, and multiple ways.[21]

The five dangers that Cohen and Rosenzweig see in an otherwise "rosy digital history revolution" include: 1) quality—how can authenticity of historical material be determined, from misspellings and faked photographs to plain inaccuracies and wrong information; 2) durability—the flipside of accessibility and flexibility, as a surprising number of historical records are being lost or failed to be preserved; 3) readability—online print presentations can take on a "non user-friendly" appearance due to hypertextuality and the inclusion of assorted videos and other additional features; 4) passivity—rather than historical deliberations and debate we get uncomplicated objective questions (true/false and multiple choice) that lead to one-way, inactive media like television; 5) inaccessibility—beyond the consumption side of the issue, such as the digital divide discussed above, this has to do with production and whether amateur historians, including students, academic historians, and teachers can compete with the well-financed commercial operations like the History Channel.[22]

The "non user-friendly" facets of readability in terms of the Internet are real. Hill has pointed out that textbooks, for all the criticism they receive, are organized, sequential, and contain content that is considered by most educators to be legitimate. When going online to search a topic, the issue of validity and reliability emerges as well as the massive amounts of information available. New skills and strategies will be needed for students to be successful in the area of reading comprehension and learning on the Internet. As Hill writes, "Students often play with the latest toys, but they are tech savvy and not information savvy."[23] For the Internet to live up to its potential it will take investment in terms of personnel and expertise to assist learners with these new technological tools.

A crossover activity for middle level learners is what three teacher educators and practitioners have called "Digital Collaborative Literacy." In its simplest form it is an online book club. But on a more multidimensional level, this particular collaborative literacy initiative combines student group activities (reading, writing, discussion, and literary analysis) with the theme of working together and getting along. Teachers select books that are focused on successful collaboration by adolescents. The arrival of recent technologies is redefining what it means to be a reader and writer. According to the researchers, through the use of wikis (the creation and editing of interlinked web pages from the Polynesian phrase "wiki-wiki" or "quick-quick"), traditional group activities such as literature circles, learning and book clubs, and reciprocal teaching have gone "virtual." Each wiki contains the basics such as book title and author, a synopsis of the book, and basic questions about how the characters did or did not work collaboratively.[24]

A number of works are suggested for using the idea of digital collaboration among youth in works of historical fiction. Two books that explore how families worked together to help Jewish friends and families during World War II are *Number the Stars* (1998) by Lois Lowery and *The Butterfly* (2000) by Patricia Polacco. Polacco has also written a Civil War book, *Pink and Say* (1994), about two soldiers—one Black and one White—who despite being from opposite worlds work together to survive. And *The Wright 3* (2006) by Blue Balliett is the creative mystery of a three sixth-graders who team up to save a Frank Lloyd Wright house from destruction.[25]

There are, in addition to the above, other potential drawbacks to the Internet. These include excessive time in non-academic chat rooms, cyber experiences involving sexual predators, social isolation, and academic dishonesty. In this last category students have been known to use search engines to locate information, but can retrieve incorrect or even bizarre responses. When asked to identify Richard Nixon in the context of his role in the 1950s as communist-hunter and Vice-President, one student in the author's class referenced Watergate. Wrong decade, wrong significance. Another student looking for the Lusitania came up with the answer "an exotic flower." The significance of the sinking of the World War I-era passenger liner was lost on the student by accessing Internet information.

While it is probably the best search engine at this time, neither teachers nor students should solely rely on Google as technology, competition, and innovation quickly change the landscape in this arena. Google or other search engines can be a beginning place for historical research, but should never be the only one. The same holds true for Amazon. While it has revolutionized the book industry, there are occasional limits as to what appears on Amazon's website due to contractual arrangements between the company and publishers.[26] Presnell's comprehensive chapter on history Internet sites, search strategies, and evaluation processes is highly recommended for teachers and students alike.[27]

The research for this book demonstrated that the Internet may not always be the best resource. The example is the episode involving the confrontation between Franklin Roosevelt and the Supreme Court discussed in the previous chapter. Information on this conflict can be found on the Internet, but three recent books on the controversy were by far the best sources on the topic. Locating primary sources through the Internet, though, is probably one of the most useful tools now available. Google and other search engines are reproducing works whose copyrights have lapsed. Beyond duplications of texts, primary sources placed on the Web are increasing exponentially. Facsimiles of artifacts, government documents (including some F.B.I field office files), photographs, and statistics are also appearing.

While obvious to most Internet users, younger adolescents may need to be reminded about basic information and protocols on the Web. The identification of the website's domain can be a critical point of departure for student searches. Website suffixes label in fairly specific terms the sphere of information in which the website is operating. But both valid and dubious sites need rigorous evaluation by students and teachers alike. It is not difficult to stumble onto sites that are sponsored by White supremacist groups who are debunkers of Martin Luther King, Jr., or deniers of the Holocaust. Obligatory questions that should be asked include: who created, hosted, and wrote the website? These questions assist students in their research to determine point of view, purposes, and agendas of the website.[28] Appropriate citations are a tool in the use of online historical investigation that also needs to be taught.

The advent of "interactive" websites is a case in point. The most heavily trafficked historical information source is Wikipedia. The criticisms of this website are the issues of authority, validity, and expertise of the contributors.[29] But even Wikipedia itself warns users that "not everything in Wikipedia is accurate, comprehensive, or unbiased." The process of student involvement in such information building activities should be encouraged. A prediction in another chapter in this book suggests that student-built textbooks may very well play a major role in the future of textbooks.

A minimum level of proficiency is necessary for students using search engines when researching about history on the Web. Schrum, Gevinson, and Rosenzweig have suggested several research guidelines for students to efficiently enhance their use of search engines. These include the use of quotation marks in a search. They report that "U.S. history" in quotation marks narrows the search from 130 million results on Google to six million. (Six million is still too many, but the advantage in using this strategy is evident.) The "advanced search" feature, if available, is always helpful—even on commercial sites like Amazon. Another suggestion is the use of multiple terms in the search boxes. The example they give is "boxer rebellion + American troops" rather than just Boxer Rebellion, which can produce unwanted websites on professional boxers like Muhammad Ali.[30]

Andrew Johnson has also set out suggestions that endorse these strategies. Calling them the "four A's," they are: 1) Accessibility (check to see if the website is still there and that load time for the material is reasonable), 2) Accuracy (do you have confidence in the website for reliability, responsibility, and trustworthiness?), 3) Appropriateness (suitability in terms of content), and 4) Appeal (do the visuals, audio if present, and narrative coalesce in a way that motivates the learner to delve further into the topic?).[31]

An innovative tool that addresses data "overload" is an information aggregator. It is an online application that allows students, but especially teachers, to sort and filter the massive amounts of new information that appear each day on the Web. Information aggregators are also known as RSS (real simple syndication). RSS feeds enable the control of the websites received. A free Web-based feed reader is Pageflakes (www.pageflakes.com). Other popular readers include Bloglines (www.bloglines.com) and Google Reader (www.google.com/reader). Middle school history teacher, Bill Ferriter, endorses the use of feed readers and uses them with his classes, especially to keep up with current events and student projects.[32] The issues of quality and reliability are still present, but the quantity issues are somewhat ameliorated.

The educational delivery system of online teaching is a final area of technology that is impacting the teaching history. While online teaching is presently employed mainly in higher education, it has begun to be used on a wider basis in selected high schools. *The Boston Globe* reported that Virtual High School, a fourteen-year-old Massachusetts-based consortium, offers 336 online courses to 13,000 students in 31 states and 34 countries. Half of Massachusetts' school districts are members of the Virtual High School network. Ambient Learning, an educational technology company, reports that two million high school students are learning online with the number expected to move to ten million by 2014. Another estimate, this one from the International Association of K–12 Online Learning, believes that ten percent of all courses will be computer-based by 2014 and 50 percent online in 2019.[33] To rephrase Pogo, who said, "We have met the enemy and it is us," a more apt phrase for online learning is "We have seen the future and it is here." And it—online education—will only be the enemy if educators make it so.

At first, distance education formats such as video connections to multiple sites were the platform of choice. It was often used with smaller or rural schools in order to offer low-enrollment courses in the sciences, higher level mathematics, and the foreign languages. But online education is rapidly replacing video transfer systems. And inevitably the move to online education will shift, in one form or another, to the middle schools. History can be an appropriate subject for online teaching with suitable support systems in place to assist the student.

An oft-quoted remark attributed to NFL quarterback Charlie Batch is what he called the "5 P's—Proper Preparation Prevents Poor Performance." This epigram holds with online teaching. For online teaching to succeed, a number of support systems must be in place. Training, resources, and careful design and development are essential. Once the domain of higher education, course syllabi in history are now critical for online teaching. The next most important aspect of designing an online course is the creation of assessment rubrics. If the platform allows, online lectures often make the personal connection that is needed in distance education. The most frequent problems in online education are technical in nature. Students will readily know when a teacher is not savvy in using the technology. A help desk for students is an absolute necessity.

The most interactive portion of online teaching is the discussion boards. These are usually an essential part of the online course experience. An outstanding resource for online teaching is a newsletter titled *Online Cl@ssroom: Ideas for Effective Online Instruction.* Both teachers and students need to be aware of appropriate and effective discussion board etiquette. Patti Shrank offers several excellent suggestions for students when engaged in discussion board activity. These include:

- Make the subject line valuable. Don't use "I Agree" or "Me too."

- Make postings concise and directly connected to the question or topic from a classmate.

- Disagree, but disagree agreeably. Do not use labels, derogatory terms, or inappropriate names toward the teacher, textbook author, or classmates. Do not use offensive language. And do not SHOUT with all CAPS.

- The teacher can miss regrettable postings. Without feeling like a "tattler" let the teacher know by flagging postings that are not adhering to good discussion board etiquette.[34]

Teachers also need direction in responding to online discussion boards. Errol Craig Sull, also from *Online Cl@ssroom*, offers these ideas:

- Remember that everyone can read your postings.

- Model in your postings what you want from your students' postings.

- Always be aware of students' vocabulary level.

- Don't be afraid to let personality and humor enter your responses.

- Use examples or experiences from your life in responses.

- Create a bank of your best responses to reuse in future classes. Often the same question will be asked in the next class.[35]

One final aspect of online teaching that often enhances the course is the opportunity for students to ask the teacher or the textbook author questions.

Authors are sometimes available to respond on conference calls. This usually impresses the adolescents as well as adults. The questions provide the teacher with information that will help them clarify content issues in the class and allow the author to receive direct feedback about their book or textbook.

Online teaching can be controversial. This issue of quality is usually at the top of the list of concerns. In their research, Ko and Rossen have found a number of advantages for teachers in online instruction that counter the "lack of quality" assumption. Instructors report that teaching online made them a better teacher—not only online, but in their face-to-face classes. In addition, since online courses leave a paper trail, teachers have the opportunity to review and reflect on student assignments and can do so through rapid and flexible communication. A final positive outcome of online teaching, according to Ko and Rossen, is the fostering of creative approaches to teaching. One example was increasing the amount of work in the online class compared to a traditional class. Students will "rise to the occasion," and accomplishing more than the conventional wisdom on online teaching considered possible.[36]

Baby Boomers and the X Generation have now been joined by what some have called the Net Generation. This would be the eleven- to thirty-year-olds, which includes adolescents. In terms of technology we have been told that they know their way around the various media better than any other generation by the fact they have grown up with it. This is certainly true if we mean they can maneuver the Web, program their cell phones, and use Facebook better than older generations. With it, though, have come criticisms. The Net Generation, it is said, does not read and are poor communicators. They are Web addicted "screenagers" who have lost their social skills. Even worse attributions have been made about them. They download music illegally, have no interests other than popular culture and their friends, and care nothing for current events or the world around them. Much of this portrayal is the result, say the critics, of too much media.

But Don Tapscott, a Canadian from both the world of business and technology, disagrees with this assessment. Leading "The Net Generation: A Strategic Investigation," a $4 million research study, Tapscott has come to different conclusions—about youth and about media. He found that Net Geners want freedom of expression in their media choices, customizing and personalizing their media choices. Net Geners want to integrate their entertainment, play, work, education, and social life. One piece of Tapscott's research found that 2,000 youth, ages 8–18, were able to squeeze 8.5 hours of electronic media use into six chronological hours—not by multitasking, but by being more adept at "switching" from one task to another. However, the study found that Net Geners are doing other things differently than what the conventional wisdom says about them. In the last twenty years they are wearing their seatbelts and using condoms more, in addition to being less likely to carry a weapon or taking part in crime. They are voting more than their predecessors did at the same age, volunteering more, using drugs less, and committing less crime. Academically their IQ scores are rising and SAT scores are stable although more students are taking the test than a generation ago.[37] These trends have implications for the classroom.

How do we tap into Tapscott's findings? Since media is not going away, educators of adolescents—the frontend of the Net Generation—need to search for ways to use media to an even greater extent. It is a matter of taking the technological "know-how" of this generation and channeling it toward those areas (history being one of them) that will enhance the learning environment. If the Net Generation truly wants to integrate their education and work and social life through media, then teachers need to match that need through how they use media in the history classroom. Postman was right about how media negatively counteracts what goes on in school. But he was also right about the need for media literacy in schools and its potential to increase learning.

The final test as to whether technology—be it the Web, online teaching, YouTube, or some other aspect of the new digital world—is working in a history classroom is when its use becomes normalized. In other words, when teachers and students forget that they are even using media in their classrooms. Technology must be highly integrated in the study of history and become as common as the microcomputers that John Goodlad saw in the schools he wrote about a quarter century ago.

Endnotes

1   Roberts, Donald F., Ulla G. Foehr, and Victoria Rideout. *Generation M: Media in the Lives of 8–18 Year-Olds.* Washington, D.C.: The Henry J. Kaiser Family Foundation, 2005.

2   Award-winning historical research site <http://www.dohistory.org> is excellent. C-SPAN has multiple websites that profile the presidents and other historical figures at <http://www.C-SPAN.org>. See the Public Broadcasting System at <http://www.pbs.org>. For TeacherTube see <www.teachertube.com>. For HippoCampus see <www.hippocampus.org>. For MIT's OpenCourseware Consortium see <http://ocw.mit.edu>.

3   Parker, Jessica K. *Teaching Tech-Savvy Kids: Bringing Digital Media Into the Classroom, Grade 5–12.* Thousand Oaks: Corwin, 2010. 1.

4   Goodlad, John. *A Place Called School.* New York: McGraw-Hill, 1984. 340.

5   Postman, Neil. *Teaching as Conserving Activity.* New York: Delacourte Press, 1979. 71–86. See also Postman, Neil. *Technopoly: The Surrender of Culture to Technology.* New York: Knopf, 1992; and *Amusing Ourselves to Death.* New York: Penguin Books, 2005.

6   Munger, Dave and Shireen Campbell. *What Every Student Should Know About Researching Online.* New York: Pearson Longman, 2007.

7   Ibid. 208–209.

8   Glanz, Jeffrey. *Teaching 101: Classroom Strategies for the Beginning Teacher.* 2ⁿᵈ ed. Thousand Oaks: Corwin, 2009. 227–39.

9   Schrum, Kelly, Alan Gevinson, and Roy Rosenzweig. *History Matters: A Student Guide to U.S. History Online.* 2ⁿᵈ ed. Boston: Bedford/St. Martin's, 2005. vii. While no single work contains all the information needed to successfully maneuver the endless intricacies of the Internet, this volume has a splendid annotated bibliography of 250 critical websites. This book has its own website <http://historymatters.gmu.edu>.

10 Google search of Franklin D. Roosevelt undertaken by the author on June 2, 2009 and August 16, 2010.

11 Piscitelli, Steve. *Study Skills: Do I Really Need to Know This Stuff?* 2ⁿᵈ ed. Upper Saddle River: Pearson/Prentice Hall, 2009. 206.

12 Neuman, W. Russell. "Appraising Information Abundance." *Chronicle of Higher Education* 2 Feb. 2010: B8–B10.

13 Friedman, Thomas. *The World is Flat: A Brief History of the Twenty-First Century.* New York: Farrar, Strauss, and Giroux, 2005.

14 Richardson, Wil. *Blogs, Wikis, Podcasts, and Other Powerful Web Tools for Classrooms.* 2ⁿᵈ ed. Thousand Oaks: Corwin, 2009. 131–36.

15 Ibid. 136–37.

16 Lee, Mal, and Winzenried, Arthur. *The Use of Instructional Technology in Schools: Lessons to be Learned.* Victoria: Australian Council for Educational Research, Ltd., 2009. 5.

17 Ibid.

18 Bauerline, Mark. *The Dumbest Generation: How the Digital Age Stupefies Young Americans and Jeopardizes Our Future.* New York: Tarcher, 2008.

19 Oppenheimer, Todd. *The Flickering Mind: The False Promise of Technology in the Classroom and How Learning Can Be Saved.* New York: Random House, 2004.

20 Lee and Winzenried, 106–107.

21 Cohen, Daniel J., and Roy Rosenzweig. *Digital History: A Guide to Gathering, Preserving, and Presenting the Past on the Web.* Philadelphia: University of Pennsylvania Press, 2006. 2–8. Note: The book can be downloaded free online at <http://chnm.edu/digitalhistory>.

22 Ibid. 8–13.

23 Hill, Rebecca. "Can Johnny Read . . . Online?" *Middle Ground.* 13.3 (2010): 16–17.

24 Kissel, Brian, Jennifer I. Hathaway, and Karen D. Wood. "Digital Collaborative Literacy: Using Wikis to Promote Social Learning and Literacy Development." *Middle School Journal* 41. 5 (2010): 58–64.

25 Ibid. See also these websites for other suggested readings: ATN Reading Lists at <http://atn-reading-lists.wikispaces.com>.; AdLIt.org at <www.adlit.org>; and Literacy Matters at <www.literacymatters.org/adlit/selecting/intro.htm>.

26 Robinson, Colin. "The Trouble With Amazon." *The Nation* 291. 5–6. (2010): 29–32.

27 Presnell, Jenny L. "History and the Internet." *The Information-Literate Historian: A Guide to Research for History Students.* New York: Oxford University Press, 2007. 136–58.

28 Schrum, Gevinson, and Rosenzweig, 4–10.

29 Ibid. 11–14.

30 Ibid. 26–29.

31   Johnson, Andrew P. *Making Connections in Elementary and Middle School Social Studies*. Thousand Oaks: Sage Publications, 2010. 301.

32   Ferriter, Bill. "How to Become a Digital Leader." *Educational Leadership* 67. 2 (2009): 90–91.

33   Bolton, Michele M. "Online High School Courses Grow in Popularity." *The Boston Globe,* 30 May 2010. Web. 2 June 2010. <http://www.boston.com/news/articles/>.

34   Shrank, Patti. "Effective Ways to Reduce Offensive and Non-Valuable Discussion Postings." *Online Cl@ssroom: Ideas for Effective Online Instruction.* October 2009. 4–5.

35   Sull, Errol C. "Creating Effective Responses to Student Discussion Postings." *Online Cl@ssroom: Ideas for Effective Online Instruction.* April 2010. 6–7.

36   Ko, Susan, and Steve Rossen. *Teaching Online: A Practical Guide.* 3rd ed. New York: Routledge, 2010. 18–20.

37   Tapscott, Don. *Grown Up Digital: How the Net Generation is Changing Your World.* New York: McGraw-Hill, 2009. 3–5, 34, 35, 85, 106, 110, 112, 248, 277, 297, and 301.

TWELVE

Professional Development:
The Imperative of Lifelong Learning

In order to remain effective in the classroom, teachers must constantly be "sharpening their professional saws" in both content and methodology. One survey of Indiana history teachers revealed, unfortunately, that only one in five stayed current in their field of American history.[1] Professional development is essential for all teachers and is now built into school calendars, re-certification and licensure on the state and national levels, and in the work of teacher organizations such as the National Education Association and the American Federation of Teachers. The form professional development takes varies from the formal to independent habits of growth practiced by teachers.

Teachers, in most cases, graduate from a college or university with a bachelor's degree where they have also earned a teaching certificate through a parallel and integrated process. While the vast majority of teacher education programs are four years in length, at one end of the teacher preparation spectrum there are a handful of five-year programs that include the masters degree with licensure. At the other end of the continuum are alternative programs for non-education degree holders who receive certification through abbreviated preparation programs. The initial degree is often called the baccalaureate. The derivation of the word baccalaureate is bachelor, and that can mean not only an unmarried man, but also a young farmer without land or experience. In other words a beginner. It is a misconception on the part of the public, and possibly to those in the profession of education, that newly minted teachers are skilled practitioners, proficient in both their subject matter and the art and science of teaching. These new teachers should indeed be prepared to assume full responsibility for a classroom or several classrooms of students. But it should be remembered that they are at the "beginning" of a professional journey, not at its destination.

Experts agree that it is those teachers, early in their careers, toward which much of professional development should be aimed. Van Hover reports that more than a half dozen studies, including several by education scholars such as Linda Darling-Hammond, call for professional development for novice teachers during their formative years. As indicated in the chapter title, veteran teachers can most certainly benefit from professional development. Not only does professional development improve instructional practice, but it also increases teacher retention rates and promotes professional and psychological well-being.[2] However, poor professional development experiences have done much damage to this critical area of teachers' lives. "Weakly conceived and poorly delivered—and without attention to how teachers learn," states van Hover, are the major causes for inadequate and unpopular experiences.[3]

The standard for professional development, according to Valli and Stout, should follow this comprehensive blueprint:

> Professional development must help teachers understand the discipline they are teaching together with the content standards and the assessment, connect teachers with adequate resources, give clear guidance on what students are expected to do, and provide a continuous and supportive framework for their reform efforts.[4]

Sykes has added five general guidelines for optimal professional development. They include a selection and design based on teacher-student learning connections, specific content in the curriculum, the examination of students learning, curricular or instructional innovation, and attention to formative and summative assessment practices.[5]

Two other recent contributions to the dialogue on professional development come from Douglas Reeves in his *Transforming Professional Development into Student Results* and Joseph Semadeni in *Taking Charge of Professional Development: A Practical Model for Your School*. Both Reeves and Semadeni agree that professional development needs to be specific in terms of both grade level and subject matter, customized for the schools in which it is undertaken, and provide the opportunity for teachers to model what they have learned. The focus is on relevancy and practicality for the teacher. Student results, the authors of these two books maintain, will follow.[6]

Reeves has captured both the possibilities and the frustrations that surround professional development:

The greatest frustration for school leaders and classroom educators is the difference between what we know and what we do. We know what effective professional learning looks like. It is intensive and sustained, it is directly relevant to the needs of teachers and students. We also know what it doesn't look like: death by Power Point, ponderous lectures from people who have not been alone with a group of students for decades, and high-decibel whining about the state of children, parents, public education, and Western civilization.[7]

Reeves's other suggestion is that professional development move from the training (a word educators still quarrel over) component to internalizing what is learned through refinement, reinforcement, and deliberate practice. Echoing Sykes above, he also advocates that all professional development should fall within four broad categories: teaching, curriculum, assessment, and leadership.[8]

Professional development on a district-wide or school-wide basis is most common. They can be positive in the growth of teachers, although content-specific activities are usually viewed as more helpful. Frequent generic professional development topics include looking at research on achievement and best practices, using research in the classroom, differentiated instruction, social justice, creating a caring community in schools, technology, and parental involvement. More history-specific examples would consist of disaggregating test data to look for common areas of concerns in the curriculum, alignment of the history curriculum both vertically and horizontally, after-school book clubs that meet each month and read a young adult history or biography, and sessions on how to improve writing in the history classroom.

Formal professional development can take place in a variety of venues. Graduate education courses are one of the most familiar. At one time some states mandated a masters degree for all teachers. This is no longer the practice. While many teachers do pursue masters degrees and beyond, some have questioned the efficacy of the degree. At a time when professional development is available through a variety of sources—mainly local school districts and regional state education agencies—universities must demonstrate their relevancy to the world of teacher practice. Reaffirming, demonstrating, and validating the usefulness of graduate education is critical if higher education is to reclaim this arena of professional service and growth that was once their singular domain.

The most increasingly popular and effective form of professional development has been the National Board for Professional Teaching Standards (NBPTS). Founded in 1987, NBPTS is a voluntary system of national certification for teachers. Licensure differs from certification in that teaching licenses are usually an entry into the profession and granted under the auspices of state departments of education through either traditional routes (colleges and universities) or nontraditional routes (state department programs or organizations such as Teach for America). All licensure routes funnel through state departments of education.

NBPTS is a series of performance-based standards that indicates mastery in a variety of teaching skills, knowledge-bases, and dispositions. Not only is a high level of teaching performance and proficiency affirmed, but most states offer significant monetary remuneration for NBPTS licensure.[9]

A week of professional development that is a week well spent is the equipping teachers receive at Advanced Placement Institutes. (The author is an alumnus of the training.) Advanced Placement (AP) has emerged over the past decade as a comprehensive approach to teaching high ability students. The forty-hour experience is content specific with American History and World History courses available at both the AP and pre-AP levels. Teachers are specially trained with intensive class work led by master teachers in the methods and content of the discipline. When taken by high school students, AP courses carry college credit at most universities if a certain test score is achieved. One study has indicated that these more challenging AP classes cause greater engagement and intellectual satisfaction by the student than regular classes.[10] And anecdotal evidence appears to suggest that AP-trained teachers transfer their expertise to non-AP classes.

There have been those who have seen reason for caution, or at least watchfulness in their opinion of this popular program. The Thomas B. Fordham Institute has published a report based on both random surveys and focus groups of Advanced Placement teachers to gauge the status of this growing component of history instruction as well as other subjects. On the positive side, the report says that 59% of teachers see the difficulty and complexity of material in AP classes remaining the same while 27% viewed it as becoming more difficult. Only 18% said their students' scores have declined in the past five years. And on that point, in contrast to most teachers' views on testing, AP teachers have confidence in the integrity of AP assessments. Approximately 90% of AP teachers believe that AP exams effectively maintain quality of the coursework and are aligned with curriculum and course objectives. In addition, 80% also regard AP exams as both motivating and helpful to students.[11]

On the concern side of the ledger, the Fordham Institute found students selected to enroll in AP for utilitarian rather than intellectual reasons—the courses looked better on their college applications. High schools were drawn to offering AP classes because it burnished their reputations and gave them greater opportunity for state and national quality recognition. Fordham also discovered that there was little screening for enrollment in AP classes, yet that is not true of all schools. Teachers thought that parents often pushed their sons and daughters into courses for which they may not have been academically prepared. Finally, socio-economic concerns are also present in the AP program. Schools of poverty (75% eligible for free or reduced price lunches) report only 25% of their students receiving a three or higher on AP exams (the score that most colleges will accept) while non-poverty schools are demonstrating a 70% pass rate.[12]

Teachers have long looked to the subject matter specialists in their fields for professional information, guidance, and advice on the subjects they are teaching. The collaboration of those who teach history to adolescents and university-based and independent historians may be one of the most under-utilized practices in professional development. But the practice itself is not new. Educator George Counts and historian Charles Beard collaborated to produce social studies teaching materials in the first half of the twentieth century.[13] For a number of reasons, historians (both academic and professional) and teachers in the K–12 setting have been diffident and at times even hostile to each other when it comes to collaboration. Thornton has tracked this "distancing" between the two groups that seems to have ruptured around the middle of the twentieth century. Thornton indicates that there was a time when historians and Progressive educators, the dominant philosophy in many normal schools and teachers colleges in the 1920s and 1930s, did work together. But then a transition occurred that began the rift between the two groups. Teachers colleges became state colleges and then grew into regional state universities. With this shift in mission, the reward system also changed and "depth rather than breadth in scholarship" became the coin of the realm. A book, article, or professional conference presentation on a specialized (and often narrow) historical topic was deemed more important than the creation of knowledge or pedagogical strategies that might be taught and used in the K–12 classroom. This phenomenon moved from the campuses to the professional organizations. The American Historical Association lost interest in the pre-collegiate teaching sector, writes Thornton, and another major historians' group, the Mississippi Valley Historical Association, discontinued its teachers' section in 1947.[14]

But Thornton acknowledges that there are curriculum historians who admit that the teachers of history and historians have more in common than either side will readily admit.[15] Although the ties have been stronger and the support greater, the Nation Endowment for the Humanities (NEH) has contributed to the melding of the two groups—historians and K–12 teachers. The NEH sponsors summer workshops that bring teachers together with historians for seminars on how increased subject matter knowledge can enhance classroom practice. These experiences prove mutually helpful in boosting the interest of teachers in their content and capturing the interest of historians in pedagogy.

A boost to the relevancy of graduate education for teachers would be the blending within masters degrees (even doctorates) of courses from both history and education. Often teachers have a choice of enrolling in a degree that is housed solely in the history department or solely in the colleges of education. While both have legitimacy, it would seem that classroom practitioners could gain more if there were degrees that were balanced between content and pedagogy. Even more helpful would be if the instructors in the graduate history classes were able to make application of their subject matter to the classrooms in which many of their students are teaching. As noted, much was lost with the disappearance of teachers colleges whose mission it was to make such connections to the classrooms where their students would be teaching. And history professors themselves could gain much by having their scholarship reach a wider audience.

While this book does advocate that teachers simultaneously develop pedagogy and subject matter expertise, teachers are also encouraged to be researchers in both areas of their professional lives. The idea that only higher education faculty can publish is false. The top-down model has not only been a factor in professional development for K–12 schools, but in the area of research and publication. Time has been a factor for middle level and high school teachers writing for professional publication. Partnering with higher education faculty in history is one option. Private and public school faculty have co-authored or been consultants on history textbooks, but the examples are rare. Teachers have much to offer in the producing, rather than being only consumers, of new knowledge in the field of history.

In the first decade of the twenty-first century, history scholars and educators participated in the New York History Teaching Collaborative that developed history lessons for classrooms in New York City and Boston. The project showed that teachers deepened their knowledge of historical content, but often needed skills in analyzing and interpreting the historical evidence. In addition, the content teachers needed for their classrooms did not always match with the expertise provided by historians. Both of these concerns can readily be addressed through careful and shared planning.[16] Using this model of professional development, historians should be called on to engage teachers in every school district in the country. While normal schools and teachers colleges have disappeared, there is no reason that colleges of education and history departments that share the same university campuses cannot find ways to work in partnership for the benefit of students, teachers in middle and high schools, historians, and teacher educators.

The Facing History and Ourselves project is another opportunity for the melding of historical content and pedagogy.[17] The treatment of the Holocaust in the curriculum of the adolescent may be one of the best examples of how professional development can impact both teachers and students. A recent study by the United States Holocaust Museum shed light on the importance of professional development as it increases teachers' knowledge and promotes the inclusion of the Holocaust writing history curriculum. The study found that the Holocaust is a well-represented component of the curricula—surprisingly more so in English than history for students in grades 6–12. The findings concluded that teachers benefit from high-quality training in Holocaust education and are therefore more likely to teach and spend more time on the subject than those who do not receive professional development on the topic.[18]

The Holocaust study also discovered that teachers employed a variety of re-sources in their classrooms. Films and firsthand accounts of the Holocaust were the most frequently used, followed by photographs, textbooks, and museums. Nearly twenty percent of the teachers were able to avail themselves and their students of museums. Museums led the list in resources for professional devel-opment on the Holocaust. These included local, state, and national museums. Professional organizations, such as the National Council for the Social Studies or the National Council for Teachers of English, were also regularly mentioned. Two-thirds of teachers and the same percentage of their students indicated they personally found the subject engaging. Teachers found the Holocaust relevant in that it promoted students' tolerance as well as their understanding of prejudice and stereotypes.[19]

Perhaps the most convincing rationale for professional development on a topic such as the Holocaust was the sources that teachers gave for their knowl-edge base on the subject. The most common source given was "informal learning not including web research" at 85%. Undergraduate coursework and high school coursework both came in at just over 50% each. Only 23% named professional development and 17% graduate coursework as supplying them with information and instructional resources for teaching about the Holocaust.[20] These results pro-vide strong evidence that subject-specific professional development is needed and can enrich history classrooms for young adults on a critical topic.

Another basic component of professional development for history teachers is the regular reading of journals that connect them to historians. A number of ex-cellent ones exist. Examples include *Social Education*, the journal of the National Council for the Social Studies, the *Magazine of History* produced by the Organi-zation of American Historians, *The Social Studies*, and *The History Teacher*. Two organizations that support the increased knowledge of history paired with activi-ties for teachers are The American Institute for History Education (www.america-ninstituteforhistory.org) and the National Council for History Education (www.nche.net). Both provide professional development opportunities, conferences, publications, and online and print resources for the classroom history teacher.

While often mixing academic and popular history, there are magazines that can add to a teacher's knowledge base. These include *American Heritage, Ameri-can History Illustrated*, and specialized publications on military history focusing on the Civil War and World War II. Beyond these historical sources, teachers should be familiar with journals of opinion. These journals span the political spectrum from the left (*American Prospect, The Nation,* and *The Progressive*), the right (*American Interest, The Weekly Standard,* and *The National Review*), and the moderate middle (*The Atlantic, The New Republic,* and *Harpers*). And they often have articles connecting history to current issues and book reviews on works of history and biography.

An attendant and strong professional development opportunity can be found each weekend in teachers' homes on cable television. C-SPAN2 provides 60 hours of book talks, interviews, and panels with non-fiction authors. A majority of the books' topics are drawn from history, biography, and politics. Bookstores and universities often host local authors for readings and book signings. They are frequently related to local and state history or past and present community figures of interest.

Educators (or students) should also not forget their local library. Visits by the author to the city library usually provide a new title or two for perusal. Unique treatments of history found during such visits have included Alan Axelrod's *The Real History of World War II: A New Look at the Past*. Axelrod enriched his narrative with sections titled "Reality Check," "Links," "Takeaway," "Alternative Takes," "Details, Details," and "Numbers." In addition there were quotes and photos with expanded text to accompany them. This approach provides the teacher with multiple discussion starters to expand on the usual material found in textbooks. Another volume referenced in an earlier chapter is a collection of one-page vignettes by Axelrod and Charles Phillips's *What Every American Should Know About American History: 225 Events that Shaped the Nation*. It provided solid and fresh insights on a variety of familiar historical figures and episodes drawn from the worlds of sports, media, literature, medicine, and (again) even gangsters.[21]

Diversity has been suggested as one of the most critical topics that should be included in professional development for teachers. James Banks, who has been called the "Father of Multicultural Education," and others have suggested several reasons why diversity is essential to professional development for teachers. The rationales fit well for those who teach history to adolescents. Such professional development helps educators examine their own personal attitudes toward diversity and acquire knowledge of the histories of diverse racial, ethnic, cultural, and language (RECL) groups. Teachers also become acquainted with RECL perspectives, understand how institutions (including schools) perpetuate stereotypes, and acquire knowledge to develop and implement instruction for all students.[22]

Specific ideas for history teachers in the arena of professional development in diversity include a content scan to identify the curriculum and textbooks that examine events primarily from the point of view of the dominant culture. The perspective of the vanquished has often been disregarded or marginalized at the expense of the victors. Examples of such events in American history would include the discovery of America, the Westward Movement, territorial acquisitions both domestic and foreign, wars and occupations, support of various revolutions and opposition to others, and the perspective of RECL groups such as African Americans and Native Americans.[23]

While subject-specific (history) professional development activities are strongly encouraged, there are also what might be termed generic experiences. Some organizations provide in-service, in-school sessions, while others hold their seminars and workshops in their home offices or campuses. These organizations have established frameworks for effective professional development and include: The National Staff Development Council (www.nsdc.org), the American Association of School Administrators (www.aasa.org), the National School Boards Association (www.nsba.org), and the Association for the Supervision and Curriculum Development (www.ascd.org). Regional K–12 accrediting bodies can also be an excellent source for professional development resources and experiences. The largest in the United States is AdvancED North Central Association Commission on Accreditation and School Improvement (www.ncacasi.org). These organizations sponsor outstanding conferences and are excellent resources for discovering potential speakers in local school districts, information, and materials.

The National Institute for Learning Development (NILD) is a not-for-profit organization whose mission is to build competence and confidence in those who desire to improve their ability to learn and their ability to help others learn. First started as a group to work exclusively with learning disabled students, the organization has broadened its mission and works with educators and other leaders in the areas of teaching skills, program development, assessment, and student evaluation, to name but a few. They also have publications such as Kathleen Richards Hopkins' *Teaching How to Learn in a What-to-Learn Culture*.[24]

An example of the work of NILD is Hopkins' survey that explores the lifelong learning attitudes and habits of teachers formulated in questions. These include:

- Are you a lover of reading, inclined to read for pleasure as well as for information? Research shows that many new teachers do not like to read. They prefer to surf the Internet or watch the news rather than read a book, newspaper, or weekly magazine.

- Are you endowed with an intellectual curiosity that searches for answers through wonder and reflection? (Albert Einstein was reported to have said, "I have no special talent. I am only passionately curious.") List the things you are curious about [in history] and let your students know that you are curious about these things.

- Are you connected to your culture through cultural literacy? Are you enthusiastic about learning and gaining new information? Such a knowledge base allows us to understand our daily newspapers, our peers, and our leaders.

- Are you confident and competent in your profession? Do you think that your college studies adequately prepared you to teach? If not, what can you do about it?[25]

Mentors are an under-used and under-appreciated resource for professional development. While mentorships are often built into teacher induction programs, these experiences are usually limited to one to three years in duration. Ideally mentoring should be a lifelong process. The relationship between mentor and teacher may not necessarily continue throughout an entire career. Often, as a teacher transitions to new assignments or develops new interests, the mentor may change. (This book is dedicated to the author's five mentors—some contributed over a lifetime while others connected for shorter periods of time.) Direct benefits of mentors include a source for professional advice and "safe" constructive criticism, an entrée into new networks, and a supportive voice of encouragement. The securing of a mentor or mentors can be an effective component of professional development for both the novice and veteran teacher. By the same token, teachers, at some stage in their careers, need to assume the role of mentor to others in the profession.

In addition to mentors, an easily forgotten resource for professional development is the expertise of fellow teachers. Laura Varlas in "Looking Within: Teachers Leading Their Own Learning" quotes the National Staff Development Council report *Professional Learning in the Learning Profession: A Status Report on Teacher Development in the U.S. and Abroad*:

> U.S. teachers perceive little control over their own professional development. In other competitive nations, such as Finland, Sweden, and Switzerland . . . teachers have substantial influence . . . on their own professional development. In Hong Kong, New Zealand, and Singapore . . . embedded, ongoing, collaborative, capacity-building professional development is the norm.[26]

Varlas also notes that teachers believe that "teacher-led professional development is more personal, more tangible." The professional development is not always in the form of in-service workshops. Teachers opening up their classrooms as demonstration models for their colleagues is also professional development.[27]

A simple but effective professional development practice is exchanging ideas with colleagues. This can be accomplished at the building or district level. McCotter found in one study that monthly meetings allowed teachers to share successes and challenges, to receive feedback from peers, and to voice support for each other. There need not be an agenda, speaker, or administrative permission or leadership to make this happen.[28] This may be counterintuitive to the need for professional development that is targeted at a specific age group, teaching strategy, or subject matter area. But this is not to say those forms of professional development preclude the informal sessions McCotter discovered.

William Van Til described in his autobiography a similar approach that began in the 1930s and continued into the 21st century. Comprised of both K–12 and higher education professionals, the gathering was known as the "Spring Conference." Meeting in Chicago each year, the group of approximately 30 educators would spend a Saturday morning sharing the issues and topics that were most on their minds.

Over lunch, four panels were structured that topically captured the professional interests of the group. A session—representing two of the panels—met Saturday afternoon, presenting to the entire group and leading a discussion. The other two panels held their session on Sunday morning. Brief talks with much interaction followed. There were no formal presentations, no papers, no minutes, no publications, and what was "said in Chicago stayed in Chicago."[29] It is a model that could be easily replicated by history teachers. A workable variation would be cross-district professional development time where history teachers talk to colleagues from other schools about common history-related teaching issues.

The final essential element of professional development is sustainability. Fullan has listed here non-negotiables for successful sustainability that for him means building capacity for change. They are competencies, resources, and motivation. Unpacked in their most practical sense competencies are the skills, knowledge, and dispositions that are developed. Resources can be anything from time to expertise to money. And motivation is when there is energy, commitment, and internal interest to improve.[30] These serve as the foundation for professional development. For teachers these are not tasks or obligations, but opportunities to grow and truly become lifelong learners. This makes professional development itself a "non-negotiable." In the eighteenth century Samuel Johnson famously stated, "When one is tired of London, one is tired of life." A modification of Johnson's statement to fit today's educators could be, "When one is tired of learning, one is tired of teaching."

The World of Practice
A Model Lesson from the Advanced Placement Classroom
by Paul Shaddox

I begin the lesson for each chapter of the textbook used in my Advanced Placement United States History class with a discussion of a "big picture" or "focus question" assigned to the students. This question is given to the students before they are assigned to read the chapter. This question is subjective in nature and is intended to require that the students create and defend a thesis. In addition to the "big picture question," the students are also given several objective questions to answer from the reading. Their instruction is to answer the objective questions and then to reflect on their responses and record how the information from the objective questions and answers might be used in creating and defending a thesis response to the subjective focus question. At this point it would be useful to look at an example from my lesson plans.

The first chapter of most U.S. History survey textbooks tells the story of the collision of the "worlds" of western Europe, the west coast of Africa, and the islands of the Caribbean and the lands from Florida to the tip of South America. I have chosen to take that idea of a "collision of worlds" and have asked students to respond to the following question:

Analyze and evaluate the effects of the "collision of worlds" on the people of Europe, Africa, and Latin-America between 1450 and 1600.

I assign the reading of Chapter 1 and I provide the students with objective questions to answer as they read. The questions are intended to give the students a large "bank" of information useful in their task of answering the "big picture question" concerning the "collision of worlds." The students are instructed to record any thought that may occur to them about how the people and events they are reading about impacted the people indigenous to those three broad regions.

At the beginning of the first lesson on Chapter 1, I will have a student read the focus question and I will explain the meaning of key terms in the question. After several students have been given the opportunity to explain back to me the basic expectations required by the wording of the question (i.e., the essay should be organized into body paragraphs with each paragraph focused on a particular set or category of facts and that the impact on the lives of the people of all three "worlds" must be judged), we begin to discuss the story of that contact. I provide talking points from a projector. Periodically, I ask an individual student to tell the class how a particular person, such as Cortez, impacted the lives of the Spanish and Aztecs. After hearing the answer, I then ask another student to tell me which one of the three main groups of people listed in the focus question benefited from the "collision" and which group may have been harmed by the "collision of worlds."

At the conclusion of the chapter, I arrange the students into small groups and assign each group the task of taking the information from their notes and separating useful facts into the following four categories: Social; Political; Economic; and Cultural.

I encourage the students to use proper nouns and to make their lists as lengthy as they are able. Once the lists have been produced, I have students from each group read the list of facts from the four categories. We discuss whether or not the facts are appropriately grouped. For example, students often use the establishment of the African slave trade by the Portuguese and the enrichment of Portugal at the cost of freedom for the Africans captured and the disruption of society on the west coast of Africa in both the social and the economic categories.

Next, I ask each group to briefly discuss the nature of the social, political, economic, and cultural changes that occurred to each of the three groups of people as a result of the "collision of worlds." Usually the students recognize that the "collision of worlds" produced profound changes in the lives of the people in all three "worlds." They also recognize through our learning process that the Europeans derived many of the benefits and suffered few of the costs of the changes while the people of Africa and the natives of the Americas shared in fewer of the benefits and bore most of the costs of the world-changing events between 1450 and 1600. At this point, they are ready to write a thesis statement.

The students are instructed to pay strict attention to the language of the question and incorporate much of that language into their thesis statement. This instruction serves the purpose of ensuring that the students remain focused on answering the question that was asked rather than "drifting" into an essay response to a different question. I show them a little trick that I learned early in my career as an AP US History teacher. It is a "pat" thesis response referred to as "Although . . . nevertheless . . ." Often, using this format, students will experience success in developing a thesis that is clear, complex, and responsive to the question asked. Quite often, the statement developed by the students will be similar to the following example:

> *The "collision of worlds" occurring between 1450 and 1600 produced profound social, political, economic, and cultural changes resulting primarily in benefits and dominance for the people of Europe and most of the costs being borne by the people of Africa and the natives of the Americas.*

Once each student has created a thesis, we work on organizing an essay around the thesis. I train my students to begin the essay with a brief background statement of no more than one or two sentences. I tell them to refer to an event preceding the scope contained in the question. In the chapter 1 question, many students make a reference to the Crusades, Marco Polo, or the quest for a trade route to Asia. This background demonstrates that the student understands that history involves an on-going process in which events of the particular time (1450–1600) are related to events that came before 1450. The next step in the introduction paragraph is to create a transition or bridging statement connecting the background information to the thesis. I teach them to focus on the question and to call attention to something in the question that will connect the background to the thesis. Often, students will see a connection between European contact with the outside world in launching the Crusades or in the travels of Marco Polo or the quest for a trade route to Asia. In one or two sentences, the students will point out that it was the European "world" that sought the contact with the people of the other two "worlds." Together, the background, transition, and thesis statement created following this method should provide the student with a very smooth introduction paragraph for this (or any) essay, making it easy for his teacher or future college professor to understand his argument. The following is an example of how a typical student response to the collision of worlds question begins:

> *In the aftermath of the Crusades, Europe began to awaken from the Dark Ages and redeveloped an interest in trade with the outside world. To facilitate lower costs for goods from the Far East, sailors employed by the Portuguese and later, the Spanish, began to search for water routes to Asia. The voyages of discovery that followed brought the people of Europe into contact with the people of coastal West Africa and the people of the Americas. The "collision of worlds" between 1450 and 1600 produced profound social, political, economic, and cultural changes resulting primarily in benefits and dominance for the people of Europe and most of the costs being borne by the people of Africa and the natives of the Americas.*

Four body paragraphs may be organized for this essay. Each paragraph should be devoted to one of the four categories of changes identified in the thesis statement. Each body paragraph should begin with a simple statement to identify the type of change that will be explored in that paragraph. I tell my students to be sure to use many proper nouns from the list of facts that they made during group work. I also caution them to be sure that the specific facts are accurately developed and that they do not contradict their thesis with their choice of facts. It is a good indication that a student might want to rethink his thesis if he finds that his facts don't support his argument. In addition to creating a topic sentence and using substantial numbers of specific and relevant facts, the students also must draw appropriate conclusions from the facts to support the thesis. The following example is typical of a competent student body paragraph devoted to social changes:

> *The collision of worlds produced significant social changes for the people of Europe, Africa, and the Americas. The Spanish developed the encomienda system which consisted of large land grants made by the King to the nobility of Spain. In the Americas, the nobles who chose to live on their new estates were referred to as the peninsulares and were recognized as the highest class in the New World social order. Beneath the peninsulares were their American-born children, the criollos. Beneath the children of the nobles were the Spanish soldiers and government officials. Socially below the people of European blood were the mixed-race Mestizo population. These people, of Spanish fathers and Native-American mothers, eventually formed the nucleus of the Latin-American version of the middle class. At the bottom of the New World society were the Native Americans, the Africans, and those of mixed African and Native American ancestry. The emergent society in the New World placed the people of European ancestry at the upper levels and the people of Native American and African origins in subservient positions, with many of them being enslaved by the Europeans.*

The final or conclusion paragraph begins with a restatement of the thesis. Sometimes, students reach a deeper understanding of their topic as a result of going through the process of writing an essay. I tell my students that it is appropriate to rephrase their thesis (while not contradicting the original statement) if they are able to clarify or elaborate on their original point. I then have them summarize the best points that were made in advancing their argument with the idea that it is good to remind the reader of the strongest points of analysis just before a grade is assigned. I then tell them to conclude with an extension statement that goes beyond the time period of the question. Many times on this question, students will choose to mention the coming English and French colonies in the New World and note how the Latin-American paradigm of European dominance would continue into the seventeenth and eighteenth centuries.

In summation, I believe that this method not only helps students to write very competent essays, it also helps them to master the "facts" about U.S. History at a high level. Most years, when I receive the results from the AP US History exam, I find that my sophomores have scored above the national average of juniors and seniors on both the essay and multiple choice portions of the test. The students who create, keep, and study all forty-one thesis statements and category outline/lists from the chapter questions rarely fail to qualify for college credit and the majority of those hard-working students score either a 4 or a 5 on the exam.

Paul Shaddox is a high school and community college instructor of United States history in Broken Arrow, Oklahoma. He has taught Advanced Placement United States history, been a consultant for the College Board, and trained thousands of his fellow teachers in the AP process.

Endnotes

1   Loewen, James W. *Lies My Teacher Told Me: Everything Your American History Textbook Got Wrong*. New York: Touchstone, 2007. 327.
2   van Hover, Stephanie. "The Professional Development of Teachers." Ed. Linda S. Levstik, and Cynthia A. Tuson. *Handbook of Research in Social Studies Education*. New York: Routledge, 2008. 354.
3   van Hover, 356.
4   Valli, L., and M. Stout. "Continuing Professional Development for Social Studies Teachers." Ed. S. Adler. *Critical Issues in Social Studies Teacher Education*. Greenwich: Information Age Publishing, 2004. 184.
5   Sykes, Gary. "Teacher and Student Learning: Strengthening their Connection." Ed. Linda Darling-Hammond and Gary Sykes. *Teaching as the Learning Profession: Handbook of Policy and Practice*. San Francisco: Jossey-Bass, 1999. 161.
6   Reeves, Douglas B. *Transforming Professional Development into Student Results*. Alexandria: Association for Supervision and Curriculum, 2010; Semadeni, Joseph H.

Taking Charge of Professional Development: A Practical Model for Your School. Alexandria: Association for Supervision and Curriculum, 2010.

7   Reeves, 23.

8   Ibid. 52–53 and 65–71.

9   See *National Board for Professional Teaching Standards* website at <http://www.nbpts.org>.

10   Blescke-Rechek, April, David Lubinski, and Camilla P. Benbow. "Meeting the Education Needs of Special Populations: Advanced Placement's Role in Developing Exceptional Human Capital." *Psychological Science* 15 (2004): 217–24.

11   Duffett, Ann, and Steve Farkas. *Growing Pains in the Advanced Placement Program: Do Tough Trade-Offs Lie Ahead?* Report by the Thomas B. Fordham Institute available at <http://www.edexcellence.net>.

12   Ibid.

13   Dennis, Lawrence J. *George S. Counts and Charles A. Beard: Collaborators for Change.* Albany: State University of New York Press, 1989.

14   Thornton, Stephen J. *Teaching Social Studies That Matters: Curriculum for Active Learning.* New York: Teachers College Press, 2005. 38.

15   Ibid. 39.

16   Turk, Diana, Rachel Mattson, Terrie Epstein, and Robert Cohen. *Teaching U.S. History: Dialogues among Social Studies Teachers and Historians.* New York: Routledge, 2010.

17   See <http://www.facinghistory.org> for workshops, materials, and other resources.

18   Donnelly, Mary Beth. "Educating Students About the Holocaust: A Survey of Teaching Practices." *Social Education* 70. 1 (2006): 51–55.

19   Ibid.

20   See the *Facing History and Ourselves* website <http://www2.facinghistory.org> for a list of seminars and resources in this exceptional Holocaust professional development organization.

21   Axelrod, Alan. *The Real History of World War II: A New Look at the Past.* New York: Sterling Publishing, 2008; and Axelrod, Alan and Charles Phillips. *What Every American Should Know about American History: 225 Events that Shaped the Nation.* 3rd ed. Avon: Adams Media, 2008.

22   Banks, James A. et al. "Education and Diversity." *Social Education* 69. 1 (2005): 36–41.

23   Ibid.

24   Hopkins, Kathleen Richards. *Teaching How to Learn in a What-to-Learn Culture.* San Francisco: Jossey-Bass, 2010. See also <http://www.nild.net> for more information on the work of the *National Institute for Learning Development*.

25   Ibid. 42–47.

26   Varlas, Laura. "Looking Within: Teachers Leading Their Own Learning." *Education Update* 52. 7 (2010): 3.

27   Ibid. 4.

28   McCotter, S. S. "Collaborative Groups as Professional Development." *Teaching and Teacher Education* 17 . 6 (2001): 685–704.

29   Van Til, William. *My Way of Looking at It.* 2nd ed. San Francisco: Caddo Gap Press, 1996. 286–87.

30   Fullan, Michael. *The Six Secrets of Change: What the Best Leaders Do to Help Their Organizations Survive and Thrive.* San Francisco, CA: Jossey-Bass, 2008. 57.

THIRTEEN

Assessment:
How Do We Know What the Students Know?

As discussed in the first chapter, the topic of assessing student learning has become the overriding issue in American education during the past decade. The centrality it now holds in classrooms, school districts, state boards of education, and national policy has become paramount. No other practice holds greater dominance in the everyday work of students and teachers or consumes the time, efforts, and conversation of educators than does assessment.

The issue of assessing individual student academic work and progress and the assessment of not only students, but entities that range from classrooms to schools to districts to states is not new. The intensity of the movement is, though. Forty years ago three thoughtful educators, Howard Kirschenbaum, Sidney Simon, and Rodney Napier, wrote a provocative book with a provocative title—*Wad-Ja-Get? The Grading Game in American Education*.[1] The history of assessment goes back even further, more than a century, to the work of educational theorists and practitioners such as Edward Thorndike and later Ralph Tyler. But the question "Wad-Ja-Get" is not just being asked of one student to another. "Wad-Ja-Get," in a bit more sophisticated jargon, is being asked by officials from Washington, D.C. to state capitols and school districts across the nation. The difference now is that assessment is no longer a "game."

There are informed skeptics and practitioners as to where the current assessment phenomenon is taking us. (Visit a teachers' lounge to confirm this.) O.L. Davis has written that "The idea of 'measuring history' can only be ludicrous."[2]

Grant and Horn have written, "Despite the best hopes and the direst predictions, we actually know very little about how history teachers and their students are responding to state-level tests."[3]

While the opinions of those who assail the current student assessment movement are many, veteran teacher-educator Arthur Ellis has written that there are compelling reasons for why we assess student progress. Students need to know how they are performing academically and so do parents. And, writes Ellis, teachers most of all need to know if their students are learning the important ideas, skills, and content in history. A final reason that Ellis gives for teachers paying attention to assessment is that it provivdes "a means of getting your students to take learning seriously, to realize that accountability is a fact of life."[4]

Few contributions to the literature on assessment fail to cite a host of studies which report the conventional wisdom that multiple techniques are needed to accurately and authentically measure student learning. In addition to standardized tests, the formative and summative assessment strategies suggested include oral evaluations, teacher observation of individual and group work, performances, and student self-evaluations. The National Council for the Social Studies in their position statement on the assessment components of the 2002 federal legislation No Child Left Behind expressed concern over the types of tests being administered. In addition, they also believed that due to the lack of "equal footing" with mathematics and literacy (primary areas for mandatory testing), history, civics, and geography were receiving less attention in the instructional day. The phrase "if it isn't tested, it isn't taught" has the potential of becoming a truism for history and the other subjects within the social studies.[5]

Five years into No Child Left Behind (NCLB), the marker many citizens and educators place on for the beginning of high-stakes testing, S.G. Grant examined the status of the movement. (High-stakes testing did not commence with NCLB, but rather its most recent iteration was an outgrowth of the standards movement that began in the early 1980s.) With mathematics and literacy the most frequently tested areas, only about half the states midway through the first decade of the 21st century conducted standards-based social studies tests. Grant views the "stakes" in high-stakes testing as being the consequences for students and teachers. Some states, like Texas and New York, are indeed high-stakes places. Students will not graduate from high school if they do not pass the tests. More states, though, use the scores toward an assessment of the schools. No states in Grant's 2007 study used test scores to dismiss teachers.[6]

Following the rationale behind testing to its logical conclusion, there should also be consequences for national and state legislators and also local school officials who strongly support this high-stakes practice. But this rarely happens. One indicator of success of state testing should be graduation rates. Yet in 2010 "Diplomas Count" data for 2006 showed a slight decrease in the graduation rate. The

2007 "Diplomas Count" figures, provided by the Editorial Projects in Education, a Bethesda, Maryland, nonprofit, show a 68.8 percent graduation rate for students earning a standard diploma. (The peak year was 1969, with a 77 percent rate.)

As always, when the data is closely examined there are reasons for both optimism and concern. Several large, urban districts had increased rates—these included Memphis, Tennessee, and Newport-Mesa, California. However, racial and ethnic gaps persist. Forty-six percent of Black students, 44 percent of Latinos, and 49 percent of Native Americans did not earn a diploma in four years. About one-fifth of the non-graduates came from the nation's 25 largest school districts including New York City, Los Angeles, and Clark County, Nevada. Such data, and other like it, appear to shed doubt on the efficacy of high-stakes testing. And yet an immediate response to the data by one education reform group, the Alliance for Excellent Education, was a call to "ramp up efforts on . . . holding schools accountable."[7]

Grant also found that high-stakes testing may not be having the wished-for impact on teachers that many policymakers have thought. Research shows curricular, instructional, and assessment decisions by teachers are less influenced by testing regimens than by the practices of individuals and groups in their own schools and districts. One rather subtle distinction is what has been called teachers "learning to live with the test, but not by it." The research, at this juncture, is not showing a broad spectrum of responses to testing mandates by teachers in their classroom practice.[8]

Cunningham and Allington remind us that assessment is part of everything we do in life—not just the classroom. From the weather to the food to products we use each day, we are assessing. While retaining the need to assess the policy of assessment itself and make their voice known, in support or dissent, educators need to discover ways to "make assessment an extension of teaching, rather than just one more chore that has to be done."[9]

In response to the question "What is assessment?," Cunningham and Allington give this reply:

> Sometimes it is easier to define something by beginning with what it is not. Assessment is *not* grading—although assessment can help you determine and support the grades you give. Assessment is *not* standardized test scores—although these scores can give you some general idea of what [students] have achieved so far. Assessment *is* collecting and analyzing data to make decisions about how [students] are performing and growing.[10]

But often the term assessment does become intertwined with the vocabulary of tests, grading, and evaluation. Oliva uses evaluation and assessment interchangeably to denote what is called the "general process of appraisal." The terms measurement and testing are then subsumed under the general classification of evaluation and assessment. Oliva does extrapolate, though, when describing the process of evaluation (assessment): There is 1) Pre-assessment where criterion-referenced tests are used as *entry-behavior tests* and *pretests*, 2) Formative Evaluation that consists of the formal and informal techniques used during instruction, and 3) Summative Evaluation, which is the assessment that takes place at the end of a lesson, unit or course. Oliva reiterates that there are multiple assessments beyond the classroom such as district, state, national (ACT, SAT, NAEP) and even international assessments.[11]

"By itself, the term assessment means little because it can mean so much."[12] So write Grant and Salinas in their exploration of assessment and accountability in social studies education. By this they mean it includes individual, class, school, state, and national assessments. As seen, assessments can also be categorized as formative, summative, criterion-referenced or just plain basic student knowledge. It can even be used outside the academic arena to measure students' social aptitude and career readiness. Concluding their review of assessment in the social studies, Grant and Salinas pessimistically assert that:

> On the one hand, a growing research base on assessment and accountability is far from sufficient. Some patterns can be seen, but they are more suggestive than definitive. On the other hand, the theoretical base on testing is even less developed. Some traditional and contemporary theories can be applied to the social studies testing context, but a well-conceived, well-supported theory specific to social studies assessment and accountability has yet to surface.[13]

Henson, striking at the heart of the assessment process, has written that "Assessment should always be tied to the needs of students. The most significant evaluation of student achievement should be the extent to which they want to know more and their ability to do so." Henson, who also acknowledges Oliva's view that terminology within assessment often becomes intertwined and not clearly defined, adds that tests, evaluations, or grades—whatever assessments may be labeled—must be viewed as instructionally useful to the students.[14]

An assessment process has been produced by Voltz, Sims, and Nelson. They have viewed the instructional cycle as including: 1) assessing students to determine what and how to teach, 2) planning instruction informed by assessment, 3) delivering instruction with embedded assessment, 4) assessing student learning outcomes, and 5) planning next steps in instruction sequence based on assessment.[15] Following this cycle reinforces both Henson's and Oliva's constructs for connecting assessment to instruction.

Assessment cannot be separated from the learning process. The "cram, test, forget" routine employed by many students is not education, nor is it assessment. The central goal, one could add the only goal, of assessment is to improve student learning and teacher instruction. Caldwell has provided a straightforward four-step process for assessment: 1) identify what is to be assessed, 2) collect evidence,

3) analyze the evidence, and 4) make a decision and act on that decision.[16] With Caldwell's model as a foundation, specific assessment practices can be put into place.

Two middle level educators, Brown and Knowles, focus the center of their attention on the idea of using assessment as a means to help adolescents become more involved in the assessing of their own learning. Aligned with the middle school philosophy, they see assessment as directed toward self-discovery, self-evaluation, and self-knowledge.[17] This is a noble goal that is probably not achievable in the current testing climate. But that does not mean it should not be kept as a goal.

With all the talk of high-stakes testing it is easy to forget that traditional grading is, arguably, assessment too. One middle level educator, Paul Barnwell, maintains that traditional grading in the classroom needs to be deemphasized. He gives a rationale for his stance and provides alternatives. Traditional grading does not truly measure learning, says Barnwell. Grades do show growth and they tend to reduce intrinsic motivation due to the emphasis on external motivation—the ubiquitous "will this count?" mindset. Traditional grading may produce compliance, but it does not produce learning. Barnwell suggests a number of simple, but apparently effective, grading alternatives. He places a student's name on 3 inch by 5 inch cards that he flips through every three days in class asking students questions. This is to assure there is no "hiding" by students. One tactic is to tell students that "green dots" on an assignment means that it has been spot checked and approved. If the assignment is incomplete or wrong a "red dot" is placed on it until the student work receives the "green dot." Another idea is to purchase inexpensive white wall paneling at a home improvement store and cut it into mini-white boards. Activities can be undertaken on them using erasable markers and wiped clean. Finally, laptops. In a history class students can search for virtual tours of historic sites or find Web pages connected to the lesson.[18]

The accusation has been made that high-stakes testing has contributed to less innovative teaching methods with more "drill and kill" activities being used. One saving grace, mentioned previously, is that history is often not one of the regularly tested areas. The downside to that fact is that social studies is often given less class time at the elementary grade level, thus depriving students of a strong foundation in history and other social science subjects. Terrie Epstein, reporting on data from several research studies, found what she has termed the "deleterious effects on teaching history as an academic discipline." The research supports the contention that high-stakes tests have encouraged some history teachers to lower the academic level of the material being taught, to be less creative in their pedagogy, and to dash through hundreds of years of history in order to cover the curriculum and potential test questions.[19] Assessment should never, as this study suggests, adversely impact student learning.

The current nature of assessment has been called into question on a number of fronts. One critique of current practices is that assessment only measures comprehension and the making of inferences as compared to having students grapple with the big ideas of subjects such as history. The point is related to "narrowing" the curriculum. The case of state frameworks, such as the Virginia Standards of Learning, directs students toward common and finite responses—listing, for example, the causes of World War I. One researcher has suggested that responses to such assessments provide no incentive for students to delve further into the subject.[20] The causes of World War I are an appropriate subject for students to learn about in an American history class. But for it to be given priority when studying this period of history to the exclusion of other content is how assessment becomes a limiting factor.

Loewen has pointed to researchers who maintain that that the sheer number of topics called for in math and science assessments is a major cause for poor comparative performance between the United States and other modern nations. Erickson indicates that this trend is especially problematic in history. Respected researchers Marzano and Kendall agree. National and state standards have proliferated in all disciplines until we are "awash in a sea of standards." They report that there are as many as 400 benchmarks (content topics) in a history course.[21]

One approach that can prove helpful to history teachers is the categorization of assessments. Drake and Nelson have created four levels or types of history assessments:

- Standardized—traditional objectives items such as multiple-choice, fill-in-the-blank, matching, and true and false.

- Alternative—any and all assessments that differ from traditional objective assessments.

- Authentic—assessments that engage students in applying historical knowledge and skills the way they are used in the real world.

- Performance—encompasses both alternative and authentic assessment.[22]

Drake and Nelson advocate for advancing students to the performance assessment level of historical literacy. By functioning at this level students demonstrate their knowledge of historical facts, themes, and ideas. They also demonstrate their ability to reason or operate at the higher levels of critical thinking when working with historical evidence. And finally students are able to communicate their historical knowledge and reasoning to a wider audience.[23]

One of the more helpful tools in assessment is rubrics. Rubrics provide well-defined categories of content and/or performance criteria by which students' academic efforts and products can be judged. It is often noted that rubrics should not be used for grading. But as seen by Oliva's comments on assessments, terminology frequently morphs into this area of instruction. Yet if rubrics are effective in student assessment in areas outside of grading, then there seems no rationale that they could not be just as effective to use in grading students. Rubrics, as will be shown, are being seen with greater regularity in a number of assessment venues. Therefore, their purpose needs to be examined and understood.

Rubrics are used in the assessment process for several reasons. One is that rubrics offer students explicit (or quite specific) "targets" to aim for as they undertake their work. Students know before they commence their work what the expectations are for the assignments. Second, rubrics provide a standard by which student work can be evaluated. While rubrics do not assure total objectivity, they do allow those assessing student work to do so with less subjectivity. Third, there is uniformity for all students within rubrics, thereby creating greater potential for equitable treatment among and between students. There are also usually fewer questions (and challenges) from students about assignments or assessments. This would support the contention that rubrics clarify assignments for students. Fourth, they can provide the opportunity for students and teachers to dialogue about content and instruction in a structured way. One study reported that a majority of teachers who were introduced to rubrics continued to use them.[24]

Ko and Rossen, in writing about online instruction, have succinctly stated the overall purpose of a rubric: "An effective rubric should be detailed enough to cover all the complexity and different aspects required to complete an assignment, but simple enough that an instructor has little trouble deciding between the higher and the lower parts of the grading range." They add that although creating useful rubrics requires significant upfront time, the investment in the final product will pay dividends when assessments are completed by the students.[25]

Another aspect of using rubrics is the need to provide students with explanations in regard to the terminology being used. What follow are examples used by the author in connection with rubric language that could be used with older adolescents in gifted and talented history classes:

Thorough is defined as carried through to completion, marked by full detail, complete in all aspects, relatively error-free in its presentation—of overall exceptional quality. If creativeness is called for in the work, such creativeness would include some, but not all, of descriptors such as original, inventive, imaginative, and innovative. Higher-order thinking skills such as evaluation, synthesis, and analysis are demonstrated. The creativeness is readily apparent and evident to the evaluator. The response went beyond what was asked for in the task, question, review, or project. Not all of these attributes must be present, but the term **thorough** indicates that several are in place.

Adequate is defined as meeting basic requirements, sufficient, satisfactory, acceptable but not exceptional. Occasional, but not serious, errors are present. If creativeness is called for in the work, it is limited and moderately original with some innovativeness present. Higher-order thinking skills are present to some extent, with application and comprehension level also evident. Not all of these attributes must be present, but the term **adequate** indicates several are in place.

Limited is defined as attempting to respond to the question, but not fully succeeding in the answer. Errors are present and detract from the response. The responses show a lack of understanding of the material and are based too heavily on the textbook. Often there is an inability to apply or comprehend the material being assessed. Expansion and additional investment in time and effort are needed.

Not every aspect of these three terms—thorough, adequate, and limited— needs to be met to reach the level of the rubric's expectation. But such explanations assist both student and teacher in the assessment process.

Integrated teaching is often advocated in the study of history. The practice calls for teachers as well as students to "up their game" in the intellectual arena. Assessing integrated learning can be even more challenging. But again, the use of rubrics can assist. Fogarty has created criteria and quality indicators within a set of generic rubrics to assess integrated learning. The five elements are relevance (real), richness (multidimensional), relatedness (connected), rigor (higher-order thinking), and recursion (transfer). His four key quality indicators are "Not Yet!" (progress, needs help, does not meet standards), "On Our Way" (developing, emerging, on the brink, almost meets standards), "This Is It!" (in the zone, competent, good job, meets standards), and "Above and Beyond!" (exceptional, superior, proficient, exceeds standards).[26] In addition to these key terms, for both criteria and especially quality indicators, it may helpful to define several of the terms. For example, what is meant by competent, proficient, or superior?

Do we know if rubrics enhance student learning? The research on rubrics is beginning to emerge. Robert Marzano, writing in 2010, has found that students tracking their own progress by using rubrics is a " hidden gem" in terms of practice. Achievement gains of 25% and higher have been reported when rubrics are incorporated in the assessment process. Again, these studies were focused on students tracking their own work. Factors, in addition to rubrics, were addressing a single goal in all the assessments and the use of differing assessments. But the third factor, and a major one, was the use of rubrics. Marzano does warn against using points instead of rubrics. But realistically, when rubrics are used in grading, they will have points assigned to them. The concern over the use of points is that a rubric in one chapter, assignment, or project may not be worth the same as a rubric in some other chapter, assignment, or project. Yet whether points are employed or not, there is no way in a history curriculum that equivalencies between and among material can be determined. But research does support the efficacy of rubrics.[27]

As discussed in an earlier chapter in terms of student involvement in textbook selection, so too there has been a call for their participation in the assessment process. Vagle has reported that a number of studies point to student involvement as one of several key factors in quality assessment. One important approach that Vagle lists is descriptive feedback. Feedback that describes learning rather than evaluates it; specificity of feedback; feedback that provides the next steps that students need to take in their learning; and feedback that is focused and manageable are all viewed as ways students can be better drawn in to the work of assessment.[28] One example of this student-focused assessment strategy, using a history example, would be a writing sample drawn from a lesson on the 1955 Montgomery Bus Boycott. Using appropriate teacher prompts, student writing samples would be produced from this event. Teachers would then provide specific strengths (or deficiencies) in the work. These could include feedback from the teacher such as: Which individuals were mentioned or "left out?" Was the chronological flow of the narrative accurate? What details from the boycott became part of the wider Civil Rights movement?

Before students assess their own work there is the question of who creates the test. Kari Smith, a Norwegian educator, has suggested that having students help write their own tests is what she terms a "complementary" form of assessment, not just an "alternative" form of assessment. (This is also formative assessment.) By complementary Smith is signifying that assessment (or tests) can be learning tools. Letting students in on the "secret" of testing and test construction is one method.[29] Smith does not grade the tests in terms of them "counting," but there is no reason why such student-created assessments could not be used in the grading process. The one reservation in terms of history assessments is the tendency for students (and sometimes teachers) to use minutiae and unimportant facts (dates and obscure names come quickly to mind) in their test creation.

For its uses and abuses, assessment can have a positive effect on students and schools. Not in the usual oversight or comparative functions of assessments that are most commonly practiced, but in showing educators what works and what doesn't work. It is often forgotten that arguably the best example of assessment took place in the years just prior to World War II. Known as the Eight Year Study, two groups of students—one attending traditional high schools and the other progressive schools—were tracked for their four years of high school and then four years of college. Comparisons were then made. Some will maintain that the progressive schools came out a bit better on most measures, including academics and social skills. Some assert that the results were at best a draw. It has been called "The Great Debate" in education between Essentialism and Progressivism. It is a debate that continues and will continue as new conceptions of teaching, learning, and measuring remain a critical component of our educational milieu.

Basic practices should always be employed in assessment. Positive comments, for example, should be used before noting the areas that need improvement. Some studies have shown that students receive negative comments to positive comments at a ratio of nine to one. Yet students need to know what they know and do not know, what they can do well and cannot do well. While students sometimes know where they stand academically, it is teachers who for the most part must provide this information. Feedback needs to be as specific as possible and delivered in a timely fashion.[30] Teachers should also be accepting of the idea of open-book tests. It can be used as a check of details, especially in history. It is not an "easy" way out for students. If they have not studied, then the use of their textbook will be of little help on a test.

Winger, a history teacher, has brought assessment back to reality with his appeal that the education establishment not lose track of what really matters in assessment. Winger notes the disconnect between school and life and the whip-lash it often causes students, not to mention teachers and parents, as they jump through a variety of "hoops of compliance and recall." Echoing the theme of relevance, Winger calls for students to apply what they learn to real-world situations and then not just ask for "remembering" but for understanding. "Understanding . . . makes learning meaningful, relevant, and enduring."[31]

In the end what history teachers need to remember is that assessment, whether formative, summative, or interim, must be balanced. A number of research studies have found that the skilled use of formative assessment has a significant and positive effect on student learning.[32] But employing such assessments takes practice, knowledge, and support in order for teachers to succeed. Schools and teachers must use tests for diagnostic purposes as well as benchmarks by which school or district-wide progress is measured. Only then will the practice of assessment live up to its promise.

The World of Practice
Using Rubrics for Assessing History Assignments
by Linda Merillat

Rubrics can be a powerful tool in the classroom. Not only can they be used to assess student performance, they can be used to clearly communicate requirements to students and to clearly delineate what constitutes excellent work from work that needs improvement.

As illustrated in Figure 1, content for a class is based on Standards and Class Outcomes—what students should be learning. As a part of class planning and design, one can ask the questions: How will I assess my students? How will I know the appropriate standards and class outcomes have been met? Ideally, assignments and assessments are designed together and stem from the content being presented. The decision to use one or more rubrics can occur at any point in the process, but the use of rubrics is most effective when the decision to use them is made early in the process and their use closely aligns with the overall class goals.

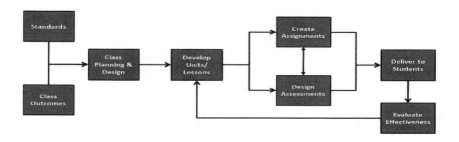

Figure 1 - Designing a Course

An Example Rubric

In general, a rubric lists criteria being evaluated, and it provides a corresponding metric for performance. There is a wide variety in the types of rubrics, the kinds of information included, and how they are used. Some examples include:

- **Checklist:** A checklist provides a list of criteria, and points can be assigned based on whether or not the item was completed.

- **Analytic Rubric:** An analytic rubric is the most common form and provides performance descriptions for each set of criteria. An example of analytic rubric is provided in Figure 2.

- **Holistic Rubric:** A holistic rubric combines several criteria and puts an emphasis on the overall performance rather than specific elements.

Category	Excellent	Good	Acceptable	Needs Improvement
Explanation of Reconstruction	The work explains why reconstruction occurred, what it was, and why it ended.	The work answers almost all of the questions about reconstruction.	The work only answers a few of the questions about reconstruction.	The work does not provide any explanation of reconstruction.
Historical Accuracy	There were no factual errors in the work, and the work was rich with factual details about real people, places, or events.	There were no factual errors, and many factual details were included about real people, places, or events.	There were no factual errors, and some factual details were included about real people, places, or events.	There were factual errors, or there were very few facts about real people, places, or events included.
Research	Research was extensive, and alternative points of view were investigated. Both primary and secondary sources were considered.	Research was appropriate, and alternative points of view were investigated.	Research was spotty and lacked depth.	Research was very limited.
Evidence and Examples	Many pieces of relevant and specific evidence or examples were presented, and the accompanying explanation clearly supported the author's position.	More than one piece of evidence or example was included, and the accompanying explanation clearly supported the author's position.	At least one piece of evidence or one example was provided to support author's position.	Evidence and examples do not apply to situation AND/OR were not explained.
Interpretation	The work includes several realistic inferences, possible situations, and thoughts that are reflective of the period.	The work includes some realistic inferences, possible situations, and thoughts that are reflective of the period.	The work includes very few realistic inferences, possible situations, and thoughts that are reflective of the period, or the ideas do not fit very well with this period.	The work includes no creative interpretation of the period.
Source Citation	All sources are cited, and all are formatted as requested.	All sources are cited, but a few are not formatted as requested.	All sources are cited, but many are not formatted as requested.	Some sources are not properly cited.

Figure 2 - Example Rubric

In an analytic rubric, as illustrated in Figure 2, categories for areas to be evaluated are listed in the first column. Different levels of performance are listed in the column headings. These descriptions tend to be unique for each rubric. For each cell of the rubric, a written description of the expected performance at a given level is provided. Some rubrics are based on four or more columns, while others are based on three. When rubrics are used for scoring, the corresponding point value for each cell may also be provided.

Creating Rubrics

Rubrics can be very difficult and time consuming to create. Developing a rubric from scratch may take 1–2 hours. In general, the steps to follow when creating a rubric are outlined below.

1. Identify the major features of the assignment to be evaluated.

2. Determine the levels of performance. Will you use 3, 4, or more columns?

3. Provide descriptive names to each level of performance. Examples of performance descriptions:

    • Top Level: Exemplary, Mastery, Advanced, Excellent, Outstanding, Fluent

    • Next Level: Proficient, Accomplished, Adept, Knowledgeable

    • Next Level: Developing, Adequate, Acceptable

    • Lowest Level: Beginning, Formative, Emerging, Limited, Needs Improvement, Unacceptable

4. Provide descriptions for each category and level of performance combination (the text for each cell).

5. If used for scoring, provide the points associated with each cell.

In many cases, rubrics are developed over a period of time. A teacher will continually update the rubric and he or she discovers what works and what doesn't work as well.

There are many resources online for creating rubrics. One of the most popular is RubiStar (http://rubistar.4teachers.org). RubiStar is a free, easy-to-use, online tool for creating rubrics based on a library of exemplar rubrics in a wide range of subject areas. Once a rubric template is selected, the teacher can customize all aspects of the rubric before printing it, downloading it, or saving it online.

Intel has also developed a tool for developing rubrics and checklists (http://www97.intel.com/en/assessingprojects/). This tool is more complicated to use, but it has rubrics and checklists that are classified by age and subject area. The exemplars provided also put a greater emphasis on higher-order thinking skills.

Effective Use of Rubrics

There are some guidelines that can be followed to improve the overall quality of a rubric:

- **Cover the Right Content:** The rubric should emphasize what the teacher really wants the students to achieve. It should cover all the essential features without putting emphasis on minor details.

- **Organize Criteria and Levels:** The number of criteria and the levels or scales of performance should be sufficient to cover the area. Too many can be confusing. Features should appear only once and not in multiple places.

- **Clearly Define Levels:** The performance descriptions in each cell should be clearly defined and be clearly distinct from one another. This is the hardest guideline to achieve. Ideally, all student work should fall within a specific cell and not between cells.

One of the greatest benefits of rubrics is as a tool to clearly communicate expectations and requirements to students. The most common approach is for the teacher to design the rubric and go over it with students early in the assignment. Providing models that illustrate the various levels of performance to students is a way to further reinforce and define expectations and requirements. Another alternative is to design the rubric with students' input. In some cases, a teacher may allow students to select what elements of the rubric to apply to their work. Students may complete the rubric for their own work or may use it to evaluate another student's work. When the same rubric is used for several assignments it can be used to track and document skill development.

Conclusion

Rubrics are a simple but powerful way to assess student learning and performance. They can be difficult and time consuming to develop, but there are several resources online that can be used to streamline the process. The benefits can be enormous. When developed well, they can inspire and motivate students to perform to their highest capability.

Linda Merillat is an Instructional Designer in the Interactive Teaching and Technology Center at Arkansas State University. She is a specialist in technology and assessment.

Endnotes

1   Kirschenbaum, Howard, Sidney B. Simon, and Rodney W Napier. *Wad-Ja-Get?: The Grading Game in American Education.* New York: Hart Publishing Company, Inc., 1971.

2   Davis, O.L. Foreword. *Measuring History: Cases of State-Level Testing Across the United States.* Ed. S.G. Grant. Greenwich: Information Age Publishing, 2006. vii.

3   Grant, S.G. and Catherine Horn. "The State of State-Level History Tests." *Measuring History.* Buffalo: SUNY, 2006. 24.

4   Ellis, Arthur K. *Teaching and Learning Elementary Social Studies.* 7th ed. Boston: Allyn and Bacon, 2002. 159.

5   "Social Studies in the Era of No Child Left Behind: A Position Statement of the National Council for the Social Studies." *Social Education* 71. 5 (2007): 284.

6   Grant, S.G. "High-Stakes Testing: How are the Social Studies Responding?" *Social Education* 71. 5 (2007): 250–54.

7   Khadaroo, Stacy Teicher. "Graduation Rate for US High-Schoolers Falls for Second Straight Year." *The Christian Science Monitor.* Web. <http://www.csmonitor.com>. 10 June 2010.

8   Grant, "High-Stakes Testing." 254. See also Segal, Avner. "Teaching History in the Age of Accountability: Measuring History or Measuring Up to It?" Grant, *Measuring History.* 105–32.

9   Cunningham, Patricia M. and Richard L. Allington. *Classrooms That Work: They Can All Read and Write.* 5th ed. Boston: Pearson, 2011. 204.

10   Ibid. 205.

11   Oliva, Peter F. *Developing the Curriculum.* 6th ed. Boston: Pearson, Allyn and Bacon, 2005. 384–87 and 398–402.

12   Grant, S.G. and Cinthia Salinas. "Assessment and Accountability in the Social Studies." Ed. Linda S. Levstik and Cynthia A. Tuson. *Handbook of Research in Social Studies Education.* New York: Routledge, 2008. 219–20.

13   Ibid. 232.

14   Henson, Kenneth T. *Curriculum Planning: Integrating Multiculturalism, Constructivism, and Educational Reform.* 4th ed. Long Grove: Waveland Press, Inc., 2010. 301, 303.

15 Voltz, Deborah L., Michel Jean Sims, and Betty Nelson. *Connecting Teachers Students and Standards: Strategies for Success in Diverse and Inclusive Classrooms.* Alexandria: Association for Supervision and Curriculum Development, 2010. 117.

16 Caldwell, J. *Reading Assessment: A Primer for Teachers and Tutors.* New York: Guilford, 2002.

17 Brown, Dave F. and Trudy Knowles. *What Every Middle School Teacher Should Know.* 2nd ed. Portsmouth, NH: Heinemann, 2007. 181–83.

18 Barnwell, Paul. "Get Away from Grading and Get Students Learning." *Middle Ground* 13. 3 (2010): 24–25.

19 Epstein, Terrie. "Research on Teaching and Learning History: Teacher Professionalization and Student Cognition and Culture." Ed. Diana Turk, Rachel Mattson, Terrie Epstein, and Robert Cohen. *Teaching U.S. History: Dialogues among Social Studies Teachers and Historians.* New York: Routledge, 2010. 191.

20 Ivey, Gay. "Texts That Matter." *Educational Leadership* 67. 6 (2010): 22.

21 Loewen, James W. *Teaching What Really Happened: How to Avoid the Tyranny of Textbooks & Get Students Excited About Doing History.* New York: Teachers College Press, 2010. 21. Also Erickson, Lynn. *Concept-Based Curriculum and Instruction.* Thousand Oaks: Sage-Corwin, 2002. 5–6, 15–16, 63–64; and Marzano, Robert and J. Kendall. "Awash in a Sea of Standards." Web.<http://www.mcrel.org/PDF/Standards/5982IR_AwashInASea.pdf>. An example of a national history standards document is *National Standards for United States History*, 1994, National Center for History in the Schools.

22 Drake, Frederick D. and Lynn R. Nelson. *Engagement in Teaching History: Theory and Practices for Middle and Secondary Teachers.* 2nd ed. Upper Saddle River: Merrill/Pearson, 2009. 114–15.

23 Ibid.

24 Glasgow, Neal A. and Cathy D. Hicks. *What Successful Teachers Do: 101 Research-Based Classroom Strategies for New and Veteran Teachers.* Thousand Oaks: Corwin Press, 2009. 70.

25 Ko, Susan and Steve Rossen. *Teaching Online: A Practical Guide.* New York: Routledge, 2010. 223–24.

26 Fogarty, Robin. *How to Integrate the Curricula.* 3rd ed. Thousand Oaks: Corwin, 2009. 121–26.

27 Marzano, Robert J. "When Students Track Their Progress." *Educational Leadership* 67. 4 (2010): 86–87.

28 Vagle, Nicole M. "Inspiring and Requiring Action." *The Teacher as Assessment Leader.* Ed. Thomas R. Guskey. Bloomington: Solution Tree Press, 2009. 205–11.

29 Smith, Kari. "From Test Takers to Test Makers." *Educational Leadership* 67. 3 (2009): 26–30. On formative assessment see also Greenstein, Laura. *What Teachers Really Need to Know About Formative Assessment.* Alexandria: Association for Supervision and Curriculum Development, 2010.

30 Glasgow and Hicks, 90, 97.

31 Winger, Terry. "Grading What Matters." *Educational Leadership* 67. 3 (2009): 73–75.

32 Heubner, Tracy A. "Balanced Assessment." *Educational Leadership* 67. 3 (2009): 85–87.

FOURTEEN

Just One or Two More Things

Not all the ideas and issues that encompass the work and joy of teaching history to adolescents can be neatly categorized into chapters. This chapter attempts to capture three traditional approaches to teaching history that did not quite fit into earlier chapters. They include the use of lecturing, incorporating humor into the classroom, and the strategy of games and simulations in education. There is also a brief conclusion at the end of the chapter.

Probably the most famous lecture in history was given by actor/economist/gadfly Ben Stein in the 1986 movie *Ferris Bueller's Day Off.* (The cost of renting, or even purchasing, this film on DVD and viewing the minute Stein is on screen is well worth the price.) Since it is within a comedy film it is, of course, not a "real" lecture. But in many ways it is quite real as all (yes, all) students have experienced some rendition of such a lecture. Before the script from which Stein worked is quoted, keep in mind that the teacher he portrays probably does not think he is giving a lecture. He asks questions, but until the very last question there is no discussion. There are pauses in his lecture, but they are not long enough for any student reflection to take place. He does attempt to connect his lecture to a current event of the day, which is important in any history class. For that he should be applauded. He just goes about it wrong. This particular film clip should be shown every year to every middle school and high school history teacher in the nation. It would do no harm for university historians to annually also view it. Here it is:

In 1930, the Republican-controlled House of Representatives endeavored to alleviate the effects of the—anyone? anyone?—Great Depression. Passed the—anyone? anyone?—the tariff bill. The Hawley-Smoot Tariff Act, which—anyone? anyone?—raised tariffs in an effort to collect more revenues for the federal government. Did it work? Anyone? Anyone know the effects? It did not work and the United States sank deeply into the Great Depression. Today we have a similar debate over this. Anyone know what this is? Class? Anyone? Anyone? Anyone seen this before, the Laffer Curve?

With no help from Stein, the efficacy of lecturing has often been questioned and used as an example of inferior pedagogy as compared to the use of small groups, real classroom discussion, and differentiated instruction strategies. The criticism is that lectures have been seen as hampering student interaction, reducing student thinking, and diminishing student contributions to the class. Yet new studies are challenging those observations and long-held views on the lecture. One study seems to indicate that lecturing may not be as adverse to student learning as was once thought. Grant found lecturing could be effective if given by master teachers who had a significant amount of content knowledge, delivered them in engaging or even entertaining ways, and incorporated examples and challenging questions.[1]

Other research seems to support Grant. Ausubel, in a dated but useful study, found that the lecture could indeed be an efficient way to teach. He recommended the use of "advance organizers" (also referred to as scaffolds or outlines). These provide intellectual frameworks to which ideas, events, and individuals can be systematically structured to connect to larger themes and generalizations.[2] Drake and Nelson have made a number of helpful suggestions as to how the lecture can be an effective tool in the classroom. They call on teachers to decide in advance the purpose of the lecture. Will it be motivational, informational, for enrichment, or summation? The need is for a "hook" or a piece of material or visual that attempts to engage students from the beginning of the lecture. This could be in the form of a story, a question, or a problem. Other elements of the lecture to be considered are the selection of language to be used, the use of illustrations and/or visuals to accompany the lecture, and the organization of the lecture with a beginning, middle, and end. Finally, Nelson and Drake encourage teachers who wish to lecture effectively to know their audience (class), be well prepared, friendly, and confident.[3]

Another area where research tells us that positive results can occur for students is when humor is used in the classroom. Humor should not be viewed as doing stand-up comedy or having a joke-for-the-day. And not all teachers have a sense of humor or are funny. However, humor can help students deal with stress and anxiety, build rapport with the teacher, generate interest on the part of the students in the class and therefore the subject matter. It should be noted that sarcasm or any attempts at humor that personally insult students—individually or as a group—should never occur.[4] Zuckerman concurs that while humor can enliven a lesson, defuse tension, and promote a positive relationship with students it should only be directed at the teacher, the content of the lesson when appropriate, or a situation. Zuckerman also quotes research that indicates that humor does indeed promote a sense of community and build relationships.[5]

There are various ways to insert humor into the classroom. A current cartoon, whether it is connected to the lesson or not, can often be a way to commence a class on the right note. A joke, if it is a good one, will work. Jokes often work better with younger adolescents than older ones. Older adolescents seem to have difficulty acknowledging humor due to peer pressure over what should be considered funny. Comical photographs or video-clips are also welcome. Teachers do need to be careful with Internet humor. Even what may seem harmless fun to some students can be embarrassing to others. A ubiquitous form of Internet humor has been photographs, supposedly not staged, of men and women dressed differently than the norm and shopping at Wal-Mart or K-Mart. The dress or behavior of some individuals in public places may reflect poverty or disabilities—not appropriate choices for humor.

Hopkins has written that two important qualities that every teacher needs are playfulness and a sense of connectedness. They are both closely related to humor. Hopkins writes that "Humor is a vital component of a thriving learning environment. The pressures of content coverage seem to have made us more serious and intense in our delivery of information to students. Nothing relieves stress like laughter."[6] Hopkins says that this is especially important for middle level students. What she calls playfulness, banter, and connecting to their interests does much to make teachers (adult role models for adolescents) advance the "crystallizing" of learning and make teachers real people to learners. And by the way, adults like humor, too.

Humor can also be positive for the teacher. McDonald and Hershman have found that "when we (teachers) can have a sense of humor about what students do, our lives become less stressful." They also advise that while adolescents may think they are adults, they are not. Not taking everything that happens seriously can make challenging days go much better. McDonald and Hershman do advise that the teacher must always be ready to transition back to the classroom activities. What at first seemed like a moment of frivolity, they advise, can easily turn into twenty minutes of chaos.[7]

One must be careful to not too closely follow the trends of today's youth. A used and maybe over-used practice in many facets of everyday life is the employment of the "top ten list." Now in its second decade of use by late-night talk show host David Letterman, the use of top ten lists seems to appear everywhere. (Although my time at Ball State University did slightly overlap with those of Mr.

Letterman's, learning how to create top ten lists was not in the institution's curriculum.) But when used selectively, creatively, and with a purpose, it can prove effective in capturing the attention of students.

The way "top ten lists" can be used, and not necessarily for humor, is as a means to allow students to gain basic factual information about historical individuals by employing comparisons and contrasts. Three examples used with modest success are the top ten differences between Thomas Jefferson and Alexander Hamilton; between W.E.B. Du Bois and Booker T. Washington; and between Martin Luther King, Jr., and Malcolm X. Students are provided the major ideas of these leaders and thinkers and also see how they differed and, at times, were similar. Students can also examine the four black leaders listed above by having students conjecture if Du Bois and Malcolm X or King and Washington were similar in their ideas and tactics. But there is always new research. In *Up From History: The Life of Booker T. Washington*, Robert Norrell posits that Washington was much more of an activist than previously portrayed in textbooks. He vigorously opposed lynching, effectively garnered financial support from northern philanthropists, and spoke openly, albeit selectively, on issues of race in both the North and the South.[8]

A third strategy once viewed as innovative, yet has fallen into only moderate use, is games and simulations. Games and simulations are especially germane to the history classroom. In 1968 James Coleman wrote that games and simulations can be a critical part of learning due to the experiences they provide students. It gives adolescents, and even younger students, an opportunity for social action that is imbedded in a social context.[9] Even John Dewey, in *Human Nature and Conduct*, concluded that games provide "fresh and deeper meanings to the usual activities of life."[10] This is true for history, in the Deweyan "learning by doing" function where there are few opportunities to make history, write history, or solve problems in the historical arena. Abt has argued that games allow students to make "a mistake in history [which is] making a wrong decision, not failing to remember a date."[11] This experiential attribute of games and simulations provides for improved student understanding of the field.

Games and simulations were quite popular in the 1960s and 1970s with a number of them being produced. Courses in universities were also taught on the classroom use of this method. One 1965 quantitative study employed a simulation experience on the causes of the Civil War. One group of eighth grade high-ability students were taught the unit using a traditional textbook approach while another group employed the simulation. The results indicated that students using the simulation demonstrated higher achievement and better attitudes toward the subject.[12]

Jerome Bruner's research, also in the 1960s, made a strong case for simulations. Using what he termed the "Cone of Experience," Bruner uses a continuum from "direct experience" through visuals to "verbal symbols." The lower end of the continuum includes "contrived experiences" of which games and simulations are a part. Bruner found that such "contrived experiences" worked well with elementary and younger adolescent students due to the reality base of the experiences.[13]

The purpose behind any game, simulation, or role-playing activity by students must be reflected on before undertaking the activity in the classroom. Koenig, as both a parent and educator, protested the inclusion of the simulation/role playing of a battle as part of a Civil War day for young adolescents. Uniforms (blue and gray) were passed out as well as wooden guns and cards that described their fate—from survived to wounded to killed. (Historical note: More soldiers during the Civil War died of dysentery than any other cause. Not a good simulation activity.) Koenig viewed the exercise as not only antithetic to the school policy on weapons, but there was a lack of clear aims, objectives, or even purpose for the activity. Students, it was reported, found it "fun." The school administration, on second thought, did not find the activity "fun" and discontinued it. Koenig then tells of the community reaction to the dropping of the activity and, after a public debate, there was a reinstatement of the reenactment. A lesson from this episode is that a reenactment is not the same as role playing. Reenactment, a legitimate activity, is mainly for the purpose of imitating a historical personage or episode. This clearly was not a reenactment. An epilogue to this case was the rejection of the idea of allowing students to reenact the historical role of pacifists during the Civil War.[14]

The Civil War role-playing episode points out the hazards of employing this valid approach to teaching (role playing) without a larger purpose in mind. Role playing, as Bigelow points out, is not just telling students, but showing them. Role playing, he writes, "can bring history-making to life in the classroom" by having students attempt to imagine themselves in circumstances of other individuals throughout history."[15] The key is the word *attempt*. As discussed earlier, empathy is a critical disposition that can in many cases be taught. We can never know what it was like to be a slave in America or a prisoner (slave) in a Nazi concentration or work camp. (Such examples of role playing these victims have occurred.) To *attempt* to role play these horrific historical situations is wrong. But, suggests Bigelow, to ask students to ponder whether they would have supported the Anti-Slavery Society in eighteenth-century America or role playing whether Columbus "discovered America" or "stole it" are both realistic and possible in the history classroom.[16]

The sophistication of games and simulations, especially in online learning, is increasing. Gibson, Aldrich, and Prensky have edited a comprehensive volume on their current status as an educational tool. Topics their volume includes are using online games and simulations to enhance skills for the 21st century, multiplayer video games, and one chapter is devoted to a reality game in U.S. history. Karen Schrier, from the Massachusetts Institute of Technology, has designed a reality game to teach critical thinking and historical inquiry through a place-based simulation of Lexington, Massachusetts, during the American Revolution.[17]

Gibson and his colleagues indicate that games and simulations have the potential to dramatically improve student motivation and education outcomes. But they are careful not to promise too much. Their research has found that games and simulations vary greatly among individuals who participate in them due to individual learning strengths and styles. They also suggest that much of the success of online games and simulations depends on good design. In fact, the difficulty in the design of games and simulations may, at this time, be the greatest barrier for its growth. Even though the editors are committed to this avenue of instruction, they state that it will not be a panacea for education's problems unless there is great creativity in their design. And finally, these gaming advocates write that simulations must walk a tightrope between authenticity and validity. It might be real and also entertaining, but does it serve an educational goal by conveying deep content through the activity?[18]

Recent research on games and simulations has confirmed the hypotheses and findings of the past few decades. Marzano has documented more than 60 studies that indicate gains in student achievement when academic games are used. Specific strategies were used to achieve these results. They included the use of inconsequential competition. This meant while there might be "winners and losers" in the game, the competition did not harm a student's grade. Another strategy was targeting essential academic content, not just playing a game for entertainment. Debriefing after the game was also found to be critical.[19]

Games specific to history can be found in two sources. *Hands-On History: American History Activities* contains eight historical topics ranging from Colonial America to the Civil Rights Movement. In "Tecumseh and the American Indian Experience," the game is "rigged" for the settlers to win, just like they did in 1809. The Jeffersonian period calls for students to examine and then make presidential decisions.[20] In *American History Simulations*, the activities are again related to a variety of periods in American history and are aimed at adolescents from younger middle school to high school.[21] The games and simulations in these two books link to major historical topics and are aligned with standards.

Online role-playing is when students become characters in a game world. (Such role-playing emerged even before online activity through the board game *Dungeons and Dragons*.) As with comic books, role-playing has been viewed as "child's play" by some. But a study from the MacArthur Foundation has suggested that role-playing is a fundamental new literacy skill. Jenkins and his colleagues have found that playing or writing about a character can offer one the capability to understand issues from multiple viewpoints, to digest information and to problem solve.[22]

The positive aspects of role-playing can be a motivator for learning. This is due to students' selecting the roles they wish to play. The various types of role-playing include costume play, online role-play boards, role-playing games, and what are known as MMORPG's (or massively multiplayer online role-playing games). In addition, role-playing is usually not graded, although feedback from the teacher and peers is provided. Finally, in role-playing there is a low risk of failure.

Conclusion

History cannot be seen as dead to adolescents, nor should the future be seen as unreal to them. Our students already live too much in the present. Just as a person with amnesia is disoriented, so too will our youth be if we allow them to amputate the memory of the past. To return to that bitterly cold evening in Minneapolis and Carl Becker's address to a group of Depression-era historians, these pages have suggested, as did Becker, the imperative to make history live for adolescents. "However accurately we may determine the 'facts' of history, the facts themselves and our interpretation of them . . . will be seen in a different perspective or a less vivid light as [we] move into the unknown future," he said. "[The] world can obviously be understood only tentatively, since it is by definition something still in the making, something as yet unfinished."[23]

This book began with the question of the importance of history. While teachers and scholars will always defend and advocate for their disciplines, the study of history is indeed important. A recent episode of this fact is most telling. When President George W. Bush refused to let National Security Advisor Condoleezza Rice testify before the 9/11 Commission on the grounds of executive privilege, a historian came to the rescue. Philip Zelikow, a University of Virginia historian and executive director of the 9/11 Commission, found a November 22, 1945 *New York Times* front-page photograph of Admiral William D. Leahy, chief of staff to presidents Roosevelt and Truman, testifying before a congressional panel investigating the attack on Pearl Harbor. When the photo was faxed to a weekly news magazine, President Bush then quickly allowed Rice to testify. History had made a difference.[24]

The suggestions in this book are by no means a comprehensive rendering of what motivated adolescent students and their teachers can accomplish through the study of history. But maybe no other approach to teaching history to adolescents is as effective as enthusiasm by the teacher. James A. Percoco in his *A Passion for the Past: Creative Teaching of U.S. History* has written that it may be a good idea to tell students, "Yes, class, I love history!"[25] And as John Dewey's major disciple, William Heard Kilpatrick, once asked, "If students take a course in history and make the grade of 'A,' but end up hating history, have they really learned history?"

Not all students will love history as much as Mr. Percoco and other history teachers. But no adolescent should leave a history classroom hating it.

Endnotes

1   Grant, S.G. *History Lessons: Teaching, Learning and Testing in U.S. History Classrooms.* New York: Taylor and Francis, 2003.

2   Ausubel, David. "The Use of Advance Organizers in Learning and Retention of Meaningful Material." *Journal of Educational Psychology* 51 (1960): 267–72.

3   Drake, Frederick D. and Lynn R. Nelson. *Engagement in Teaching History: Theory and Practice for Middle and Secondary Teachers.* 2nd ed. Upper Saddle River: Merrill/Pearson, 2005. 67.

4   Glasgow, Neal A. and Cathy D. Hicks. *What Successful Teachers Do: 101 Research-Based Classroom Strategies for New and Veteran Teachers.* Thousand Oaks: Corwin Press, 2009. 3–4.

5   Zuckerman, June Trop. *From Lesson Plans to Power Struggle, Grades 6–12: Classroom Management Strategies for New Teachers.* Thousand Oaks, CA: Corwin, 2009. 16–17.

6   Hopkins, Kathleen Richards. *Teaching How to Learn in a What-to-Learn Culture.* San Francisco: Jossey-Bass, 2010. 47–48.

7   McDonald, Emma S. and Dyan M. Hershman. *Classrooms That Spark! Recharge and Revive Your Teaching.* San Francisco: Jossey-Bass, 2010. 46.

8   Norrell, Robert J. *Up From History: The Life of Booker T. Washington.* Cambridge: The Belknap Press of Harvard University, 2009.

9   Coleman, James S. Preface. *Simulation Games in Learning.* Ed. Sarane S. Boocock and E.O. Schild. Beverly Hills: Sage Publications, 1968. 7–10.

10   Dewey, John. *Human Nature and Conduct.* New York: Henry Holt, 1922. 162.

11   Abt, Clark C. "Games for Learning: Some Problems of Teaching Social Studies in Elementary and Secondary Schools." *Simulation Games in Learning.* Ed. Sarane S. Boocock and E.O. Schild. Beverly Hills: Sage Publications, 1968. 65–66.

12   Baker, Eugene H. "A Pre-Civil War Simulation for Teaching American History." *Simulation Games in Learning.* Ed. Sarane S. Boocock and E.O. Schild. Beverly Hills: Sage Publications, 1968. 135–42.

13   Bruner, Jerome. *Toward a Theory of Instruction.* Cambridge: Harvard University Press, 1966.

14   Koenig, Karen Park. "It Was So Much Fun! I Died of Massive Blood Loss!" *Rethinking Education* 23. 4 (2009).

15   Bigelow, Bill. *A People's History for the Classroom.* Milwaukee: Rethinking Schools Ltd., 2008. 3–4.

16   Ibid.

17   Schrier, Karen. "Reliving History with 'Reliving the Revolution': Designing Augmented Reality Games to Teach the Critical Thinking of History." Gibson, David, Aldrich Clark and Marc Prensky, Eds. *Games and Simulations in Online Learning: Research and Development Frameworks.* Hershey: Information Science Publishing, 2007. 250–60.

18   Gibson, David, Aldrich Clark and Marc Prensky, Eds. *Games and Simulations in Online Learning: Research and Development Frameworks.* Hershey: Information Science Publishing. 2007.

19 Marzano, Robert J. "Using Games to Enhance Student Achievement." *Educational Leadership* 76. 5 (2010): 71–72.

20 Sundem, Garth. *Hands-On History: American History Activities.* Huntington Beach: Shell Education, 2007.

21 Fischer, Max. *American History Simulations.* Westminster: Teacher Created Resources, 2004.

22 See Jenkins, Henry. *Confronting the Challenges of Participatory Culture: Education for the 21ˢᵗ Century.* The John D. and Catherine T. MacArthur Foundation, 2006, at <http://digitallearning.macfound.org>.

23 Becker, Carl. "Everyman His Own Historian." *The American Historical Review* 37. 2 (1932): 236.

24 Bryant, James A. "The Fax About History." *Phi Delta Kappan* 86. 10 (2005): 754–56.

25 Percoco, James A. *A Passion for the Past: Creative Teaching of U.S. History.* Portsmouth: Heinemann, 1998. 5.

Index

Adolescent Cultures, School & Society

Joseph L. DeVitis & Linda Irwin-DeVitis
GENERAL EDITORS

As schools struggle to redefine and restructure themselves, they need to be cognizant of the new realities of adolescents. Thus, this series of monographs and textbooks is committed to depicting the variety of adolescent cultures that exist in today's post-industrial societies. It is intended to be a primarily qualitative research, practice, and policy series devoted to contextual interpretation and analysis that encompasses a broad range of interdisciplinary critique. In addition, this series will seek to provide a pragmatic, pro-active response to the current backlash of conservatism that continues to dominate political discourse, practice, and policy. This series seeks to address issues of curriculum theory and practice; multicultural education; aggression and violence; the media and arts; school dropouts; homeless and runaway youth; alienated youth; at-risk adolescent populations; family structures and parental involvement; and race, ethnicity, class, and gender studies.

Send proposals and manuscripts to the general editors at:

Joseph L. DeVitis & Linda Irwin-DeVitis
Darden College of Education
Old Dominion University
Norfolk, VA 23503

To order other books in this series, please contact our Customer Service Department at:

(800) 770-LANG (within the U.S.)
(212) 647-7706 (outside the U.S.)
(212) 647-7707 FAX

or browse online by series at:

WWW.PETERLANG.COM